AGAINST
US

AGAINST US

US

THE NEW FACE OF AMERICA'S ENEMIES IN THE MUSLIM WORLD

JIM SCIUTTO

HARMONY BOOKS

NEW YORK

Copyright © 2008 by Jim Sciutto

Published in the United States by Harmony Books, an imprint of
the Crown Publishing Group, a division of Random House, Inc.,
New York.
www.crownpublishing.com

Harmony Books is a registered trademark and the Harmony Books colophon
is a trademark of Random House, Inc.

Library of Congress Cataloging-in-Publication Data

Sciutto, Jim
    Against us: the new face of America's enemies in the Muslim world / Jim Sciutto.
    1. Anti-Americanism—Middle East.   2. United States—Foreign public opinion,
Middle Eastern.   3. Public opinion—Middle East.   4. Middle East—Foreign
relations—United States.   5. United States—Foreign relations—Middle East.
I. Title.
    DS63.2.U5S313 2008
    303.48'27301767—dc22

                                                                                2008014971

ISBN 978-0-307-40688-0

Printed in the United States of America

Design by Level C

10 9 8 7 6 5 4 3 2 1

First Edition

In memory of my mother,
Elizabeth Higgins Sciutto,
for the inspiration and the drive to write

CONTENTS

	Introduction	ix
ONE	Jordan *The Terrorist with a Marketing Major*	I
TWO	Lebanon *Christians for Hezbollah*	31
THREE	Egypt *The Forgotten Democratic Hero*	63
FOUR	Iraq *Stanch the Bleeding*	95
FIVE	Iran *Deaf to America*	127
SIX	The UK *Baghdad Comes to Birmingham*	161
SEVEN	Afghanistan *An Afghan Girl's Wildest Dreams*	193
EIGHT	Saudi Arabia *The Jihadi Turned Electrician*	219
EPILOGUE	Pakistan	247
	Acknowledgments	253
	Index	257

INTRODUCTION

F OR FIVE YEARS, I've lived in Notting Hill—
home to fashion boutiques, gourmet delicatessens,
Park Avenue rents, and half a dozen guys planning for martyrdom. My neighbors are terrorists. I found out the first
time in July 2005. After attempting and failing to blow
themselves up on the London subway, three young British
Muslims were captured in an apartment just down the
street from me and right around the corner from the Travel
Book Shop, where Hugh Grant's character worked in the
movie *Notting Hill*. In perfect Notting Hill style, I'd sped
by their place on my Vespa coming back from the gym just
before the police swooped in. When the ABC desk called
me with the news, I went to the scene still wearing my
sneakers and sweats.

The story quickly burst the posh, hip, and *safe* bubble I
had created for myself in London. Through all the wars and
terror attacks overseas, I had imagined my neighborhood as
a terror-free zone. Standing there on the corner of Lancaster
and Portobello Roads that morning, I could see my favorite
place for brunch, my favorite Italian restaurant, and my
gym. It was like finding out that the next nineteen hijackers were living in the West Village.

London's collective sense of security had already been shattered two weeks earlier, when four other British men detonated bombs on three subway trains and a bus across the capital. Those attackers had been successful, killing fifty-two people and themselves. As an American, I marveled at Britain's calm. London was shocked but not frozen. The buses and trains started running again almost immediately. Friends kept their dinner dates that night. Londoners proudly recalled the Second World War: We survived the blitz, we can survive this. But this time the threat came from home. Britain's own people were killing their fellow citizens. And these were good British boys, with jobs, families, favorite soccer teams, and unmistakably British accents.

There would be other chilling reminders of this threat every few months. In August 2006, a plot was uncovered in Waltham Forest, East London, to blow up half a dozen airliners over the Atlantic using chemicals carried on board in soda bottles. If the alleged planners had been successful, they would have killed thousands: a 9/11 over the sea. In February 2007, Scotland Yard foiled a plan in Birmingham to kidnap and behead British Muslim soldiers returning from Iraq and Afghanistan. Several newspapers shared a single headline for the story: BAGHDAD COMES TO BIRMINGHAM.

Each plot seemed more sinister than the last. In July 2007, two men tried to detonate car bombs outside two London nightclubs. When the bombs failed, they drove ten hours to Scotland to set themselves on fire outside the departure terminal at Glasgow International Airport. Like the Birmingham suspects, they had intended to bring Iraqi-like violence home to the British people. But this conspiracy had a new twist: the attackers were doctors. And they were my neighbors as well. Two of them had addresses just down the street from me, again, in idyllic Notting Hill.

What worried me was that the hate—against Britain, against America, against the West (they make little distinction)—had become a part of the fabric of everyday life. In early 2002, I had embarked on an educational tour of the Arab World as a foreign correspondent for ABC News. After 9/11, I knew we had dangerous enemies in the region. But they were, I thought, easily identifiable: terrorists, radical imams, infiltrators from faraway places. One hundred assignments later, from the Caucasus in the north, down through Afghanistan and Iran, the Persian Gulf, and into the Middle East, I was changed, even floored. In Afghanistan and Jordan I'd met Al-Qaeda fighters who told me it was their dream to kill me. That was no surprise. But for everyone from Egyptian democracy activists to Iraqis who had once supported the U.S. invasion to "pro-western" Lebanese lawmakers, America seemed to have perfected some sort of perverse art in alienating people.

I'd already spent several years in Asia after college, so I'd learned to shed any conceit that Americans were always, or even usually, perceived as the good guys. People in many countries can remember a time when they were up and we were down, and long for history to repeat itself. I also knew that anti-Americanism is a convenient tool for governments. The United States as foreign menace is a nice distraction from poverty, corruption, and utter failure at home. Still, among Muslims there is something distinct and demoralizing about their anti-American sentiment. Many Muslims I've met have long believed that the United States is trying to control their lives, nearly always with the worst intentions. They don't blame me personally. They usually make the distinction between the American people and their politicians (though that distinction is fading). But they do treat me as America's official spokesman, or as its defense attorney in an international court of public opinion where the facts as we see them don't matter much. Here, the September 11 attacks were a joint plot of the CIA and Israeli intelligence. Violence in Iraq is not failed policy, but a deliberate American plan to occupy Muslim land and steal oil. The Israel-Lebanon War was a brazen attempt by the United States and Israel to send a violent message to Muslims by killing Lebanese civilians. Such assumptions extend even to native-born European Muslims. Among many British Muslims, the July 7 London subway bombers weren't murderers, but innocent young men framed by the police (though they'll often add that Britain deserved the attacks anyway).

After seven years of reporting on this subject, I came to an unsettling truth: The Al-Qaeda-inspired view of an evil America bent on destroying Islam has moved from the fringe to the mainstream. Today, America's enemies are not the wild-eyed radicals I had imagined, but are often moderates—and many of those whom we thought were our friends are now some of our most virulent detractors.

Positive views of America—already anemic—have grown slimmer and slimmer. A 2007 poll by the U.S.-based Program on International Policy Attitudes in four Muslim countries (Egypt, Morocco, Pakistan, and Indonesia) found that 79 percent believe the United States seeks to "weaken and divide the Islamic world." Strong majorities (64 percent on average) even believe it is a U.S. goal to "spread Christianity in the region."

Between 2002 and 2007, the Pew Global Attitudes Project found that the number of people who rated the United States favorably declined in twenty-six of thirty-three countries. By 2007, in nine countries less than 30 percent of the population rated the United States positively. Eight of them were predominantly Muslim: Turkey, Pakistan, Palestine, Morocco, Jordan, Egypt, Malaysia, and Indonesia (Argentina was the odd man out).

In more than thirty years as a pollster, Andrew Kohut, the president and director of the Pew Research Center, has said he could find no frame of reference for the current decline.

"We don't have any experience with this. We never got the breadth of discontent with America as we have now," he said. "In other countries, it's disappointment, resentment, envy. Among Muslims, it ranges from strong dislike to hatred."

Increasingly, negative views of America as a country are extending to the American people. Another Pew poll found that fewer than one-third of Egyptians, Moroccans, Palestinians, Pakistanis, and Turks have a favorable view of Americans, characterizing us as greedy, violent, and immoral.

Just after 9/11, President Bush declared nations around the world "with us or against us" in the war on terror. Now those in the Muslim world are against us in greater numbers than ever before—and they have a new face. A remarkable variety of people—normal people—believe the United States intentionally obstructs rather than promotes progress. Al-Qaeda may be losing the military campaign, but, in considerable ways, it is winning the ideological war.

"Al-Qaeda's ideological claims now have credibility, that the West is waging war against Islam," said Fawaz Gerges, a longtime Middle East analyst. "There is a crusading spirit in the West. It helps shape the Muslim view that the U.S. is trying to control their lives. The U.S. is convinced Al-Qaeda is an evildoer. Al-Qaeda has convinced Muslims that the U.S. is an evildoer too."

As an American, I found myself eager to raise the alarm at how deeply our image has been damaged and search for ways to repair it. I found some of the answers by getting to know some of the people who see every event of their lives affected—stage-managed, even—by the United States. For Iraqis, every car bombing has an American imprint. For Palestinians, it's every foot of the wall Israel has built along the border of the West Bank. For Afghans, it's the electricity that's still off most of the day. We have no connection to them, but they feel every connection to us. Their anger is as real as their humanity. These people aren't monsters. Through the profiles that follow, I hope to show how average people buy the conspiracy theories, answer "yes" when asked if America is seeking to weaken the Muslim world, and place more hope in holy war than in America.

In the eyes of many Muslims, America is the victim of its own mistakes. The United States has lost its moral compass across the region. For them, the gap between what we preach and what we do has always been wide, but today it is unbridgeable. The Iraq War was the worst advertisement for American intervention. Torture matters. Guantanamo and Abu Ghraib matter. Our relationships with dictatorships matter too. My Muslim friends laugh when we call Saudi Arabia and Egypt "moderate" regimes. This is why dissidents in Egypt today see their cause as stronger without America than with it. "Without you getting involved," a young Egyptian pro-democracy blogger told me, "we'd be fighting just [Egyptian President Hosni] Mubarak, not Mubarak *and* America."

There is a strange contradiction at the root of much of the hate: while they resent us, many Muslims remain in awe of American power—so much so that they believe U.S. failures in Iraq, Afghanistan, or the occupied territories were America's intention all along. Nothing else could explain the disparity between American promises and performance. As a result, the Iraqi trauma surgeon I've known since the invasion of Baghdad doesn't credit America for the calm after the surge. After five years of piecing together the war's victims, he is convinced America planned the mayhem from the start. He even believes the United States was behind many of the suicide bombings. To him, regardless of who's responsible, the deaths of more than 150,000 Iraqis (as estimated by the World Health Organization through 2006) was too high a price for his country to pay. Abu Ghraib and Guantanamo are nothing compared to what Al-Qaeda has done, but, held up against America's own standards, they are the crimes that have come to define us.

This feeling of being under attack has helped solidify a new Muslim identity—a new cause—of its own. Anti-Americanism is a form of Middle Eastern nationalism that transcends borders, even religion. That's why I easily found Christians in Lebanon who revere Hezbollah as devoutly as Shiite Muslims; they see it as resistance against American imperialism. Across the region and even among Muslims in Europe, hating America has become a modern-day youth movement. Hippies didn't trust anyone over thirty. Muslims have learned not to trust anything American.

As Americans, we can react self-righteously. I've lost my cool in dozens of café debates with Muslim friends. But that will not bring us closer to winning them over. The truth is, they see a different set of facts and a different world. Looking far past 9/11 and into the next presidency, Americans can wish the hostility away or look for the elements of it we can address. We had opportunities to turn the tide of hate: after 9/11, when much of the region unanimously opposed Al-Qaeda's brand of violent nihilism, and again in 2005, when elections in Iraq, Palestine, Lebanon,

Egypt, and the Gulf states gave some hope that the United States might be on to something.

Polling consistently shows that Muslims' priorities mirror ours: family, economic opportunity, reform, and a political system they can participate in. It's just that today they see America as standing in the way of those values, rather than promoting them. To us, freedom means elections. To many Arab Muslims, freedom means freedom from American influence.

There are ways we can save ourselves, I've been told, to turn the tide of hate. Sometimes the solutions are straightforward, such as putting roofs over the heads of students in Afghanistan or getting pro-democracy campaigners released from Egyptian prisons. More often they are long-term and complicated.

"Many Muslims are still deeply enamored of America the idea," said Gerges.

There's the hope. Today, though, America the reality is a disappointment and a threat. This is the new philosophy—the new cause uniting disparate people in disparate places. America is the aggressor, the real impediment to peace, the enemy. And those standing up against us are not just masked gunmen in far-off desert hideouts. They are graduate students in Lebanon, democracy campaigners in Egypt, doctors in Iraq, and those young men in my neighborhood of Notting Hill. Their attitude toward the United States—and Americans—comes from years of living as unwilling subjects of our foreign policy. Their insight into our country is at times grounded in profound wisdom and experience. At other times it's based on pure bunk. But seeing through their eyes will help us understand their vision as well as America's position in the post-9/11, post-Iraq, post–George Bush world.

AGAINST
US

O N E

JORDAN

THE TERRORIST WITH A
MARKETING MAJOR

YILDAR SAT DOWN quietly on the bunk bed opposite me and lowered the volume on a television playing music videos. Extending his hand politely, he told me
he was a marketing major, two years short of finishing his
degree at Amman University. In his Nike sweatshirt and
scruffy red beard, he could have been just another college
student in another messy apartment, except that I was in
Jordan's highest-security prison and Yildar was serving
time for fighting and killing American soldiers in Iraq. He
explained that the United States was waging war against
Islam in Iraq, and it was his duty as a Muslim to fight.

"America has many enemies," he said, "and anybody
who hates America considers Iraq his home."

In late 2006, I became the first American reporter allowed
inside the maximum-security Swaqa prison, south of
Amman. For a jail holding prisoners on a par with the worst
offenders at Guantanamo, it is surprisingly easy to get to.
Take a short drive south of the capital—on the same highway that takes hundreds of tourists to the exalted cliff-face
ruins of Petra each day—and there it is by the side of the
road. From a distance it looks more like a cheap hotel than a
jail, surrounded by whitewashed concrete walls trimmed in

a playful royal blue. Decorating the grounds are meager gardens etched into the dirt, with miniature groves of scraggly fruit trees and geraniums blooming in pots made from old paint-thinner cans. Nearby, a wobbly picnic umbrella provided shade from the glaring desert sunshine for a handful of guards slouching in plastic chairs. As our car pulled up, they self-consciously snapped to attention. The single padlock on the gate was open and we went inside.

I had been expecting gulag-level security: a phalanx of well-armed guards, a clanging of metal partitions behind me. Swaqa is, after all, reserved for some of the gravest threats to the Jordanian regime and to America. Abu Musab al-Zarqawi, the late leader of Al-Qaeda in Iraq, was a prisoner in the 1990s, jailed at the time for plotting to overthrow the Jordanian monarchy. Today, Swaqa holds dozens of convicted terrorists, alongside a thousand other hardened criminals: armed robbers, murderers, and rapists. A Libyan named Salem bin Suweid is here. He was sentenced to death for executing American diplomat Lawrence Foley in the driveway of his home in Amman in 2002. And there is Azmi al-Jayousi, a Jordanian convicted of planning a massive chemical weapons attack in Amman against targets including the U.S. Embassy. American and Jordanian intelligence officials estimated he would have killed thousands if he'd succeeded. I was surrounded by an aspiring Al-Qaeda hall of fame.

As I waited to enter the cell blocks that morning, I was hoping I would meet men who were enemies of the United States long before the Iraq invasion. I imagined a jihadist nuthouse—full of psychotic holy warriors, "dead-enders" in Donald Rumsfeld's words, who would have volunteered for jihad whether the United States invaded Iraq or not. But from the moment I met Yildar—the first of many jihadis I would encounter in the region—I knew I had found something more worrisome: Yildar and many other young volunteers for holy war like him were surprisingly normal. They came from families that weren't particularly religious. They had fairly comfortable backgrounds. And their motivation—a feeling that their culture was under assault by the West—was, to them, fact, not fantasy.

Here in Jordan, the revelation was particularly jarring. The Royal Hashemite Kingdom of Jordan—with a reform-minded king and peaceful relations with Israel—is meant to be an island of moderation in a sea of extremism. The reality is far different. Even America's allies can be havens for its enemies. And what bothered me more was that the hate was mundane. In their eyes, it was purely logical. I'd hoped to find nutcases, but the guys I met were average. They were average in every way, except for the fact that they were so swayed by their convictions that they were willing to die for them.

I arrived at Swaqa at lunchtime, apparently the happiest time of day in a maximum-security prison. As huge pots of meat stew and rice with flatbread stacked on top made their way through the halls, the building perked up. Prison workers hurried with smiles on their faces; prisoners gathered into unruly queues. I found myself in the middle of a mob. I thought I was the attraction—a strange American visitor—until I realized it was the food they were after. I was amazed, and a little frightened, at how relaxed a scene it was. Prisoners wandered in large groups outnumbering the guards. This was no Guantanamo, with a maze of steel cages, but a big concrete dormitory. The windows were large, covered with a thin metal grill. The painted walls reminded me of grade school: dark blue on the bottom, paler blue on top. I vaguely remembered that the color blue was supposed to have a calming effect. I clung to the thought. Every fifty yards or so, a metal gate divided the long corridor into separate cell blocks. As I walked along, I peeked into the cells through simple wooden doors—no sliding bars, Alcatraz-style. The prisoners looked back with bemused smiles. The cells themselves were spacious shared rooms with about a dozen beds apiece. And each bunk boasted a personal touch: handwoven blankets, pictures of Indian movie stars pasted to the walls, hot pots for making tea, and television sets pumping out an incessant din of the latest Arabic pop hits. Swaqa seemed more like a jihadist fraternity house than a high-level detention center.

I wondered who was in control. A few months earlier, in February 2006, inmates loyal to Al-Qaeda had taken over Swaqa and two other high-security prisons during violent clashes with Jordanian security forces. In one of the prisons, they managed to take several police officers hostage. They broadcast their demands live on Arab satellite networks, using smuggled-in cell phones. They wanted to stop the executions of bin Suweid, the murderer of American diplomat Lawrence Foley, and al-Jayousi, the man behind the chemical attack plot. The standoff lasted for fourteen hours. Jordanian officials never confirmed how they gained the hostages' release, but the siege was an embarrassment for the government. I knew part of the reason they allowed me inside was to prove they were back in charge again.

The uprising was a reminder that Al-Qaeda is more powerful in Jordan than many are aware. Jordan is held up as a model of gradualist reform and sometimes bold initiatives. King Abdullah has championed a more secular legal system and more-modern schools, even building a Jordanian prep school modeled on his American alma mater, Deerfield Academy, in the middle of the Jordanian desert. His wife,

Queen Rania, has championed women's rights, a tough sell among conservative Muslims. Jordan's intelligence service was one of the CIA's most trusted partners in the Arab world, with a reputation for getting prisoners to talk using methods that, according to some, would not be acceptable under U.S. law. But Jordan continues to have one of the most developed extremist movements in all of the Middle East. Surveys show surprising admiration for Zarqawi, a hometown boy from the village of Zarqa, south of Amman. Zarqawi's support persisted even after he organized horrific suicide bombings at three Amman hotels in 2005 that killed sixty people, most of them Jordanians. A 2005 survey by the Pew Research Center found that 100 percent of Jordanians viewed Jews unfavorably—the highest level in all of the Middle East.

Jordan raises difficult questions for the United States. For fifty years, Washington has backed King Hussein and now his son King Abdullah, holding them up as paragons of progress and liberalization and showering them with aid and diplomatic support. What Washington has received in return is questionable.

The inmates' ability to take over several maximum-security prisons simultaneously demonstrated their numbers and raised suspicions that they had sympathizers among the guards. The mayhem was not lost on the twenty-four-hour Arab news networks. Scenes of rioting inmates in U.S.-allied Jordan had the makings of an exciting, David-versus-Goliath storyline. Touring the cell blocks that day, I had a more immediate concern. Who really had the upper hand?

Today the warden smiled as he welcomed me into his grand office for an obligatory cup of tea. Ali was a career policeman. On the walls were awards for exemplary service and a gargantuan portrait of King Abdullah—symbols of loyalty to a regime that has many enemies inside and outside the prison. Ali looked calm and confident in his perfectly pressed uniform. He resembled a London policeman minus the funny hat: blue shirt with shiny epaulettes, an array of ribbons on his lapel, and creased black pants. He smoked as he fiddled with a brand-new Dell desktop computer, which I guessed had been paid for with my tax money.

He wanted to know why an American reporter wanted to be alone with convicted terrorists. "These guys are crazy," he said. "Real Islamist crackpots." I told him I could never think of meeting face-to-face with insurgents in Iraq. There I would be a target (for kidnapping or worse). But here, in the relative safety of the prison, I had my chance.

Smiling and shaking his head as if to say I didn't know what I was getting into, the warden said I was welcome to speak with them. But the prison's chief interrogator, who acted as my guide, said I had to get permission from one more person. The prison had another hierarchy independent of the warden. The former insurgents are the prison celebrities, commanding the respect of fellow inmates and even some of the guards, who still spoke of Zarqawi with grudging respect. I was told that the current prison boss was a middle-aged terrorist named Abdullah, who was convicted of blowing up movie theaters in Afghanistan. The inmates called him their *emir*—"prince" in Arabic. "Godfather" would have fit better.

Abdullah agreed to meet with us in a guard's office, a comfortable room befitting his stature here: a desk, a leather couch, and coveted air-conditioning. He walked into the room with the air of a mafia don, without a guard or handcuffs. No one, in fact, seemed to be wearing handcuffs here—and there were certainly none of the leg irons or orange jumpsuits of Guantanamo. With a charming smile, Abdullah said, *"Ehlen-wah-sahlen"*—"welcome"— and sat down quietly next to me, fingering his prayer beads. He was short and chubby, and moved around the room with the deliberate pace of a man with time to burn—in his case, another fifteen years. He exuded confidence and comfort: an easy smile, a glint in his eye. I wondered how he managed to stay so well groomed in prison: manicured fingernails, close-cropped beard, carefully pressed white robe. His refined appearance belied his crime: recruiting young men to blow up movie theater audiences for indulging in a form of entertainment he saw as an affront to Islam. I pictured his victims: Afghan men who would have seen a movie ticket as a small luxury. I imagined them enjoying the sights and sounds, and then would come fire, smoke, and chaos.

"Where are you from?" he asked. When I said New York, I watched for his reaction. Whenever I meet Al-Qaeda members, I sense their grim satisfaction at the fact that my home was the scene of Al-Qaeda's greatest triumph. Something approaching, "You know what we can do. I don't have to explain this to you." I saw his eyes light up, then our conversation turned to more mundane things. He had four children. His family visited him several times a week, bringing him home-cooked food and new photographs of the kids. They have special rooms for that here: wide, cafeteria-style halls for quality time with the family, another perquisite I'd never imagined in a prison for terrorists. I wondered if the emir's privileges included conjugal visits. I later found out they did.

My interrogator friend was getting impatient. Looking around the room with the smile of someone about to tell a good joke, he asked me, "Do you want to know what his bombers were like?"

"One of his bombers walked into the theater," he said, "but he had a problem. When he brought *his* bomb into the cinema, he actually liked the movie. It was an Indian film and he couldn't get enough of it. So he decided to stick around for a while, the bomb under his seat between his legs. He was laughing. He was singing along to the songs. He was flirting with the Indian female star." Even the emir was smiling now. "And then he lit a cigarette. Boom!" The bomb went off, blowing off the bomber's legs. One theater destroyed. One dense bomber horribly injured. They all laughed. Everyone, apparently, likes a good war story.

After a few minutes, Abdullah turned toward the doorway and gave an approving nod. Yildar and another prisoner he introduced as Mustafa walked in. Each was disarmingly polite. At about five-feet-eight and chubby, Yildar cut anything but an intimidating figure. He was noticeably awkward, like the kid chosen last in gym class. And with light, freckled skin and reddish hair, he looked more European than Middle Eastern. He would have fit right in at an American shopping mall, with his lazy gait and baggy jeans. Looking at his sweatshirt again, I thought how Nike would shudder to see its logo worn proudly at Swaqa.

We were not allowed to film inside the maximum-security wing, so we sat down in an empty cell in a medium-security wing housing the common criminals. Surrounded by the murderers and rapists, I felt oddly comfortable with the terrorists. For the moment, they felt less threatening. I would have been an ideal target for them in Baghdad, but here I was their chance to preach to an American audience.

Leaning back on the bed, Yildar told me his path to the

insurgency began on a bus. Just after the invasion in 2003, he simply hopped the express from Amman to Fallujah to join the new holy war against the Americans. There was no mysterious and sophisticated underground network orchestrated by Al-Qaeda, but just a teenager and twenty bucks. Yildar didn't join Al-Qaeda. What he joined was a makeshift army of volunteers.

"Al-Qaeda is not an open restaurant," Yildar told me. "Not everyone can join. They choose special people. Al-Qaeda is not interested in having just anyone."

I was most interested in *why* he chose to fight. He told me his decision had been fairly spontaneous. Growing up in Jordan, he did not frequent a radical mosque, and his family was not religiously conservative. But when he saw Americans invading a Muslim country, he told me he was surprised by how viscerally he reacted. He was sick and angry. He said he and his fellow fighters saw themselves not as terrorists, but as defenders of Muslims against a vast and highly coordinated assault on their faith and culture by the United States, of which the clearest demonstration was the Iraq invasion. He entered Iraq just as the Bush administration's case for war was disintegrating in the fruitless search for weapons of mass destruction.

The U.S.-led invasion became a siren call to young Muslim men. Yildar was one of thousands to volunteer for jihad in Iraq. In April 2006, the National Intelligence Estimate, a compilation of reports and analysis by thirteen American intelligence agencies, found that the war was now the main recruiting vehicle for new Islamic extremists, the cause célèbre for jihadists worldwide. Extremist groups use the Internet to motivate recruits, communicating through a vast network of websites. Their favorite publicity tools are the increasingly well-produced videos of insurgent attacks

on U.S. soldiers. While they share an ideology with Al-
Qaeda, they are independent of the organization itself and
outside the direction of Osama bin Laden and his deputies.
In this sense, what brought Yildar to Iraq was less a formal,
from-the-top-down terror organization than a grassroots
Islamist movement. Imagine a jihadist version of Outward
Bound.

The Iraq war inspired a youth movement with appeal
across the Middle East. Wherever I traveled, I found eager
recruits and proud veterans, in a jail like Swaqa and even
right out in the open. In neighboring Syria, I encountered
one former insurgent serving—and still serving today—in
the Syrian army. He was a twenty-nine-year-old soldier
named Mohammed.

Like Yildar, Mohammed was the product of a relatively
liberal, middle class upbringing. His family lived in Damascus, his father a school teacher teaching Arabic, his mother
a housewife. All six of his siblings, including the girls, went
to college. Mohammed studied psychology and had started
a master's course before he went to Iraq. His family was
educated and laid back. He and his brothers and sisters
dated, drank alcohol, and dressed as they liked.

I communicated with Mohammed on his cell phone
from his home in Aleppo in the summer of 2007. At the
time, a friend asked me how I'd tracked him down. Was he
speaking to me on a secure telephone line? A satellite
phone from a cave in the Syrian mountains? I told my
friend that wasn't necessary. Mohammed, unlike Yildar, is
a free man.

When I asked him what had led him to fight, he reeled off
a lengthy list of talking points. He had thought this
through.

"My first reason is a religious one, but the fact that it's

religious does not in any way mean Islamic," he said. "I would have done it if I was Christian or Buddhist or Jewish. Religious teaching says one always must defend one's land. So that was the religious motive, but not necessarily an Islamic one."

Mohammed didn't see himself as a religious fanatic, but as a young man with political convictions. I would hear similar arguments from young people in Lebanon or Egypt, or even from British Muslims in the UK. The battle wasn't about Islam purely as a faith, but as a political entity to be defended.

Ayaan Hirsi, a Muslim member of the Dutch parliament, has described Islamic radicalism as a political ideology, not just a religious one. She bases this in part on her view that Islam has yet to accept the secular state as superseding the religious one. Islam has not had a reformation. Her views are anathema to many Muslims. In 2004, Hirsi and a prominent Dutch film director, Theo van Gogh, made a short film titled *Submission*, about the abuse of women in Islam. Later that year, van Gogh was shot and killed in front of dozens of witnesses on a busy Amsterdam street. Hirsi lives now under constant death threats. Raising the alarm from within can carry a heavy price.

Mohammed, however, sees the threat as coming from the outside. This is the West attacking Islam—pursuing its own interests at the expense of those of Muslims, and at the expense of its own principles.

"The invasion was injustice being brought on Arabs once again," he said. "All of us have grown up learning about injustice brought on Palestine. My generation was never able to do anything about that. This was the chance for me and my generation to take up the cause and take on the root cause, which is America and its support for Israel."

The perceived oppression of the Palestinian people by Israel and America is a rallying cry throughout the Muslim world, cited as an explanation for just about everything that is going wrong in the region. I often tell Arab friends that it absolves Arab people of any responsibility for bettering their lives. Still, Mohammed and others like him feel that by backing Israel as well as disliked Arab regimes such as Egypt, Saudi Arabia, and Kuwait, the United States shares responsibility for those regimes' failures.

"American interests dictate that these regimes stay in power," Mohammed said. "There is a belief that by our going to Iraq and humiliating the U.S. there, ultimately, America will be less able to pressure these various Arab governments, and so people might have more of a say in how their own lives are run, and improve their livelihood."

Mohammed saw the fight as policy with an articulated goal. He was not running to Iraq to die and claim his seventy-two virgins. He, like many others, believed he was volunteering to make a real, measurable difference in geopolitical terms.

"The West operates on the law of the jungle," he said. "Although I don't accept that law, I thought, 'Well, fine, if that's what the West believes in, then let's go to Iraq and try to humiliate America, and make a stand, and perhaps by [our] making a stand, America will take the Arab people more seriously, and not take them for granted as they usually do.'"

How they fought was just as revealing as why. Yildar was not bent on becoming a martyr. He told me he hadn't gone to Iraq to die, but to take on the Americans. In fact, he whispered to me that he was scared—scared to death, in fact, of American firepower. He admitted he felt useless at times, confronting sophisticated tanks and helicopters with just a machine gun. The U.S. army was an intimidating opponent.

"At the beginning, we didn't confront the soldiers," he said. "The war started basically with American airstrikes and tank attacks, so we mainly faced helicopters and tanks. We barely saw American soldiers in the streets. They were mostly behind or inside the tanks, out of our reach. Frankly, I was happy when I didn't have to fight them up close. I'm not sure I would have survived."

Mohammed was scared as well. It was immediately clear that this wouldn't be a boys' adventure.

"We were on our way to Baghdad with more than ninety jihadis on board," Mohammed told me. "I remember I was listening to a report on the BBC's Arabic service about an antiwar protest in Damascus, when at that exact moment our bus was hit by [he thinks] American missiles." He said eighty-seven of those on board were killed. He survived with minor injuries to his hands and forehead, as well as a newfound resolve to fight.

"We were far outmatched by American firepower," he said. "And a lot of the weapons America was using in Iraq were experimental, as if America was trying out its latest military gadgets on the mujahideen."

This is one of many popular myths among jihadis, part of a wider collection of conspiracy theories in the region, highlighted by the most elaborate: that the United States and Israel staged 9/11 to justify the invasions of Afghanistan and Iraq. They're built on a deep-seated belief in America's nefarious intentions, and on profound awe at America's technological prowess. In reality, many things in the U.S. arsenal might appear like "experimental weapons" to inexperienced jihadis on the ground—a deadly accurate and eerily silent, satellite-guided bomb from a high-flying and unseen jet, for instance. Still, these myths are enduring and another sign of just how bad they think we are.

"When I went to Iraq, I went thinking I would probably not return to my family," said Mohammed. "But this was an attempt to bring back a certain amount of dignity which we lacked."

I had encountered reluctant martyrs before. In Saudi Arabia, a soccer team from Jeddah crossed into Iraq together, volunteering for jihad as a single unit. When they arrived, their commanders groomed them as suicide bombers. But they didn't want to blow themselves up. They wanted to take shots at American soldiers. Realizing they were headed for martyrdom, they turned around and went home, where they were captured by Saudi intelligence. Like vacationers disappointed with a package tour, they complained to their Saudi interrogators that jihad had let them down.

Listening to Yildar and Mohammed, I searched for signs of madness, or at least evidence that their motivations were nonsensical. They were middle-class young men who had uprooted themselves to fight a far better armed army in a foreign country. They were killers of U.S. soldiers, one imprisoned for his crime, the other running free. But they were not rampaging Islamic fundamentalists. They were boys on what had become an unexceptional mission.

The author Robert Pape did a comprehensive study of suicide campaigns from 1980 to 2003—including those in Lebanon, Chechnya, Sri Lanka, Turkey, Kashmir, and the occupied territories. In his book *Dying to Win: The Strategic Logic of Suicide Terrorism* (Random House, 2006), he found that terror attacks occured almost exclusively in the context of foreign military occupation. He argues that even Al-Qaeda fits the pattern. One of its objectives was the removal of U.S. forces from the Arabian Peninsula—a goal

Al-Qaeda ostensibly achieved when the United States withdrew those forces in 2003. Inspired by the U.S. invasion of Iraq, Yildar and Mohammed had many counterparts in different parts of the world.

Both first arrived in the early days of the insurgency, when it was still a loose group of fighters. "Who told you what to do? Who gave you the orders?" I asked Yildar. "There wasn't much organization when the Americans invaded Iraq. There wasn't a top commander at the beginning." But as the months passed just after the invasion, Yildar watched the insurgency develop from a makeshift collection of former Iraqi soldiers, Al-Qaeda members, and foreign volunteers into something more coordinated. In the late summer of 2003, an Iraqi army officer dismissed by the Americans took command of Yildar's unit. This commander began organizing fighters into a more professional force. He established fighting units and a chain of command, and arranged for a steady flow of arms and ammunition. Keeping the combatants armed was not difficult in Iraq. The country was littered with arms caches left behind by the Iraqi military. Some interpreted this as a sign that the Iraqi army had been laying the groundwork for a postwar insurgency long before the invasion. Iraqi military units hid their weapons in countless stashes across the country to be retrieved—and used with great effect—after "formal combat operations" had ended.

I had seen hints of what was in store while embedded with U.S. Special Forces during the invasion. We were the first American forces to enter Kirkuk the day the city fell in early April 2003—racing in with little more than a firefight. A few days later we went by an abandoned training camp used by the Fedayeen Saddam, Saddam Hussein's elite death squad. By the time we arrived, the fighters had

melted into the city, leaving behind their elaborate cos-
tumes: ski masks, Saddam Hussein lapel pins, and black
helmets seemingly inspired by Darth Vader. Even their
shooting targets were shaped like U.S. soldiers. But they
had not left behind a single weapon. At the time, Saddam's
most feared fighting unit looked to have been a paper tiger,
but once the insurgency began, many of the same Fedayeen
Saddam served as Yildar's fellow fighters and commanders.

The insurgents had other help. Yildar said they received
generous support from Iraqi civilians, including food,
money, and housing. I said they must have contributed out
of fear, but Yildar said their support was voluntary.

"We got all of this because we were fighting in the name
of Allah," he said. "And if you are [taking part] in jihad,
God will take care of you."

Gradually the insurgency became more international.
Yildar met fellow fighters from all over the world: the
Middle East, France, and Britain. He said he'd even fought
alongside two Muslims who he believed were American.

"Were you amazed to see Americans fighting Americans?" I asked him. "Yes," he replied. "One of the American insurgents told me he had a brother in the U.S. Army
who didn't want to fight in Iraq because he knew his
brother was [an insurgent] on the other side." His story
could be a battlefield myth, though the U.S. military says it
is possible that some insurgents lived in America at one
time. European intelligence agencies have broken up several terror cells that recruited European Muslims to fight in
Iraq.

Mohammed was battle-tested in Iraq. He says he fought
more than two dozen engagements with U.S. forces in and
around Baghdad.

"What really shocked me was to see the Iraqi army not

even willing to put up a fight," he said. "The burden of resistance was on the shoulders of the mujahideen."

His job was to fire rocket-propelled grenades (RPGs) at U.S. tanks and armored vehicles.

"I believe I killed Americans when I hit several tanks," Mohammed said. His claim is impossible to verify. Was this a jihadi's bravado? Still, I wondered which of the young men and women on the growing roster of American military dead might be there as a result of his actions.

"We would hit the tanks," he said. "Each would require several hits before we destroyed it."

Mohammed said he and the other fighters believed the tank crews would usually survive the strikes, but stay inside rather than risk capture, even as the tanks burned.

"We heard gossip that Americans were terrified of being captured," he said. "Because they'd heard we would cut them up. Apparently the Americans even believed we would eat the bodies of captured soldiers."

Their view of the battlefield was filled with the urban legends of war. One rumor was that many U.S. soldiers were illegal immigrants from Latin America who were given citizenship in exchange for fighting in Iraq. Mohammed said he and others saw them as mercenaries, so they took special satisfaction in killing soldiers they believed were Latino. Another claim made by former insurgents and repeated on Islamist websites is that the United States covered up many battlefield casualties, reducing the official American death toll.

"At the end of every battle, the Americans would do their best to erase any sign of an American army presence," he said. "When there were casualties, they would make sure nothing was left behind. We even saw Americans picking up shoelaces."

This claim gained some currency in the mainstream. Muslim friends have asked me why I thought the Bush administration banned photographs of military coffins returning home. It is one more uncorroborated rumor, but it is also a measure of diminishing American credibility.

Mohammed said he looked at American soldiers with pity.

"When I saw bodies of Americans, I felt bad for them— bad because they were coming to Iraq because of Bush's policies and Bush's big lie about weapons of mass destruction," he said. "But we had a duty to defend the country, defend Muslims, and if that meant fighting them and killing them, then so be it."

Yildar left Iraq in late 2003 and returned home, a hero to the few friends he told about his experience. I asked him directly if he believed he killed American soldiers; he refused to answer. With his Jordanian interrogators listening, I sensed he didn't want to dig himself a deeper legal hole. In 2004, acting on a tip, Jordanian police arrested him and sent him to Swaqa. But his sentence seemed better suited for a shoplifter than for a former insurgent. When I met him, he was six months away from completing a two-year term.

Mohammed left Iraq in 2003 as well. But, unlike Yildar, he was able to return to his life in Jordan unpunished. He says he got away with a swift questioning by Syrian security forces.

"I wasn't berated," he said. "They just wanted to know my reasons for going to Iraq."

In the end, he was told that he might better serve his country by staying at home.

"Because Syria might be the next target," he added.

At the time, that was not an outlandish prospect. In the

view of some in the Middle East and the United States, Syria—with its untested president, Bashar Assad, and weak military—was a "low-hanging fruit," an easy grab in the short-lived euphoria following swift victory in Iraq. "Perhaps I wouldn't have to leave home for this next chance to fight the Americans," Mohammed said.

If Yildar and Mohammed were low-level fighters, the next man I met at Swaqa, Mustafa, was far more senior. According to U.S. and Jordanian intelligence, he was one of a tight circle of lieutenants to Abu Musab al-Zarqawi. His job was to recruit and train fighters for Al-Qaeda in Iraq, some of the most devoted and ruthless members of the insurgency. His demeanor was every bit as intimidating as the charges against him. Tall and imposing, he had the build and face of a boxer, his nose crooked and scarred. He was darker-skinned than Yildar, with a scraggly beard and a muscular physique. I was prepared to interview a thug. But I found him far more calculating.

As we sat down on adjacent prison bunk beds, Mustafa looked back at me with the calm, emotionless stare I recognized from other encounters with captured Al-Qaeda fighters. In a northern Afghan prison just after the war, one of them had told me with a smile that, as an American, I deserved to die. It is a look of both complete confidence and unmistakable disdain. I sensed that Mustafa saw me as someone who had no understanding of the true order of things. As an American, I'd learned early in encounters like this to abandon any natural assumption that we're seen as the good guys. Men like Mustafa never considered any such notion as that we had invaded Iraq to bring about democracy, or that we had a system of government to aspire to. I was looking at someone who saw America simply as the enemy, and an enemy on an irreversible downward spiral, hurtling toward a fate ordained by God. Even after years of traveling the Middle East, it is still a difficult adjustment for me to make. I knew he was someone the United States had lost long before the Iraq invasion, but I worried that the war might have made him stronger. He was a recruiter for Al-Qaeda, and our invasion had given him the ultimate recruiting tool.

Mustafa, like any good propagandist, understood the power of a widely distributed sound bite. And so an interview with an American reporter might serve some purpose. In that sense, for the moment, we served each other's interests. And that's how he and I—an American from New York and an Al-Qaeda recruiter from Jordan—found ourselves sitting across from each other in a maximum-security prison, on gaily decorated, floral-patterned bedspreads.

After several years of detention by the Jordanians, Americans, and Iraqis, interrogations had became sport for Mustafa. When I began by asking him how he had recruited foreigners to fight in Iraq, he accused me of being a CIA agent: "This question is an investigator's question. It's a CIA question." Conspiracy theory number one for jihadis: all American reporters are working for the U.S. government.

Mustafa had the odd distinction of having been arrested by both Saddam Hussein and the American military. Mustafa went to Iraq before the U.S. invasion to fight Saddam's regime, one of a hardened group of Islamists who saw Iraq as far too secular and a target for regime change, Al-Qaeda-style. Regardless of suggestions by the Bush administration, Saddam Hussein was on the Al-Qaeda hit list. Sitting there next to this veteran of two Iraq insurgencies, I realized that there was a moment before the war when he and the U.S. government shared a common goal in Iraq.

"I was accused of being involved with Al-Qaeda," he

said. "So I was arrested by Saddam Hussein's forces before the war. They accused me of being the link between Abu Musab al-Zarqawi and the other Iraqis."

After the invasion, Mustafa was one of the thousands of prisoners Saddam freed from prison in an effort to spark chaos. In Mustafa's case, the tactic worked. U.S. forces became his new target, and Abu Musab al-Zarqawi, the soon-to-be leader of Al-Qaeda in Iraq, his new commander.

"The Iraqi people saw the Americans killing their kids, their wives, and then they saw Zarqawi killing the ones who were killing their kids and wives," he said. "He was fighting the American occupation."

Mustafa said the war had made his job as a recruiter easy. The U.S. invasion was a powerful rallying cry.

"Fighters from Saudi Arabia and from Jordan and from Syria believe that the Americans came to Iraq not only because they wanted to remove Saddam and fight Iraqis. They believed that Iraq was the gateway to their own countries," he said. "Bush claims that he is fighting for justice; I don't think even his wife believes that. No one believes America wants to establish democracy and stability in the region."

The suspicions are endemic. In the occupied territories, the belief is Israeli settlements are part of a U.S.-sanctioned policy to oppress the Palestinians. In Afghanistan, some are beginning to see the widening terrorist violence as part of an American plot to extend the occupation. As an American, I learned to drop any expectation that people would give us the benefit of the doubt.

Equally as motivating as the occupation itself were accounts of American atrocities in Iraq. For an Al-Qaeda recruiter, the killings at Haditha and the prisoner abuse at Abu Ghraib were powerful motivational tools. Photographs and accounts were widely distributed on Islamist websites. They were shared in mosques by radical and moderate imams alike. And they became the source of café conversation across the Muslim world. To Americans, they were mistakes deserving of outrage and perhaps criminal charges, but otherwise they were simply a sad by-product of war. To Mustafa's recruits, they were not exceptions, but the rule—official U.S. policy.

"I was witness to a clash between the mujahideen and the Americans," Mustafa told me, his voice growing louder. "One Iraqi fighter threw two bombs at an American vehicle, and then he managed to run away. The Americans' response was so ugly. They shot and killed innocent people who were not involved in the attack. This makes us all feel that we are part of the conflict."

Iraq is played by a skewed set of rules. Just as the United States can win the vast majority of engagements but still lose the war, U.S. soldiers can also take every precaution to limit civilian casualties—against an enemy that explicitly targets civilians—but still be perceived as equally brutal, and not just clumsily so, but intentionally.

The military would soon add the ultimate badge of courage to Mustafa's résumé. He was a prisoner at Abu Ghraib during the height of prisoner abuse there in 2003 and 2004. Abu Ghraib was a seminal event in cementing opposition to the invasion. Today the images of Muslim prisoners hooded, stripped naked, and threatened by dogs—with American soldiers smiling at their side—remain powerful.

Pointing to his scars, Mustafa claimed he was beaten and tortured, citing a long list of now-familiar techniques: waterboarding, sleep deprivation, extreme cold, and (unforgettably for him) public humiliation. In one of the most devastating photographs of abuse at Abu Ghraib—the "human pyramid" of naked men—Mustafa could point himself out right there next to a smiling Lynndie England. Mustafa now had unassailable "street cred" among young potential recruits.

Americans back home might debate how much sleep they would lose over Mustafa's harsh treatment. But sitting next to him in a prison cell in Jordan, I could feel how his hatred had been intensified by his experience.

"Anyone who faces the American occupation and American torture would hate them," he said. "Personally, wouldn't you, if you had been treated that way?"

The connection between torture and terrorism is another theme debated in the Middle East. Some trace today's jihadist movement back to the 1960s dungeons of Nasser's Egypt, where Islamists were tortured and even killed. How, the Egyptian prisoners asked, could fellow Muslims willfully harm them? Their answer was that their guards and the leaders behind them were not really Muslims at all. Since some Muslims interpret certain passages of the Koran as saying that the blood of non-Muslims can be shed, the groundwork for jihad was laid. Mustafa had been lost long before his time at Abu Ghraib, but I wondered if we needed to give him any more convincing.

Abu Ghraib further polarized debate over the invasion in the Muslim world, convincing even some moderates that the United States was there to destroy rather than build a country. But, on the ground, the war was changing in even more dramatic ways. This was no longer solely a battle between insurgents and coalition forces, but an increasingly self-destructive civil war—with some insurgent groups targeting Iraqis in a deliberate and ultimately successful attempt to foment civil war: Shiites killing Sunnis, Sunnis killing Shiites.

When I asked the former fighters if today's Iraq resembled what they had fought for, I watched their confidence wane.

Mustafa, who is a Sunni, blamed the Shiites.

"[The Shiites] think that they have a right to Baghdad," he said. "So they think they can get their right by taking revenge on any Sunni. That is how the conflict started between the Sunnis and the Shiites." His answer was predictable. But when I asked him about Al-Qaeda's ruthless slaughter of Shiites, in part to spark revenge attacks and perpetuate the cycle of violence, he fell uncharacteristically silent.

Mohammed was proud of performing his duty, but gravely disappointed with the results, frustrated as the unified and heroic mujahideen he had imagined disintegrated into infighting between competing factions.

"When I first went to Iraq, it was one enemy," he said. "But within that month it was no longer one enemy but many enemies: different units of the Iraqi army fighting each other, different segments of the Iraqi population fighting each other. This was a Sunni-Shiite battle."

He had seen the early signs of what Iraq would become.

"In the end, they weren't fighting with the Americans, but just to survive," he said. "There was no longer a reason for me to stay."

When I asked Yildar if this was what he was fighting for, he responded with surprising candor and some defensiveness.

"Of course not, this was not our aim," he said. "But it happened because of other Arab countries' involvement in Iraq. Iran, Syria, and others all believe that they have claims on Iraq."

I smiled at the thought that this was one point on which Yildar and the White House agreed.

Would a new White House administration sap their will to fight? How much of a difference would it make in the eyes of these young jihadis when President Bush, the lightning rod of anti-American emotions in the Middle East, left office? These questions were central to my own fears about America's future in the region. New leaders might disavow Bush's foreign policy, but U.S. troops would remain in Iraq and Afghanistan long after he left office.

"In 2003, my anger was mainly at the Bush administration for taking America to war in Iraq," Mohammed told me. "It wasn't against Americans, but then, to our surprise, Bush gets reelected [in 2004]. Americans had seen the atrocities being committed in Iraq. What option do we have but to feel hatred toward Americans?"

In Mohammed's view, the legacy of both the man and the policy is enduring. The debate over withdrawal from Iraq leaves future American leaders with a Hobson's choice: stay and prolong a loathed occupation of a Muslim land, or leave and condemn the country to a chaotic future that many in the region will blame on the United States.

"Withdrawal is not enough now," Mohammed told me in the summer of 2007, as the first Republicans were starting to abandon President Bush's position on the war. "What's the point of withdrawing and leaving a country completely destroyed? America needs to wake up and stop acting as the world's policeman. America should take a back seat now."

So what would make a difference? "First, Americans need to make an unequivocal apology to the Iraqi people," he said.

"Second, solve Israel-Palestine in a just way," he said. "As long as that doesn't get resolved, nothing gets resolved in the region."

Here was a former insurgent, from a country known to

sponsor terrorism in Lebanon and Iraq, repeating the arguments made by diplomats in Europe and even in America. Again, Mohammed did not believe he was fighting for a return of a Muslim caliphate across Muslim lands; he believed he was fighting for a change in policy.

"The onus is on the Americans to take the initiative," he said. "If the Americans want us to be more positive toward them, it's on the Americans to take that initiative first, and to show us with their actions that this love is reciprocal."

I did not expect "love" to work its way into a former insurgent's diatribe against America. But many Muslims I meet have immensely complex feelings about America: resentment mixed with admiration turned sour by deep disappointment. For me, this is cause for both worry and hope—worry that the United States has lost something valuable, and hope that it may still gain it back. It adds urgency to the battle in places where our admirers still outnumber our detractors, such as Afghanistan and, to a surprising degree, Iran.

Still, there are many in the region, including Mohammed, who have little confidence America will ever get it right.

"This is all talk because whatever America does, it will not succeed for two reasons," he said. "For one, America views people in this part of the world as eighth-class citizens. They're only a source of wealth and strategic needs for America. Their only function is to provide wealth for America, and America does not see any reason these people should have any control over their own resources. Second, America has reached its peak and is probably on its way down, so whatever it does, it might be too late."

The United States is fighting dual enemies: a loss of faith

both in American intentions and in the power of American influence.

THE SUN WAS shining as I left Swaqa. An endless blue sky stretched out over the prison grounds and the desert beyond. On the back of my notebook, I quickly jotted down the rough arithmetic of the insurgency. Jordan holds about one hundred captured insurgents. U.S.- and Iraqi-run prisons in Iraq hold several hundred more. Several dozen captured fighters are held in their home countries, such as Saudi Arabia and Kuwait. The U.S. military estimates that thousands more have been killed in fighting in Iraq. But intelligence analysts estimate that each year thousands of new volunteers replace them. Today the math is not in our favor. Terrorism was never a zero-sum game. And if many of the volunteers are like Yildar or Mohammed, the pool of new recruits for jihad is frighteningly large.

On leaving the prison, I returned to a thought that had frightened me since I first arrived in the Middle East four years earlier. From the moment a U.S.-led invasion of Iraq became a possibility, I had witnessed firsthand every stage of the gathering conflict: the ominous prewar warnings of a great Muslim backlash, the excitement after the lightning-quick invasion, the bungled nation-building, the immense chaos of civil war, and the fragile calm after the American troop surge. I worried that the best-case scenario was a low-level war. Now I wanted to know whether the war was going to follow me home. Had the war inspired a new generation of men and women to kill Americans—whether we were traveling the world or walking the streets of Washington and New York? U.S. and European intelligence agencies had already answered yes, concluding in intelligence reports that the Iraq War had expanded the appeal of jihad.

For me, the troublesome model was the Soviet invasion of Afghanistan. For the last twenty years we have been able to trace almost every major terrorist attack back to the last great Western military misadventure in the Muslim world. Al-Qaeda's senior leaders built their reputations fighting the Soviets. Al-Qaeda itself was incubated during the occupation, aided by the United States. Since then, the architects of the September 11 attacks, the Madrid train bombings, and the Bali nightclub explosion all received training in Afghan terror camps. In the future, how many terror attacks will we be able to trace back to Iraq?

To me, after meeting Yildar, Mohammed, and Mustafa, Iraq was beginning to look like my generation's Afghanistan. The question seemed to be not whether the war would follow me, but how far. European intelligence agencies were intently focused on tracking the movement of jihadis from Iraq westward. They had already thwarted attacks in Europe planned by militants originating in Iraq. Other former insurgents had staged attacks in Algeria and Lebanon. Would these three jihadis be a danger again someday?

Mustafa faced another eighteen years imprisoned in Swaqa. But before the end of our interview, he left me with a parting threat: "If today we see explosions in Iraq, tomorrow we will see explosions in Jordan and in Syria and beyond." He clearly relished the chance to convey a frightening message.

Mohammed was a free man. With bravado, he vowed he'd do it all over again.

"Any other country, if it was invaded by the U.S., I'd do exactly the same thing," he said. "It doesn't have to be an

Arab nation. If it's being unfairly attacked by America, I'd do the same thing. It's a matter of principle."

Yildar was set to be released in just six months. Like many captured insurgents, he served a prison sentence that was shorter than an American soldier's tour of duty in Iraq. As I left, I asked him what he would do when he was released. He checked to see if the guards were listening, and then whispered to me, "I will keep fighting."

That's the rallying cry for many young Muslims: To live free of America, we must fight.

LEBANON

CHRISTIANS FOR HEZBOLLAH

WHEN I VISITED them just before Christmas 2007, half the members of the Lebanese parliament were prisoners—albeit in a "jail" with turn-down service, satellite TV, and the best spa in Beirut. The politicians, all members of the pro-democracy camp, had become permanent guests at the Intercontinental Hotel, taking refuge from a spate of violence. Between 2005 and 2007, more than half a dozen pro-democracy politicians were blown up on the streets of the Lebanese capital—whittling down their majority in parliament one car bomb at a time. Twenty years after the end of Lebanon's bloody civil war, politics is still street warfare.

Inside, the men lived behind layers of security and away from their families, leaving the building only for parliamentary sessions, and then they traveled in huge armored convoys. Forty grown men whiled away the days conducting some government business, but otherwise they played cards, drank coffee, and watched television. One of the MPs, Mohammed Kabbani, told me he'd never had time before to watch TV. Now he had seen all six seasons of *24* on DVD.

"I'd better not be here for season seven," he told me and laughed.

They had a cushy captivity, but they had real reason to be scared. I was there for the first assassination in the series. On Valentine's Day 2005, a massive car bomb killed Rafik Hariri, a former prime minister turned billionaire business-man, who led the pro-democracy bloc. It was the biggest car-bomb explosion I had ever seen, bigger than anything I'd witnessed in thirteen trips to Iraq. It left such a huge crater in the street that at first investigators thought the explosives had been buried under the pavement. The blast shattered windows for several blocks around, and left the streets covered with a layer of broken glass. Hariri's heavily armored limousine sat in the middle of the street, burned, broken against the force of the blast, as fragile as a child's toy.

His death sparked another street battle, but this one was a contest in pure numbers: Who could pull more people into the streets to demonstrate their support? The pro-western faction, led by Hariri, or the groups aligned with Iran and Syria, represented by Hezbollah?

The pro-democracy gatherings began with Hariri's funeral, on February 16, 2005. I wandered among the hun-dreds of thousands of Lebanese who had flooded the streets to honor a man they described as a national hero. Church bells rang in unison with a Muslim call to prayer. The funeral was a Muslim ceremony, but the crowd, like Lebanon, was a mix of Shiite and Sunni Muslims, Chris-tians, and Druze. They had fought each other viciously in the civil war. On that day the mourners were united in their anger at Syria, whom they blamed for his murder. I heard men chanting, "We want our revenge on [Syrian pres-ident] Bashar Assad!"

I met Nayla Moawad, a Lebanese politician whose husband, René Moawad, was himself assassinated by a car bomb in 1989, just seventeen days after being elected president. In Lebanon, death and politics go hand in hand.

"I think there is a genuine feeling among most of the Lebanese, a feeling of being fed up," she told me. "We are fed up with repression. We are fed up with humiliation. We want to rule ourselves."

Mixing among the crowd, I believed her. There was excitement and purpose in the air. I remember thinking that this was what a 1960s civil rights march must have felt like: a sense that this is our time.

A young mother holding the hand of her ten-year-old son told me, "It's a historic moment. I even took my son out of school because I didn't want him to miss history."

This was a special cut of Lebanese society: educated, relatively well off, many with foreign, especially American, passports. Some looked lifted from the pages of glossy magazines: jet-black hair, flashy sunglasses, the latest fashions. After the protest, many walked toward some of the sparkling new cafés on Martyrs' Square. It once marked the "green line" between warring militias during the civil war. Now it is full of fine restaurants and expensive boutiques housed in turn-of-the-century buildings, carefully restored by Hariri. Inside an outlet of Paul, the famous Parisian café, I ordered a latte surrounded by people still wearing the red-and-white scarves representing the flag of Lebanon. It was the best-dressed protest I had ever seen.

The protests quickly captured the imagination of American officials and journalists. The demonstration fit right in, it seemed, with other democratic victories in the Middle East and beyond: the "Rose Revolution" in Georgia, named after the red roses protesters gave government soldiers; the "Orange Revolution" in the Ukraine, named for the orange flags that came to identify anti-Russian protesters; and what some had taken to calling the "Purple Revolution" in Iraq, after the purple ink used to stain the thumbs of voters in Iraq's national elections just a few weeks earlier. There was even a "Tulip Revolution" in Kyrgyzstan. It was U.S. Undersecretary of State for Global Affairs Paula Dobriansky who gave Lebanon's protest its name: the "Cedar Revolution," after the cedar tree at the center of the Lebanese flag. Lebanon, it seemed, was yearning for an anti-Syrian, pro-American democracy.

But we'd spoken too quickly. The next month, it was the green flag of Hezbollah that dominated the streets. Just a block from the anti-Syrian protests, Hezbollah held its own demonstration with the contradictory message: for Syria and against American interference in Lebanon.

Hezbollah supporters flooded into downtown Beirut. Roads from Hezbollah neighborhoods in the south were jammed with traffic. City streets were swollen with people. By early afternoon, Hezbollah followers outnumbered the Cedar Revolution.

This was a different crowd. Many women were wearing the veil; many men had long beards. Hezbollah fighters dressed in black were out in equal numbers with Lebanese police. Many of these supporters would not be going to Café Paul afterward for lattes.

I asked one woman what brought her there.

"We don't want the interference of the U.S., of Israel, of France, of any country," she told me.

America? There it was. Syria was not the villain. It was American policy in the Middle East. And for Hezbollah, the Cedar Revolution was a western creation, not their fight.

The rallying cry for Hezbollah leader Sheikh Hassan Nasrallah, who was making a rare visit to central Beirut from the Hezbollah stronghold in the south, was a loud "Down with America."

"We will defeat the Americans and their fleets if they come to Lebanon," he shouted from a stage overlooking the vast crowd.

I stood in the middle of the crowd to take in its sheer size. It was overwhelming, almost suffocating. This was Hezbollah's "million-man march" and unlike other aspiring "million man" rallies in the United States, this one actually hit its target.

Which was the real Lebanon? These two crowds seemed to be the dividing line. The Cedar Revolution set—liberal-minded, pro-American, anti-Syrian, and peaceful—versus the Hezbollah faithful: Shiite Muslim, religiously conservative, for Syria and against America.

But I was wrong a second time. Hezbollah's message of resistance to America appealed beyond their Shiite power base. Among the Hezbollah supporters that day was a young woman who looked as though she had taken a wrong turn. She was Christian, with grandparents in California and a college degree from Canada. She was westernized in both her dress and social views, but she, like Nasrallah, saw her country's real enemy far away in America.

"Basically, the U.S. wants to take Lebanon officially under its wing, to become its protector," said twenty-four-year-old Sara. "The U.S. has not learned from its mistakes, in the same way as it never learned from the mistakes of Vietnam. All these have been the result of the imperial arrogance."

Here in Lebanon, I was discovering something new: anti-Americanism not as a religious cause, but as a pan-Arab nationalist movement—our people against yours, our nations against your superpower. There was some truth to this contrarian view of Hezbollah. Lebanon is the only majority-Muslim state with a system based on power-sharing with a Christian minority. And here was part of that minority, throwing its support firmly behind what I'd thought was a purely Shiite Muslim cause.

"The Cedar Revolution was American-inspired bull-shit," she said.

Ironically, Sara looks like the cover girl for the Cedar Revolution set. She wears Diesel jeans and hip T-shirts. With her light eyes and wavy brown hair and her feature-less North American accent, she could easily be identified as an American. Like many Lebanese who can afford it, she went to college abroad, studying computer science and English literature in Canada. Today she is a graduate stu-dent, studying Israeli military strategy. And war is never far from her mind.

"Israel says Arabs never lose an opportunity to lose an opportunity," she told me. "I find this phrase applies more to the Israelis and the Americans."

Sara makes no distinction between Israel and America. To her, Israel serves as a proxy for the United States, a tool of American policy in the Muslim world. And so every Israeli invasion or bombing run might just as well have been delivered by the American military. This is a common view in the region. For many Muslims, Israel is the face of American policy in the Middle East.

Sara is confident in her views, but she is not fearless about the consequences. She hopes someday to study for a PhD in North America, so from the beginning she asked me not to use her real name, and I haven't.

Like every young Lebanese today, she is a child of con-flict. She was born March 23, 1983, the halfway point in the Lebanese civil war and one year into the eighteen-year Israeli occupation of southern Lebanon.

Beirut was then a city of explosive ethnic and religious fault lines. Her family was divided by the war. Their home was in Christian East Beirut, but her father's business—a clothing store—was in Muslim West Beirut, which was then dominated by Sunni Muslims and Palestinians. Violating the division was dangerous.

"They used to kill people by their ID. They would look at your religion and slit your throat if you weren't the right one," she said.

For their family's economic survival, her father stayed with their shop. He had to navigate a volatile mix of competing gangs. Palestinian and Lebanese militias collected protection money. The civil war was a confusing, multi-sided fight. Muslim, Christian, and Druze militias fought each other and internally, factions of each group fought among themselves. Lebanon's deadly divisions were all around them. Even the Christian community was divided between Maronite Catholics and Armenian Orthodox Christians, such as Sara's family.

"My family was not religious in any real sense of the word," she said. "But Christianity was always an important element in the equation of national identity."

During the war, Sara was a child, but she retains vivid memories.

"My memories of the civil war are quite detailed, but not in any way chronological," she said. "I remember the sounds of the bombs and I remember running, almost on a daily basis, to seek shelter in an underground storage depot across the street, and, on one occasion, seeing a tank run over a car that did not heed its warning to get out of its way.

"I remember that bombs and shells hit our building many times," she said. "One hit our kitchen."

The war was all around her, but in a uniquely Lebanese way, people made their lives within it. The fighting followed a bizarre rhythm.

"For me, at that young age, the war felt like a game," she said. "It felt strange to be listening to announcements on the radio that the shelling would resume on such-and-such a day at precisely such-and-such an hour. It did not feel as if the war was 'natural,' but rather an artificial act, a play, put together by a bunch of politicians."

She received an early education in the violent divisions at the root of the fighting. From the outside, the civil war was portrayed as largely Christian versus Muslim. But like nearly everything in the Middle East, the conflict was more complicated. There were Christian, Shia, Sunni, Druze, and Palestinian factions, as well as international involvement by the United States, the Soviet Union, Israel, and more. Over the course of the war, just about every faction had betrayed just about everyone else. Sara remembers the division and hatred. Lebanon's communities were segregated, like some Middle Eastern version of the antebellum South.

"I grew up on extremely hateful and condescending talk about Muslims," she said. "Having never met a Muslim, I drew pictures in my mind of what a Muslim would look like, and entertained vivid images of how he would act. Needless to say, they were all images of filth, poverty—as if poverty was a crime and as if there was anything inherently Muslim about poverty!—and violence."

Today, Sara sees her youthful prejudice as analogous to the way she believes Americans view Muslims today.

"They entertain and teach their children similar ideas

about innate Muslim proneness to violence, theft, disrespect for human rights," she said.

Lebanon's Christians were divided as well, between the
Phalange of Bachir Gemayal and forces loyal to Michel
Aoun, a general in the Lebanese army.

"While they were bombing the civilians under each
other's control, parents in the neighborhood, who were
being bombed, were debating who was the more righteous
one," Sara said.

It was only after the civil war that Sara was able to visit
Muslim West Beirut for the first time. Even within the glaring diversity of Beirut, she had never met a Muslim before.

"I wasn't actively prejudiced. It was more that I had genuine lack of knowledge [about Muslims]," she said. "The
breaking point came after I started to come face-to-face
with Muslims in real-life situations."

Her first encounter with Hezbollah changed her impression for good. She was a seventh-grade student at the
Armenian Evangelical School, when a group of Hezbollah
representatives visited to make a presentation at the school
assembly. This was an emotional time in Lebanon. On
April 18, 1996, Israelis returned fire from Hezbollah fighters and struck the headquarters of the Fijian battalion of
UN peacekeepers in Qana, a small village near the southern city of Tyre. Hundreds of civilians had taken shelter
there, and more than a hundred were killed, according to
UN estimates. Israel accused Hezbollah of using civilians
as human shields. A subsequent investigation by the UN
secretary-general's military adviser found it unlikely the
shelling was accidental. Among Lebanese, Muslims and
Christian alike, the attack became known as the Qana
Massacre.

The Hezbollah representatives had come to show the

students—young Christian girls just entering their teens—
what they were fighting for. This was a remarkable stop on
a Hezbollah propaganda tour. Being there, in the middle of
Christian East Beirut at a Christian evangelical school, was
something like the IRA entering a British school in Northern Ireland during the height of "the troubles" in the 1980s.
But anger at the Qana attack extended beyond Lebanon's
Muslim community.

"I remember the presentation began with the historical
timeline of Israeli occupation, accompanied by images of
destruction and insight into what life was like in the occupation zone—the arrests, the torture, the killings," she said.

Then came the images of the Qana attack.

"There were images of scattered and maimed bodies,"
she said. "They were shocking. I had never seen anything
like it."

Qana has an emotional place in Lebanese hearts and
minds. Some have described it to me as a small-scale version of the September 11 attacks: proof that Israel was willing to kill civilians and to do so, many Lebanese believed,
intentionally. Since Israel had American support, this was
an American crime as well. The pictures Hezbollah showed
that day had their intended effect on this thirteen-year-old
Christian girl. When Hezbollah gave out yellow ribbons to
the children as a reminder of the attack—like the American flag pins many public figures wore in the United States
after 9/11—most of the children removed them. But Sara
kept hers.

"I went home wearing it, and kept it for many years," she
said.

Hezbollah gave her something else that day. They put a
human face on the Muslims she had grown up to hate.
They were real, and they had a mission.

"I started challenging those—including my family—who uttered such condescending talk," Sara said, full of righteous fervor. "Gradually, I started forcing them to admit that people are people, that Muslims do not differ in any way from us, and that the anger and hatred should be directed at foreign leaders and not at Lebanese people, and definitely not based on religion or lower social status."

Sara exchanged one hatred for another that day, replacing the admittedly ignorant hostility she'd felt toward Muslims with a deep-seated resentment of Israel and America. This was more than an adolescent burst of conscience. Sara found something attractive and right in Hezbollah's political message. The key is resistance, to Israel and to Israel's chief ally, America.

An American, hearing the name Hezbollah, hears *terrorism*. A Lebanese hears *resistance*. Hezbollah wears the label with an extra dose of pride because its resistance has been successful. In the eyes of many Arabs inside and outside of Lebanon, Hezbollah has the unique distinction of being the only Arab fighting force to defeat Israel—twice—first by driving Israeli forces out of Lebanon in 2000 after an eighteen-year occupation of southern Lebanon, and then by holding their own in the 2006 Israel-Lebanon war. Describing Hezbollah today, Sara adopts the language of a party manifesto.

"I support it because it is a resistance," Sara said. "And resistance to the oppressor—whatever the nature of the oppression, be it economic, national, or otherwise—is not only a right but also a duty for all peoples. I support Hezbollah because I think that only through the actions of the oppressed will there be an awakening in the countries where the fate of the oppressed, the weak, and the poor is decided upon."

Hezbollah, or "Party of God," was founded in 1982 by Shiite Muslim clerics. Earlier that year the Israeli army had invaded Lebanon, aiming to destroy Palestinian forces which had taken up bases in southern Lebanon and were staging attacks on Israel. Some Lebanese initially welcomed Israeli forces. Yasser Arafat's PLO had become a state within a state, upsetting many ordinary Lebanese. But as the invasion turned into what would become an eighteen-year occupation, the initial welcome faded.

At first, Hezbollah was just one of many factions in the civil war. Inspired by the Iranian revolution three years earlier, its leaders dreamed of establishing an Islamic state in Lebanon. But, over time, Hezbollah became focused on driving Israeli forces out of Lebanon. It soon had the United States in its sights as well. U.S. Marines had entered Lebanon in 1982 as part of a multinational force in Lebanon—the first sizable U.S. military deployment since the Vietnam War. Their mission was to help stabilize Beirut, but the Marines found themselves under fire from several factions.

Hezbollah's attack was the biggest and boldest. On October 23, 1983, a suicide bomber drove a truck packed with 12,000 pounds of explosives into the U.S. Marine barracks near the airport in Beirut. That attack killed 241 American servicemen, the deadliest day for the marines since the battle of Iwo Jima in World War II. U.S. officials said at the time it was the largest non-nuclear blast ever deliberately detonated. Seconds later, another suicide bomber attacked a French military barracks, killing fifty-eight troops.

The bombings put Hezbollah on the map for Lebanon and for America. They also set a new standard for spectacular terror attacks, a model that helped inspire Al-Qaeda. Looking at Hezbollah's tactics in the years that followed, it's hard to imagine clearer examples of pure terrorism.

Throughout the civil war, the group would continue to gain international notoriety by taking western hostages. They captured and held several journalists, sometimes for years. In 1989, Hezbollah kidnapped U.S. Marine lieutenant colonel William R. Higgins, later filming and releasing pictures of his hanging body to the media—again setting an early standard for Al-Qaeda-linked groups. They staged attacks abroad as well. In the 1990s, Hezbollah carried out two bombings outside the Israeli embassy and a Jewish center in Buenos Aires, Argentina. Together, those attacks killed more than a hundred people.

Sara does not, however, single out Hezbollah's brutality from the violence perpetrated by any of a number of armed groups during the civil war.

"What's the difference between Hezbollah bombing Marines and U.S. battleships shelling the mountains around Beirut?" she asks.

More broadly, she believes the United States has been guilty of worse, in Iraq, Palestine, and Lebanon. Sara and I have very different definitions of terrorism. Here is a Christian girl equating Hezbollah's acts of terrorism—suicide bombings, kidnappings, and videotaped hangings—with military action.

There is a schoolyard logic to this. When I bring up Hezbollah's terror attacks to some Lebanese—or mention Hamas's suicide bombings to Palestinians, or Iraqi insurgents' roadside bombs to Iraqis—they raise the issue of American attacks that have killed civilians: the invasion of Iraq itself, as well as any number of bombing runs or raids that produced "collateral damage," even if the civilian deaths were unintentional casualties (a concession few here make easily). Our mistakes, in effect, justify Hezbollah's and other terror groups' raison d'être.

But there is also a deep philosophical difference. Terror attacks, even to this young Christian, are seen as the only way—and therefore an acceptable way—for a small force to challenge American military might, which they believe the United States exercises without moral or legal authority. Terror attacks that intentionally rather than accidentally kill civilians, the logic goes, are unfortunate, but not damning, considering Hezbollah's noble cause. I learned to dismiss the thought that support for terrorism arises purely from a misguided interpretation of Islam.

In Lebanon, it was Hezbollah's attacks on the occupying Israeli forces that truly defined it. Hezbollah was credited with forcing Israel's slow withdrawal—first to a so-called security zone in the south and then out of the country entirely in 2000.

Some Israeli leaders would later acknowledge it was the occupation that had given rise to this new and formidable enemy. "When we entered Lebanon . . . there was no Hezbollah," said former prime minister Ehud Barak. Yitzhak Rabin, the Israeli prime minister assassinated in 1995, decried how the invasion had "let the Shiite genie out of the bottle."

Sara gloats at Israel's troubles, again sounding like a Hezbollah propagandist.

"Hezbollah demonstrated what the oppressed can do if they set it in their minds to fight and die for a cause rather than live on their knees, and because it has demonstrated to the peoples of the world the power of the weak and the weakness of the powerful," Sara said.

The words sounded as if they had been lifted from an Osama bin Laden video. I wanted to dismiss them as the musings of a somewhat sanctimonious young student activist. But the logic—like the perception of Hezbollah as resistance fighters rather than terrorists—is commonplace. It is again that paradoxical combination of hating American power and grudgingly respecting it, if only in the sense that the United States controls everything without regard for Muslims' needs.

After the civil war, Hezbollah began to transform itself from a terrorist group to the full-fledged political organization that it is today. By then it had abandoned its goal of establishing an Islamic state, realizing that the idea was a nonstarter for the vast majority of Lebanese. Instead it focused on driving out Israeli forces as well as creating a powerful, conservative religious political bloc representing Lebanon's Shiite Muslims. Hezbollah released the last of its Western hostages in 1992.

Since then, Hezbollah has certainly kept its military wing, with thousands of well-trained and highly disciplined fighters. When I was on assignment covering the huge Hezbollah demonstrations in central Beirut in 2005, Hezbollah fighters outnumbered policemen. They were the law. When we tried to film Nasrallah near the podium, six men dressed head-to-toe in black surrounded my camera crew and me, and forced us into the lobby of a nearby building.

"What do you think you are doing?" one of them shouted at us in Arabic.

As the guards locked the lobby doors, they told us we had put the leader's life in danger. I've been detained and harassed for filming in several Middle Eastern countries. I doubted this was going to be more than a detention for show. American reporters are too much trouble to hang on to. But I marveled at their sense of authority and control.

The guards made several calls on their cell phones. After an hour, I watched their faces relax. They smiled and offered me tea, then took our tape and sent us back into the crowd. We were free, but their point was made: Hezbollah was in charge here.

Today, Hezbollah is more than a militia. It has twelve serving members of parliament and a huge network of social support. Its welfare program may be its greatest political asset. Hezbollah runs schools, free health clinics, and job-training programs. In the wake of the 2006 war, Hezbollah has even served as a sort of insurance company, handing out millions of dollars to Lebanese whose homes were destroyed. The going rate: $14,000 per house, $10,000 if the occupants were renters. It's believed that much of the money comes from Iran.

In effect, Hezbollah is doing what the Lebanese government has often failed to do. And, throughout, it has earned a reputation for avoiding the corruption that infects the official state system. It may come as a surprise to Americans, but to Lebanese, Hezbollah is not just clean—it is the *only* clean party. And that is one way it has expanded its support outside its Shiite Muslim base to include Christians.

"I believe Hezbollah is not corrupt at all," Sara told me. "I would prefer them any day over the ruling bunch."

I told her those were brave words, coming from a western-minded Christian woman. Hezbollah is a paragon of fundamentalist Islam. In Hezbollah-controlled areas, no woman walks around without a veil. In more fanatical times, men threw acid in the faces of bareheaded Muslim women. Outward expressions of conservatism persist today. In 2006, Taiwan donated SUVs to mine-clearance teams in southern Lebanon. When Hezbollah fighters found they were inscribed with the words LOVE FROM TAIWAN, they demanded that the word LOVE be scraped off—to preserve proper Islamic morals, they said. Nevertheless,

Sara sees Hezbollah as devoutly nonsectarian, in favor of a Lebanon for all of Lebanon's religions and sects—even more so than what she refers to as "so-called pro-democracy" groups. Sara sounds willfully naïve in her trust, but she is not alone. One of the largest Christian parties, the Free Patriotic Movement of Michel Aoun, has put its faith in Hezbollah as well, joining forces with it to form one of the country's most powerful political blocs.

"Hezbollah just wants their share," she said. "But I don't believe they want a Shiite state. If Hezbollah wanted to impose Islamic rule on all of us, they could have done it by now."

This is a matter of faith, not just in Hezbollah and the resistance it represents, but also in its revered leader, Hassan Nasrallah.

Today, Nasrallah, whose name means "Victory of God," has been elevated to a special status above other Lebanese politicians, analogous in some degree to the way Pope John Paul II was revered as both a religious leader and as the man who stood up to the Soviet Union.

"I would trust Nasrallah over any other Lebanese or Arab politician. Lebanese politics revolves around petty, insignificant issues, certainly not comparable in any way to resistance against Zionism, which is deeply entrenched in the Arab/Muslim soul," she said.

Nasrallah's views, like Hezbollah itself, are more complicated than the caricature. He has harshly criticized the Taliban. In an interview with Robin Wright of the *Washington Post* in July 2006, he called it "the worst, the most dangerous thing that this Islamic revival has encountered." He has also condemned the beheading of hostages by Al-Qaeda in Iraq, saying, "It is unacceptable, it is forbidden, to harm the innocent." He continued, however, to support suicide attacks targeting Israeli civilians, and Hezbollah continued to fire rockets indiscriminately at Israeli cities.

In this sense, his views reflect the attitude of many in the Muslim world, who make a distinction between terror attacks, such as 9/11, and what they call the "resistance," such as Hezbollah rocket attacks on Israel.

"I think he's a very charismatic leader. Very. Unlike any we have seen in the Arab world since Gamal Abdel Nasser. I would even say he is far superior to Nasser," she said.

By the age of twenty-four, Sara had lived all but six years of her life in war. So where did this budding anti-American firebrand escape the violence? America. The source of all evil in the Muslim world was also, apparently, a great place to live and learn. In 2008 she was applying to PhD programs at Columbia and MIT and considering spending time with her grandparents, who live in California. She wanted to study all the things we'd been talking about for months: comparative politics with a focus on the Middle East. She had already earned a college degree in Canada.

She finds the idea that you shouldn't criticize the United States just because you're studying there "ridiculous."

"Should Americans not criticize their own government too, then? Or does that argument only apply to foreigners?" She went further. "This is intellectual terrorism, pure and simple.

"I think of America positively in ways that have nothing to do with politics, like freedom of speech," she said.

This is a distinction many young Arabs make without any feeling of hypocrisy. They do retain admiration for many parts of the American system, including education. America still has some of the best universities in the world, in their view. And there's something almost opportunistic about their willingness to go to America despite their political hostility: *If we can use the American system to make us stronger against America,* they seem to think, *what could be better?*

Sara arrived in North America for the first time in late August 2001: an eighteen-year-old Lebanese, Christian, anti-American college freshman on the eve of 9/11. Her views of the attacks would be as contradictory as her views of America itself.

Ask someone in the Middle East where they were on 9/11, and they will know just as well as any American. As in the United States, it is the Arab world's equivalent of Pearl Harbor, but for different reasons. For Sara, it is the day that the United States elevated the war on the Muslim world to a higher, more fearsome level. She had been a student for just a few days when the planes hit the towers.

"The instantaneous reaction, upon seeing the planes hitting the buildings, was one of shock, disgust, and more generally a feeling of inability to comprehend what I had actually seen," she said.

This didn't surprise me. Despite numerous stories, I have met few people in the region who actually cheered at first sight of the towers coming down. Even some of the most resentful Muslims describe real revulsion that day. But with time to digest the events over the next several weeks, her feelings changed. She felt less compassion and more righteous indignation.

"There most certainly was this sense of agreement with the necessity of turning the world's and the American people's attention to U.S. foreign policy and its monumental, disastrous impact on the lives of the people of the Middle East, and if anything, this attack certainly did aspire to do so and arguably succeeded at it to some extent," she said.

Her coolness was unsettling. "The realization was also there that what was needed was action rather than mere words and protests against [American] injustices," she said.

Thus it was that a Christian in North America, studying at a North American university, found the rationale of the attackers logical. She agreed the method was horrible, "murderous and sinister." But in the same breath she said, "I did see the need for the U.S. to get a taste of its own medicine."

Now, seven years later, her criticism of the attacks is more practical than principled. She sees 9/11 as a failed strategy rather than evil for evil's sake. The plotters did have an admirable goal; they just failed to achieve it.

"Extremely accurate and successful as it might have been, 9/11 in fact delivered a crushing blow to any genuine Arab and Muslim aspirations for bringing about the American awakening that I referred to," she said.

For one thing, America brought the war to the Muslim world with the invasions of Afghanistan and Iraq. Like many Muslims, Sara sees Israel's hand in that strategy, especially in the invasion of Iraq. But the more fundamental change, in her view, was one chief component of President George W. Bush's war on terror—the most important part of the "with us or against us" mantra—that the United States now saw all terrorist groups, regardless of ideology, as the same.

"What 9/11 also did was lend support to the practical elimination of any distinction between resistance and 'terrorism.'" She added quotes in the air for emphasis as she spoke. "In other words, the delegitimization of resistance movements like the Palestinian resistance, Hezbollah, and the legitimization of what I would call state terrorism—all in the name of the global fight against terror."

Sara had hoped 9/11 would awaken America to its failed policy in the Middle East, but in her view the attacks back-fired, bringing even worse misfortune on the Muslim world, including America's new commitment to eliminating Hezbollah as a fighting force.

Traveling in Canada and the United States after 9/11, Sara sensed that people treated her differently, especially on her first visit to the States.

"The whole process of being forced to have facial shots taken in a security screening area in one terminal, then having to make my way to another terminal, made me feel as if I had been to the U.S. on a 'terror'-related trip," she said.

New immigration rules have been an enormous source of bitterness for Muslims. After 9/11, U.S. immigration officers began fingerprinting and photographing foreign arrivals. American embassies in Muslim countries added face-to-face interviews and waits as long as several weeks. The increased visa difficulty—coupled with the perception that foreign students were less welcome—helped spark a drop in the number of international students in the United States, particularly from the Middle East. According to the International Institute of Education, applications from the Middle East fell 10 percent in the 2002–2003 school year and 9 percent in 2003–2004. Some countries, such as Saudi Arabia, Pakistan, and the United Arab Emirates, experienced declines near 30 percent. Enrollment only began to rebound in 2007. For Sara, the visa restrictions meant the United States was practicing racial profiling on a massive scale.

As a regular traveler to the Middle East, I often raise red flags at U.S. immigration, which gives me a glimpse of small but revealing aspects of the new security procedures.

When I was flying home to New York from London for Christmas in 2005, a United Airlines check-in agent noticed an Iraq visa stamp in my passport. Her face fell. She waved to a security officer who escorted me away from the check-in desk, down a hallway, up a few flights of stairs, and down another hallway to a special room with an armed guard outside the door. Inside, I saw six other passengers, all of whom appeared to be of Arab or South Asian descent, and half a dozen police officers rummaging through their luggage. When my turn came, the officers gave my belongings the most extensive inspection I'd ever seen. They unpacked and inspected everything in my bag, sniffed every toiletry item, and even unrolled my socks, sticking their hands inside each one. The search took a full hour. I missed my flight. I shrugged my shoulders at the other passengers sympathetically. They looked back with almost satisfied expressions, as if to say, *Now you see what we have to go through.*

When Sara applied for a visa to visit the United States, she was given an additional interview because she was traveling on a Lebanese passport.

"What appalled me was not so much the fact that I was to be subject to further questioning in a separate area, but that, upon reading my name and finding out I was of Armenian and therefore Christian origin, the interviewing official immediately approved of my visa," she said. "I could not help but link the two. It was too obvious to go unnoticed."

The difference, she believed, was her religion. More and more, America's reaction to 9/11 reminded Sara of the crisis in Lebanon. She recognized the same politics of division she had grown up with during the civil war. In her view, American politicians were using the attacks to create a new enemy of the state, far more widespread than Al-Qaeda. Despite the denials and President Bush's quick retraction of his description of the war as a "crusade," this was in Sara's view us-against-them at its worst.

"What I could not wrap my head around was how so many people in the U.S. could not see this abuse and cheered for the hate-fest that would soon be initiated," she said. "I came to the conclusion that this, too, was a case of politicians riding the wave of identity politics, manipulating people's sensitivities to their own ends."

She saw it in ways many Americans might miss. She had grown up in a country where identity politics played themselves out in a fifteen-year civil war. She recognized the signs. One was the sudden clamp-down on visas from the Arab world. The changes were cloaked in procedural terms, but the results were political: young Muslim men were more dangerous and so they were less welcome. To Sara, it reminded her of the ID checks to which competing militias had subjected her father during the war.

The other shifts were rhetorical. She heard people making distinctions between religions that had formerly been politically incorrect even to imply. It became acceptable, for instance, for Americans to say that violence was part of Islam. There were subtle changes in language as well. In Iraq and Afghanistan, the U.S. military began calling every opposing fighter a terrorist, regardless of whether they targeted American forces, which was justified in her view, or civilians, which she saw as unacceptable. American officials called Egypt, Saudi Arabia, and Jordan, which she considered dictatorships, "moderate" regimes, while Hezbollah, which she saw as an honest representative of the Lebanese people, was an ally of Al-Qaeda.

Waged under the false pretenses of a WMD threat and

unable to secure the promise of democracy, the Iraq War was, to her, the ultimate abomination. And as the occupation took a long and bloody turn, Sara, like many Muslims in the region, took grim satisfaction in American losses. Just as she approved of Hezbollah's attacks on Israeli soldiers during the Israeli occupation of Lebanon, she views the Iraqi insurgency as resistance, not terrorism.

"You can say I feel the U.S. deserves the beating it has received there," she said.

For a time she hoped that the Iraq War would make America rethink its policy in a way that 9/11 had failed to do. But as the war dragged into its fifth year and the U.S. sent in more troops rather than withdrawing, she reached a different conclusion. To her, it seems that America *needs* war.

"The U.S. has not learned, and will not learn for some time to come, from 9/11 and all that followed it," she said.

That is where she stood in March 2005, facing a choice between the American-backed Cedar Revolution and the pro-Hezbollah protests. She did want a revolution, but her heroes were Hezbollah.

"I was all for storming the palace gates," she said. "I was hoping Hezbollah would continue and pick up the momentum and just do something and be done with it."

You wanted a coup? I asked her. Yes, she answered. "If we can't use force, then we won't have any leverage on the political level," she explained.

The 2006 Israel-Lebanon war gave her more proof. On July 12, 2006, a little more than a year after the Hezbollah demonstration, Hezbollah fighters attacked an Israeli patrol on the Israeli side of the Lebanese-Israeli border, killing three soldiers, injuring two more, and taking two others captive. Five more Israeli soldiers were killed when the Israeli military attempted a rescue. Cross-border attacks were common. Hezbollah had used captured soldiers in the past, often successfully, as leverage for the exchange of prisoners held by Israel. The attacks settled into a rhythm. It's widely believed that the two sides even negotiated "ground rules," establishing accepted levels of retaliation for each kind of attack. To Sara and other Hezbollah supporters, the Hezbollah operation fell under those ground rules. For Israel, eight soldiers killed and two held captive was a step too far. Israel responded with a massive air campaign and a small ground invasion. The Israel-Lebanon war was underway.

Sara was one year into graduate school in Beirut when the bombing began. She and her family retreated to their home in Mount Lebanon—a safe distance from southern Beirut, Hezbollah's stronghold and the chief target of Israeli bombing. From her balcony she could see the bombs falling on Beirut and the smoke rising. It was a violent pyrotechnic display. From her balcony perch, she became an underground war reporter.

"I was so angry during the war, so I tried to channel the anger through blogging," she said. "The western media didn't really cover all the details of what was happening."

Sara's blog became a popular source for the latest news of the bombing. She soon had 1,000 unique hits a day, sparking a vibrant interaction between her reports and users' comments. Lebanese outside the country asked about their neighborhoods. Others vented about what she and her readers saw as Israeli and American war crimes. Reading her entries today, I sense she was scared.

(I'm paraphrasing Sara's blog entry to protect her identity.) July 23: "People were watching the World Cup a couple weeks ago, lighting off fireworks. Now they're scared about what's coming. They're hoarding food and supplies. Kids used to show off political party banners on their cars. Now the only cars on the roads are ones taking people out of town. My father's business is closed."

On her blog, she made it clear who she believed was responsible: (again paraphrasing) "The U.S. sent in weapons without hiding it. Take them and use them, despite all the civilians who are being killed. It wouldn't have made me as angry if the targets were buildings and roads. But people are being killed, so how would the U.S. expect us to react?"

At the start of the war, I was 150 miles off the coast of Lebanon in Cyprus. ABC News had sent me there to follow the exodus of Lebanese and foreigners fleeing the fighting on a giant flotilla of cruise liners and U.S. Navy ships. It was one of the largest mass evacuations by the U.S. military since the Second World War, a huge, supremely coordinated exodus, paid for by the U.S. government and offered free to thousands of people. To many Lebanese, it was a silly gift. In their view, the U.S.-supplied bombs and aircraft were destroying Lebanon on the one hand, while U.S. ships were carrying the victims away. Still, the people on those ships were the fortunate ones. Some had lined up for days for the opportunity, leaving their homes, possessions, and jobs behind.

The scene was painfully familiar to one American in particular. I met Joseph Ciccipio, an American who had been held hostage by the Palestinian terrorist group Islamic Jihad for five years during the civil war. He was now being forced to flee the country again.

"Everything exploded overnight," he said. "Everything came to an end, died overnight."

Joseph had been freed in 1991. After he and his wife Elham were reunited, they returned to Lebanon many times, thinking war had ended for good. The violence was bringing back the worst memories.

"We thought that we had paid the price. I mean, Lebanon went through a lot and I don't know why our destiny is always to pay the price."

In Beirut, Sara became increasingly nervous that her home was no longer out of the line of fire. General Michel Aoun, a Christian ally of Hezbollah, lived just five minutes away. She could hear Israeli military drones flying overhead.

"There were drones all over the place, and then I realized maybe they suspected Nasrallah was hiding with General Aoun," she said. "I could hear them twenty-four-seven."

I moved from Cyprus to the northern Israeli town of Metulah, situated in the mountains on the Israeli-Lebanese border. During peaceful times, it is a spa town. During the war, it was a staging ground for attacks on Hezbollah positions. We followed an Israeli tank across the border into Lebanon. The combat was raging, door-to-door fighting pitting armored Israeli units against entrenched Hezbollah foot soldiers. Israeli officials claimed the ground offensive was accomplishing its goal of stopping Hezbollah rocket attacks. But the rockets kept falling, a record of 151 in a single day. Two rockets missed my camera crew by just fifty yards.

Israel summoned its military might. Inside a military intelligence center, we saw how Israeli forces had developed 3-D models of nearly every structure in southern Lebanon, including Nasrallah's home, which they destroyed from the air. But it was the fighting on the ground—street-to-street and in difficult mountain terrain—that was deadliest for the

Israelis. Israeli newspapers were filled with the faces of soldiers killed in the Hezbollah stronghold of Bint Jbail. We visited the home of one of them in Haifa, as relatives mourned a twenty-one-year-old soldier named Liran Sandia.

Marieka, Liran's aunt, told me, "Liran wanted to go and study. Boys are going into the army in order that we can survive."

Both sides saw this as a fight for survival. When a UN-brokered cease-fire came into effect on August 14, Sara, like many Hezbollah supporters, considered it a heroic victory for underdog Hezbollah against its far better armed opponents, as well as a moral comeuppance for Israel and America.

"The U.S. found nothing unbecoming about isolating and even waging a war—through its ally/policeman in the region, Israel—against broad portions of Lebanese who have refused to abide by the American vision for and strategy towards Lebanon," she said.

"The U.S. position is that nothing—other than U.S. interests—matters," she said. I would hear the same lament from Egypt to Iran to Britain.

I saw Sara a year later, just before Christmas 2007. We met outside the campus of the Lebanese American University (LAU), where she was completing a graduate degree. Beirut's two best universities have "American" in their names: LAU and the American University Beirut. They look like islands of North American collegial bliss in Lebanon—red brick buildings surrounding green courtyards. Peter Jennings received an honorary degree from AUB. Whenever I have been on assignment in Beirut, AUB and

LAU have always been the perfect places to find English-speaking, western-minded interviewees when we were in need of a particular voice for a segment on the evening news. Sara looked the part, but did not fit the profile.

Sipping coffee at a campus café, she and I discussed the future of relations between America and the Muslim world. While she sees the United States as the villain, she does not see it as the leader of one side in a West-versus-East clash of civilizations. That gave me hope. We weren't condemned to war by character or culture. Here in front of me was someone who seemed to share so much with me, not just in the way we looked, but in what we considered important: education, freedom of expression, democracy.

"I do not believe in the theories of a cultural clash between the Islamic and western/Christian worlds. The conflict is a political one," she said.

It is political, but politics run wild, a global version of what she grew up with and still lives with in Lebanon. She saw new evidence every day. The previous May, an unknown group called Fatah al-Islam took over the Nahr al-Bared refugee camp near Tripoli. Comprising Sunni militants, it was formed in the Palestinian refugee camps in southern Lebanon, with suspected Al-Qaeda backing. Sensing the threat, Hezbollah joined forces with the Christian-controlled Lebanese army to confront the group. Hezbollah and Al-Qaeda are not allies. Hezbollah not only opposes Al-Qaeda, but fears it. That fact, Sara argued, proved President Bush's "with us or against us" argument false. People can support Hezbollah and oppose Al-Qaeda. The groups are different, not only in name, but also in their goals. Sara believes the United States should recognize and exploit that difference.

"Does America approach this issue from a strictly ide-ological view, or do you, in the absence of any viable alter-native, adopt a pragmatic stance and say 'the enemy of my enemy is my friend'?" she asked me.

Election time was gearing up in the United States, but Sara did not believe a new administration would change American policy toward Lebanon. She heard candidates publicly reaffirm their support of Israel. She did not believe Democratic promises to withdraw U.S. forces from Iraq.

"The mess did not start with the Bush administration and will not end with it," she said. "When we look at the track record of U.S. policies in the region, we cannot help but feel that whether it is the neocons or the liberals, the Republicans or the Democrats, for us, it will only be more of the same."

The "mess" in the Middle East, as Sara sees it, is based on a sense of imperial superiority. To her the change must come in the West, not in the Muslim world—an end to the assumption that the West has something to teach Lebanon. To her, Hezbollah has both the track record—in success-fully beating the Israelis—and the conviction to help bring about that change. The sense of America as the evil "man behind the curtain" is endemic in the region. The implicit denial of personal responsibility is exasperating; I reminded her that the Lebanese have killed many of their own. But the ultimate conclusion was still demoralizing: Somehow, for Sara, a Shiite Muslim, religiously conservative militant group had her best interests at heart more than many Christian Lebanese politicians and certainly more than America.

The jihadis I met in Jordan had already overcome the car-icature of wild-eyed religious nuts. Now I'd met someone who blew the entire profile out of the water. She is Christian. She has not lost a loved one at the hands of Israeli or U.S. forces. She has lived an Americanized lifestyle, received an American education, and wants to live and study in America. Here, America's battle for hearts and minds was a *political* contest, and America appeared to be losing it.

THREE

EGYPT

THE FORGOTTEN DEMOCRATIC HERO

MEETING WITH GAMEELA Ismail, the wife of
Egypt's jailed opposition leader, Ayman Nour, was
like entering a real-life version of a 1960s spy movie. Our
first conversation took place at the Café Ibis in the Nile
Hilton, an aging riverfront hotel in the heart of Cairo.
The lobby was full of potential Hollywood extras, unsmiling men in dark suits and nervous ladies with hair stacked
high on their heads. The scattered potted plants and
wooden partitions were perfect for "tails" to hide behind. I
half-imagined a lithe Sean Connery wandering around the
corner.

Gameela arrived a half hour late, looking tired and har-
ried but still energetic. A former news anchor for Egyptian
television, she is tall and pretty, with stylishly coiffed
shoulder-length black hair and fine features that suggest
both Arab royalty and Mediterranean aristocracy. She was
dressed smartly but casually, in a peach top and blue jeans.

As Gameela and I spoke, she scoured nearby tables for
agents of Egypt's ubiquitous security services.

"The hotel is infiltrated," she told me.

This is getting out of hand, I thought. I expected a hidden
director to shout "Cut!" But I learned quickly that the

spies here are as real as her husband's two-years-and-counting imprisonment. A few days earlier, Gameela had run smack into them after she met with a U.S. congressional delegation.

"I told the delegation, 'Once we step out of the café now, we're going to be filmed,'" she said.

Sure enough, one of those unsmiling men in dark suits jumped up as they left the café, capturing their exit on a video camera. Gameela immediately protested, first to the cameraman, then to the hotel staff.

"I said, 'You're not going to terrorize me this way. I'm meeting with representatives of the people. I'm not doing anything wrong.' We are always on the defensive."

She was stunned the Americans didn't protest as well.

"They weren't surprised," she said. "They were passive."

Gameela believes the Egyptian authorities use such images to portray her and her husband as puppets of America, rather than as a home-grown Egyptian political phenomenon. Such is the contradictory position of the United States with respect to its old ally Egypt: Here America plays the dual role of biggest foreign-aid donor and interfering foreign menace. The day after Gameela met with the American delegation, the front page of the ruling party's mouthpiece displayed large photographs of them together, next to a long article about the opposition's deepening ties with the American government. The ploy had worked.

I was quickly getting a taste of the life of an opposition figure in Egypt. The boldest opponents, Gameela's husband Ayman among them, face imprisonment, beating, and sometimes death. For others, reputations are sullied. "American agent" is a favorite charge. "Intellectual marines" (as in U.S. Marines) is another. Phone lines are tapped, every step is followed by security agents. The more

I met with Gameela and other dissidents, the easier it was to spot the security service agents lurking around Cairo. They always seemed to be in character, loitering outside opposition headquarters in cheap dark suits, with cigarettes glued to their fingers. When I caught their glance, I thought I detected a wry smile, which seemed to say, "We both know I'm watching you."

"Does all this scare you?" I asked Gameela.

"It used to," she said. "It's strange now. Things that would have terrified me years ago don't anymore, because we lost everything."

Gameela blames America. Yet Egypt is America's closest friend in the region in many respects—the first to recognize Israel, a longtime recipient of U.S. aid, an early participant in the "war on terror." The Egyptian government, after all, has an Islamist problem of its own in the Muslim Brotherhood, the philosophical forebears of Al-Qaeda and a massive political, social, and religious force. But Egypt is also a dictatorship, largely reviled by its own people. I've covered half a dozen peace conferences in the sunny Red Sea resort of Sharm el-Sheikh, but I've always found Egypt far from peace at home. And like Palestinians who see America behind every Israeli military strike, Egyptians see America behind every successive year they live under Hosni Mubarak. Through Gameela, Ayman, and other democratic campaigners, I'd see what American support for Egypt costs us in credibility and hope.

Gameela has become her husband's public face and voice while he sits in a cell in south Cairo's Tura Mazraa prison, cut off from his wife, his two sons, and his career as a lawyer and politician. Only his family and lawyers are allowed to visit him. He cannot speak on the telephone. In 2006 the warden banned him from writing as well, thereby forcing his wife to smuggle out handwritten notes to his relatives and friends.

Officially, Ayman Nour is in jail for falsifying signatures on petitions submitted to register his opposition political party. He and his supporters named it El Ghad, or "the Tomorrow Party," launching it in late 2004 with a reformist message and hopes of competing in the following year's national elections. Few Egyptians believe the charges against him. In reality, he's in jail for turning a quixotic presidential campaign against Mubarak—a campaign encouraged and inspired by the United States—into a respectable challenge. Too respectable, it turns out, to be tolerated in Egypt.

"Mubarak saw him as a big, big threat," Gameela explained. "And that's why things moved very quickly against us."

She has paid a professional price herself. She once hosted one of Egypt's most popular current-affairs shows for young people, taking on issues that concerned them: their politics, the costs of housing, and higher education. The show was canceled in early 2005 after she participated in her first opposition demonstration. Since then, she's fought hard to return to the air, but friends have told her quietly it's not going to happen. She's applied to other Arab-language networks (Qatar-based Al Jazeera, Saudi-owned Al Arabiya, and others), but they have all rejected her.

"What really shocked me is the position of the non-Egyptian channels. They'd offered me jobs in the past but this time, no answer," she said. "Any Arab channel with an office in Egypt is under the control of state security."

Gameela's new full-time job is fighting for her husband's release—in court and in public.

Their assault on the Egyptian government began in earnest in early 2005. It was a time of unprecedented hope in

Egypt, inspired in part by surprising democratic progress in
nearby Iraq. Iraq had just held its first elections in fifty years,
with a turnout far beyond the expectations of many inside
and outside the country. The purple thumbs of Iraqi voters,
bearing the ink used to prevent multiple trips to the ballot
box, quickly became an icon of the democratic aspirations of
Iraqis even in the face of violence. Egypt was the next in line
to succumb to a new dynamic in the Middle East.

Kuwait was preparing to grant women the right to vote
for the first time. Even Saudi Arabia, easily one of the
region's least democratic countries, held municipal elections, also for the first time. Egypt appeared to be the most
reform-minded. There was going to be an election for the
head of state, the first here in fifty years as well. Everyone
knew Mubarak would find a way to win. But simply putting the most powerful job on the line was groundbreaking.

Ayman Nour's supporters believed they had a candidate
whose run might at least chip away at President Hosni
Mubarak's grip on power, which was unchallenged for
twenty-four years. Some commentators predicted Nour
could win 20 or even 30 percent of the vote—a symbolic
defeat for Mubarak, though even the most optimistic knew
the government would never actually permit a loss.

Describing their euphoria at the time, Gameela teared up
for a moment before she caught herself.

"If you came here two years ago . . ." she said.

"Excitement?" I asked.

"Yes, the curve was up here, at its peak."

It was an exceptional time in Egypt. It seemed an entirely
new future was in the making. But Ayman Nour was fighting an entrenched political system that was loath to allow
the opposition to grow. In January 2005, just three months
after registering his party, Ayman was charged with forging

his petitions. Egyptian police arrested him and sent him immediately to jail. From behind bars, Nour kept up pressure on the government, furiously publishing critical articles and using his time in jail to draw unprecedented attention to his cause inside and outside of Egypt. He succeeded and quickly became a recognizable face of the opposition.

U.S. officials exerted pressure on the Egyptian government to release him. In his second inaugural speech, in January 2005, President Bush had put himself firmly on the side of democratic reform from Iraq to Saudi Arabia to Kuwait to Egypt, with a grand promise: "All who live in tyranny and hopelessness can know: the United States will not ignore your oppression, or excuse your oppressors. When you stand for your liberty, we will stand with you." In February 2005, Secretary of State Condoleezza Rice abruptly canceled a trip to Egypt. By March, Egypt had relented and released Nour. The Egyptian government also announced that presidential elections in the fall would for the first time be open to opposition candidates. It was a momentous turnaround. Nour believed the path to challenging the government was finally open to him.

In June 2005, Rice made her visit to Egypt, but used it to make a bold speech at the American University in Cairo:

"There are those who say that democracy leads to chaos, or conflict, or terror. In fact, the opposite is true. Ladies and gentlemen, across the Middle East today, millions of citizens are voicing their aspirations for liberty and for democracy, demanding freedom for themselves and democracy for their countries. To these courageous men and women, I say today: all free nations will stand with you as you secure the blessings of your own liberty."

It was an unprecedented public call delivered within sight of the sprawling home of President Mubarak. Rice also found time to meet face-to-face with Mubarak's challenger, Ayman Nour.

"At the end of the meeting," Gameela said, "Rice shook hands with him and said 'Don't worry.'

"They said they were supporting democracy and reform," she said. "[The administration] made those very courageous statements that actually gave hope not just to Ayman, but to most of the modern and new opposition in Egypt, who thought that, finally, the United States was stepping back from supporting dictatorships and dictators."

She paused, then added, "This was our utmost hope."

Egypt's fledgling opposition was emboldened. And there was a new development: growing cooperation between secularist opposition parties, such as Ayman's, and Islamist parties, led by the Muslim Brotherhood. The Brotherhood is a powerful political and social force. Like Hezbollah in Lebanon, it is more than a political party, providing social services to millions of Egyptians through its interlocking network of mosques, schools, hospitals, foundations, and social clubs.

Now the Brotherhood and the secular pro-democracy parties were working together, holding joint protests and coordinating election strategies. It was an odd partnership philosophically, but it made sense politically. Each side knew it was too weak to make gains against the ruling party alone. Though the Muslim Brotherhood had denounced violence for thirty years, the combination unsettled some in the United States. But Islamist parties in other countries such as Indonesia and Pakistan had risen and fallen not on their religious agenda, but on bread-and-butter issues like schools and jobs. Would the Brotherhood behave differently with a voice in government?

For all their legendary political cynicism, some Egyptians

allowed themselves to believe things might be changing ever so slightly for the better. It was invigorating to see President Mubarak's power challenged.

Soon political activists gained unlikely but powerful brothers-in-arms in Egypt's judges. An alliance of judges favoring greater judicial independence surprised the Mubarak government by lambasting its election plans as unlawful. In resounding meetings, first in Alexandria and then in Cairo, they declared they would not serve as "false witnesses" to the September presidential poll and November parliamentary elections. They were demanding something extraordinary here: independently supervised elections.

When they were unable to push the regime in the courts, the judges took their battle to the streets.

"This gave us a lot of encouragement," Gameela said. "It let us escalate, let us go and encourage the people, go down to the streets and demonstrate and call for what we think is good for this country, but under the table many things are happening that you can't see."

As the September election approached, it became clear the vote was rigged. The government delayed passing electoral rules until May. Campaigning was limited to less than three weeks. Opposition candidates had restricted access to the broadcast media. The judges and other opposition parties were encouraging a boycott. By election day, only Ayman Nour and one other opposition candidate remained.

Many Egyptian voters were also skeptical. Turnout was dismal. Less than a quarter of 32 million registered voters cast ballots according to the official count, which many believed was inflated. Hosni Mubarak received a Saddam Hussein–like 88.571 percent of the vote, and Ayman Nour 7.3 percent. Despite his imprisonment, rampant harassment, and widespread tampering, half a million Egyptians had voted for Nour. Some outside observers estimated he actually won twice as many votes.

Why had an opposition figure with little chance of winning attracted the government's attention? Many Egyptians believe it was less about the father than about his son Gamal. At eighty years of age and in failing health (rumors of cancer abound), President Mubarak has been grooming his son Gamal as heir. It is not lost on Ayman's supporters that he and Gamal are the same age.

"It's very clear that the age is decisive in this battle," Gameela told me. "And they are both 100 percent Egyptian. Ayman was raised in Egypt by an Egyptian family. He's married to an Egyptian, involved in politics since he was a student, popular as a member of parliament." These are many of the same qualities that Mubarak's own party has touted in Gamal.

The government would take a more severe blow in parliamentary elections two months later. For some opposition parties, this was the real battle. No one expected President Mubarak to give up power, but they might be able to whittle down his majority in parliament. The first of three rounds was a spirited, wide-open campaign, with little government interference. The ruling National Democratic Party won 68 percent of the seats, down from 90 percent. The Muslim Brotherhood won 20 percent of the seats, despite running a relatively small number of candidates.

The government was shocked. In the second round, it responded with force, arresting more than a thousand members of the Muslim Brotherhood and unleashing gangs of thugs on opposition supporters and on voters themselves. According to Shadi Hamid of the Project on Middle East

Democracy, roving teams of NDP supporters, often armed with machetes, sticks, and Molotov cocktails, attacked voters, blocked election monitors from entering polling stations, detained judges, and robbed ballot boxes. "It became clear why Egyptians use the Arabic word *ma'raka*, which means 'battle,' instead of 'campaign,'" said Mr. Hamid.

A violent crackdown in response to unfavorable election results was not new to the Arab world—or, indeed, to an American ally in the Arab world. After Islamists did unexpectedly well in parliamentary elections in Jordan in 1989, King Hussein instituted a new law limiting the number of opposition seats. Nearly twenty years and many pro-democracy speeches later, the law is still on the books.

But this was supposed to be a different time in Egypt and in the region. The pledges by President Bush and Secretary Rice to support democracy struck a chord. Now, however, the administration was quiet. On December 1, after more than ten days of violence and the arrests of the Muslim Brotherhood activists, State Department spokesman Sean McCormack told reporters, "We have not received, at this point, any indication that the Egyptian government isn't interested in having peaceful, free, and fair elections."

The Brotherhood's strong showing posed a problem for the Bush administration. The results were uncomfortable for Washington. Despite renouncing violence and focusing more on democratic reform and social issues, the Muslim Brotherhood was still viewed by many policymakers as a hard-line Islamist party. The results, like Hamas's election victory in Palestinian elections less than two months later, were testing the American commitment to democracy in the region.

It would be tested again three months after the presidential election. On Christmas Eve 2005, Nour was sentenced to five years in prison, convicted on the year-old charge of forging signatures on petitions submitted to register his "Tomorrow" party.

Human Rights Watch declared the trial "a terrible advertisement for President Mubarak's supposed reform agenda." The list of violations made the proceedings seem like little more than a show trial. The initial session was held in a small courtroom, where most of the seats were taken up by members of the security services. The judge denied most defense requests, including a chance to view the documents containing the signatures Nour allegedly forged. In one session, the judge overruled all defense questions to witnesses as irrelevant. Nour spent the week before the verdict in a hospital bed, weakened by a hunger strike he had initiated to protest his detention.

The White House released a statement on the day of Nour's conviction, saying only that the administration was "deeply troubled." "The conviction of Mr. Nour . . . calls into question Egypt's commitment to democracy, freedom, and the rule of law," it read. But by her next visit to Egypt in February 2006, Secretary Rice did not mention Nour's name in public. Gameela and others wondered if the administration was applying pressure behind the scenes. As the distance between public pronouncements grew longer and Ayman's time in prison dragged on, their doubts grew. Either Washington wasn't pushing hard, or its demands were falling on deaf ears.

"After the situation with Ayman, the impression with everyone here is that they're playing," she said. "They're both playing. And they have their own calculations, very old calculations, and it's not going to change."

For Gameela and other dissidents, 2005 was a lost

moment for America in Egypt—a catastrophic disappointment as their high hopes for change backed by American support came crashing down to earth.

"The problem is that it really was such a good moment," she said. "Everyone on the left and the right, we all started believing."

I asked her if she blamed America for her husband's continuing imprisonment. She answered with an emphatic "Yes."

America would seem to have the influence necessary to force change. The U.S. embassy in Egypt is the largest in the Middle East and, in fact, one of the largest in the world, with a staff of 500 Americans and 1,500 Egyptians. And the United States is by far Egypt's biggest foreign donor, supplying nearly $2 billion per year in economic and military aid. After meeting with Gameela in Cairo in July 2007, I traveled to Sharm el-Sheikh to cover a visit by Secretary of State Rice and Defense Secretary Robert Gates, where the two announced they would be extending U.S. military aid to Egypt for another ten years.

Throughout Ayman's imprisonment, American officials both from the embassy and from Washington have been constantly available to Gameela—available, she says, but not at all useful.

"I always hear this classic question at the end of every meeting. 'So do you think we can do anything?'" she told me, shaking her head and emitting a long sigh.

"Do you ever want to wring their necks?" I asked.

She hesitated and crafted a diplomatic response.

"I always tell them, 'You know what you are able to do. I can't tell you what to do,'" she said. "I mean, they know everything, I don't need to meet with them because they know everything. It all adds up to nothing. There's no progress."

Egypt is a strange ally. It can be one of America's more aggressive detractors, not only allowing anti-American hatred but encouraging it. I learned that from my very first trip in 2004. I had come to interview victims of torture in Egyptian prisons. As they were describing their beating at an anti-government protest, I noticed that a protest against the Iraq War, full of anti-American stunts including burning the American flag, went ahead without a hitch. The arrangement seemed to be clear: direct your criticism abroad—or more specifically at America—and you will have the government's blessing; direct it at the government, and you will pay a price.

"We can stage—in a minute—a demonstration against America outside Cairo's biggest mosque on Friday," Gameela said. "We can be allowed to march down the street in huge numbers if we want, *if* it's going to be anti-American."

This became eminently clear to Gameela and her husband during their election campaign, when the pro-government party first began slurring them as "agents of America."

"They had banners everywhere saying that 'Ayman is Rice's boyfriend,' or that he was the son of Madeleine Albright, or the puppet of Bush," she said. "And they burned the American flag in the middle of the square in front of his [election] headquarters to show that Ayman is the betrayer of Egypt and the tool of America in this region."

Rice herself is a particularly popular target. Gameela and others have told me they are convinced that photographs of Secretary Rice in government-controlled newspapers show her skin color a shade or two darker than in real life. I didn't believe her until I looked at some of the photographs myself.

"They hate Rice here," she said. "They are so racist."

Dismissing the dissidents as American imports is an easy way for the Egyptian government to undermine the opposition's popular support, as well as to distract attention from the government's own failures. But Gameela and other members of the opposition see something more strategic. In Egypt, anti-Americanism, with violent Islamism at its extreme, is a useful foil. It is part of the grand bargain offered to the United States from Pakistan to Saudi Arabia to Egypt. Egyptian leaders are saying, in effect, "We may not be perfect, but the alternative is much worse."

"The Egyptian regime uses this anti-western hate as a 'ghost' for the American administration, saying, 'You see, people are so anti-American. They hate Americans, so we are the key to stability,'" Gameela said. "'You have to put all your trust and confidence in us. The alternative would be the Islamists.'"

Egypt made the same argument to justify wide-ranging and brutal crackdowns on the Muslim Brotherhood in 2005 and again in 2007. Many Egyptians considered it the worst crackdown since the days of Gamal Abdel Nasser. Nasser's onslaught famously culminated with the execution of Sayid Qutb, the leading intellectual of the Brotherhood. Qutb is considered one of the most influential Muslim thinkers of all time, enhanced by what many (including Al-Qaeda) saw as his martyrdom.

Today, Gameela is allowed to see Ayman about once every three weeks. She and other visitors are made to walk the full mile from the gate to the prison building. Inside, she finds her husband slowly wasting away. At forty-three, he has the health problems of a man twenty years older, suffering from severe diabetes and heart problems. Gameela believes the stress of prison life has made him worse. Limited movement has caused damage in his joints, and his eyesight is slowly failing. Her efforts now are focused on getting him released for health reasons.

"He's deteriorating. But his situation is much better than thousands of others," she said.

"At least people are aware he's there," I replied.

"Yes," she said. "Other people are so forgotten."

Gameela told the story of a man who was in prison so long that when he was released they had to cut him out of his cell because the door had rusted shut. The accounts sound apocryphal. But I had heard enough firsthand to know the risk was real. I reminded myself that Ayman Nour was once a darling of the U.S. administration as well, held up as proof that after the Iraq invasion, democracy was blooming in the Arab world. But for Gameela there was only disappointment and an innocent man behind bars.

Ayman is forbidden to meet with journalists, so I went to see the prison for myself. Tura is a short drive from downtown Cairo. On the way, we passed by the military reviewing stand where Egyptian president Anwar Sadat was gunned down in 1981. It is a fitting landmark. Tura also holds one of the key architects of the assassination, Sayid Imam al-Sharif, the founder of the Egyptian Islamic Jihad. The attack was one of the first salvos in the global jihad. Al-Sharif later fled to Afghanistan, where he teamed up with Osama bin Laden. He also wrote the definitive text on the religious justification of terrorism, *Foundations of Preparation for Holy War*, the unofficial bible of jihad, before famously recanting it in 2007. Now the two opponents of Mubarak's regime—one violent, one peaceful—pass their days in cells a few yards apart.

The prison is surrounded by vast apartment complexes

and fields of garbage. Garbage disposal is free-form in the capital; any field or river or vacant lot will do. As we neared the jail, we pulled over to ask a man for directions. He was banging at some rubble with a hammer, trying to liberate a piece of iron rebar poking out of a chunk of concrete. I couldn't imagine a small shard of scrap metal was worth the effort, but he banged away undaunted and smiled as he told us the jail was just around the corner.

From the outside, Tura Mazraa seems innocuous. The neat, high walls are decorated with a playful motif of rippling blue waves, incongruous with the dusty, 110-degree heat. Through the gate, I could see green fields between the prison buildings. Relatives lined up carrying plastic bags filled with flatbread and fruit. A handful of guards looked relaxed as they mixed with the visitors hiding from the sun under a corrugated metal shade.

For many, the reality on the inside is far different. The Egyptian authorities are known to be ruthlessly creative in "breaking" prisoners. That's why many here believe the U.S. government has sent some of its hardest terror suspects to Egyptian prisons for questioning.

I had met face-to-face with survivors of torture. Manal, a thirty-two-year-old film director, told me policemen surrounded her on the street during an anti-government demonstration and drove her to a jail packed with women and children.

"They handcuffed me, punched me in the face, insulted me, and threatened to change the charge to adultery," she said.

Charging women with sex crimes is a favorite tactic. Threaten a woman with the loss of her reputation, and she may confess to less damaging political crimes.

"I was hurting," Manal told me. "It was very hard."

Wael, who at thirty had already served six jail terms for political activism, was arrested at the same demonstration. He was held for eight weeks without charge, stripped naked, and beaten.

"There was every type of torture one can imagine, beatings, electric shocks," he said. "Everything you heard of in Abu Ghraib happens in Egypt. We have five thousand Abu Ghraibs."

Abu Ghraib may have faded in Americans' minds, but in Egypt and other Arab countries, the pictures of American soldiers mistreating Muslim prisoners are still a powerful symbol of American hypocrisy. Hearing Wael and others mention the scandal, I always sense a measure of disappointment as well. Despite the near-universal disapproval of American policy in the Arab world, from its support of Israel to the invasion of Iraq, many still expect the United States to observe a higher standard than do their own decrepit regimes. Abu Ghraib was seen as evidence that the U.S. government was no better than their own.

Standing outside Tura prison that summer day, I was in no danger of the kind of mistreatment my interview subjects faced. Still, simply being there was against the law. There are some things the Egyptians don't want American journalists to report.

For months, Gameela gave me updates on his case. Time and again, Egyptian courts rejected Ayman's appeal for release. Gameela was frustrated but not hopeless. And she was still indefatigably proud. With a gleam in her eye, she told me how, through sheer toughness, Ayman had earned the grudging respect of his own prison guards.

"One of them told me that Ayman is worse than any of the prisoners they've met. He's telling me that the Muslim brothers are polite compared to my husband," she said.

"They never saw someone write and complain every morning, writing resolutions for this and amendments to that.

"Every morning," she said. "He is a factory of ideas."

"Does it make you proud?" I asked.

"Yes of course," she said. "He's a struggler. I'm a struggler. I'm proud because I know his spirits are high, but if he is released and he does this, the next day they'll put him back." With a hint of resignation, she added, "I know my husband is not going to get off the scene, that he's not going to shut up."

The Egyptian government seems aware of this as well. In making her appeals for her husband's release on health grounds, Gameela has had to sign numerous documents promising she will take him straight to the hospital and then for treatment outside Egypt.

"They want him out of the country," she said. "Suffering physically and psychologically.

"I talk with senior people, people he had relationships with, government ministers," she said. "They tell me, 'I'm very sorry about what's happening with him.'"

They shake their heads and blame it on presidential whims.

"Do any of them stand up for him?" I asked.

"No," she said, rubbing her palms together. "They wash their hands of it."

She believes the United States is guilty of the same.

"If the U.S. administration were serious and genuine [about getting him out]," she said, "Ayman would have been at home a year ago."

WITH EGYPT'S MOST prominent opposition figure behind bars, some of the vocal sympathizers have migrated from the political sphere to cyberspace, where free expression survives, dodging and weaving to avoid government interference. That's where I met Wael Abbas for the first time (not to be confused with the activist I met who had been tortured). He is the thirty-four-year-old behind Misr Digital, an irreverent, often caustic, chronicle of government abuse.

"All political parties are playing on the sentiments of Egyptians, using the fact that most Egyptians are illiterate," he said. "I want to give people the real picture, reality, so in the end they will make the right choice based on facts, not on sentiments. I don't want them to be drugged by either verses from the Koran or political tactics."

He is one of an estimated 6,000 active bloggers in this country of 80 million people. Bloggers have earned themselves power in the political debate that surpasses their numbers. Today they act as political machinery for the opposition, advertising the times and places of demonstrations in advance, and as its conscience, speaking their minds against the government and chronicling the state's abuses in a way the mainstream media and many political leaders cannot.

I was hoping to find less resentment of America among Egypt's bloggers. They are younger, hipper, more in touch with western styles and technology. Wael himself has visited the States several times, often on NGO-sponsored cultural exchanges. I found something more troubling. America hadn't dashed their hopes; it had never given them hope at all. We couldn't lose a generation we never had in the first place.

Wael does more than post a blog. His mission is to capture government abuses on camera—sometimes on a still camera, sometimes on video, sometimes on his cell phone—and show them to the world. Wael's website is a political *Candid Camera* for the Internet generation—and, he hopes, a despot's nightmare.

His specialty is to publicize police abuse of opposition protesters and detainees, on the street and in police stations. Wael gave me an inside look at Tura prison, where Nour is serving his sentence. My stomach turned as I watched his videos for the first time. What they depicted was unsettling not just for the violence, but even more so for the enjoyment the torturers appeared to be taking in their victims' suffering.

In one, a woman who appeared to be in her late twenties is hog-tied to a broomstick suspended between two chairs. Her arms and legs are swung over the top, the backs of her knees resting on the stick, leaving her body hanging like an animal on a barbecue spit. Pretty and vulnerable, she is screaming, pleading with her torturers to stop. Another video captures the same woman from a different angle. She's still wearing her jewelry. Tears stream down her face.

In another clip, I saw a young man in what looks like a jail cell. A policeman in uniform brings his nose inches from the victim's and yells at him, laughing in between outbursts. You can hear laughing in the background as well. Then he slaps the victim repeatedly across the face—back and forth. This is meant to demean him as much as to cause pain. The slaps get harder. The victim falls to the ground.

Slapping is sport for the Egyptian police. In video after video, victims young and old are lined up against a wall and slapped—sometimes on their faces, sometimes on the backs of their heads.

"Slapping on the back of the head is very humiliating in Egypt," Wael explained. "It reminds people of the way you treat a donkey, slapping them on the back of the neck to get them moving. It's treating a person like an animal."

One policeman uses such force that he knocks a victim to the ground in one blow. Sometimes the police use their hands, sometimes a long, flexible baton, like a thick version of a jockey's whip.

They beat men and women with equal force. One video shows a woman being hit repeatedly with a baton, while a second woman stands in the background, apparently forced to watch. The beaten woman screams. The second woman sobs uncontrollably. There is a sick flair for performance. The policemen laugh. They pause for effect between blows.

Amazingly, it is the abusers themselves who supply Wael with the images, capturing the abuse on their cell-phone cameras and sending them in anonymously. And so the torturers and their witness have an odd symbiotic relationship: Wael exposes their crimes, and the police enjoy a grotesque, YouTube-era power trip.

"It's because they are sick," Wael told me. "Remember, these are shot for the pleasure of officers themselves."

The police seem to have little real fear of punishment of any kind. It made me wonder if Mubarak is the Pinochet of our time—a leader deemed too important in a wider struggle—the Cold War then, the war on terror now—to criticize the Egyptian government's alleged crimes.

"I am of no value to the Americans, but Mubarak is of value," Wael told me. "He is protecting America's interests, like peace with Israel."

For a time the bloggers survived outside the reach of Egyptian authorities. As the police and security forces focused on the traditional opposition, the bloggers retained their voice. During the election fight of 2005, the bloggers joined opposition newspapers, such as *Al-Wafd* and *Al-Dustour*, in covering opposition protests that were largely absent from the official pro-government media. Bloggers vowed to cover the candidates and protests that others would not, posting accounts and pictures on the Internet.

"No journalists dared cover the opposition events," Wael said. "We believed in the people's right to know, so bloggers took matters into their own hands."

Wael had already chronicled police abuse behind closed doors. Now, as the government's tactics became more openly aggressive, Wael took to videotaping police abuse in the streets. The targets were the Muslim Brotherhood, Ayman Nour's Tomorrow Party, and another secular opposition group known simply by the Arabic word *Kifaya*, meaning "enough." Kifaya staged the first-ever anti-Mubarak protest in Egypt, in late 2004. A hundred supporters stood on the steps of the Supreme Court, their mouths covered in yellow tape with KIFAYA written on it in bold black letters.

Now, rather than suppressing coverage of the protests, security forces began to disrupt them actively.

"They hired thugs to break up the crowds, paying them three dollars," Wael explained. He spoke to one, who told him that the violence was sport as much as a job.

"They were told they were free to do anything and the police would protect them," he said. "They would not interfere, and so they stole laptops, cameras, they beat women, anything."

The new tactics turned Wael from an online political event publicist into an underground chronicler of state-sponsored abuse. Some of the violence was deadly. Thirteen people were killed during parliamentary elections in 2005, each death reported on Wael's blog. In the official media they were often reported as accidents—the results of tear gas and rubber bullets—but Wael knew better.

His entry the day before the election read, "The referendum is not for us to have our say, but for them to crush/ beat us."

And they did. Wael's blog became a clearinghouse for accounts of attacks and abuse. Protesters reported stories of police and hooligans breaking bones, stealing valuables, and sexually harassing women. They tore women's clothes and groped their bodies. Their tactics were adolescent but humiliating.

As the bloggers' following grew, the authorities began harassing them with the same ferocity normally reserved for members of the mainstream opposition like Ayman Nour. The mysterious Hollywood world of tails and phone taps extended its reach into the blogosphere.

We arranged to meet at the Kentucky Fried Chicken on Tahrir Square. The KFC is a favorite meeting place for young people in Cairo. As in so many Middle Eastern cities, U.S. brands somehow escape the shadow of America's radioactive image. Nearby is the posh, expatriate-favored neighborhood of Garden City. This is still, in many ways, the old heart of the capital, home to the massive American embassy and the American University in Cairo, the college of choice for the country's secular elite. It's where wealthy Egyptians and foreigners used to live, work, and play. There were buildings that would fit right into New York—ornate, late-nineteenth-century architecture, but rundown today— an Egyptian SoHo, with small cafés and a few bars. Ayman Nour's party has its headquarters here. Members of the Muslim Brotherhood often meet at the legendary Italian chocolate shop, Groppi's. Egypt's young intellectuals and political activists, including the bloggers, gravitate toward the Greek Club, a monument to Egypt's once-thriving community of Greek businessmen. The signs of Cairo's cosmopolitan past are everywhere. Across the street is a Lebanese tourism office; next to that, a French bistro.

As we sat down and ordered Egyptian Stella beers, Wael pointed out Egypt's myriad political insurgents gathering in small groups at the tables around us. There were the bloggers, and next to them the unreformed Socialists and Communists. It was an open house of political movements, living and dead.

But it was also a magnet for plainclothes security agents who lurked outside. Wael quickly ticked off the ways he'd been harassed: the phone taps, the undercover tails, the accusations distributed in the media that he's on the CIA payroll.

"I feel that I'm followed," he said, sipping his beer. "My phone is definitely bugged. I hear interference on the line, not an old-fashioned click but static, buzz, interference."

Egyptian security agents take particular interest when he visits America. When he returned from a fellowship in Washington with Freedom House (an organization promoting democracy worldwide), he noticed security agents there to meet him. How did he know?

"It's a combination of things," he said. "It's strangers looking at you like they know you, and men following you, chatting into walkie-talkies."

For Wael, dodging his minders is like a game.

"I've gotten some experience in the last few years," he said with a touch of bravado. "It comes naturally to me. I try not to look like a suspect to them. I act careless, then I jump off the main streets down little alleys, which I know better than they do."

Then he leaned in closer and added with a cryptic twist, "I have other techniques I don't want to reveal."

I knew this wasn't melodrama when I saw the agents again as we left the café, but I couldn't shake the Hollywood feel.

Still, the risk Wael faces is depressingly real. Another Egyptian blogger was convicted in 2007 and sentenced to four years in prison for alleged crimes including insulting Islam and President Mubarak. Like Wael, Abdel Kareem Nabil, a twenty-two-year-old former student at Egypt's Al-Azhar University, had been a strident critic both of President Mubarak and of Islamist extremists. He had criticized his own university for encouraging religious extremism, calling it in his blog a "university of terrorism."

Wael remained a free man, but his diatribes against the government have earned him a new form of punishment designed specifically for the Internet generation: the Web smear campaign. On pro-government websites, Wael has been called a closet homosexual, a secret Catholic, and an American agent sent by the CIA to foment a Georgian-style people's revolution against the government.

"They chose to smear my reputation," he said. "But I don't think anyone believes it."

I asked him if he feared worse—that a prison term might be next.

"I'm worried about getting arrested all the time," he said. "You can never predict what the government will do. Kareem was not participating in demonstrations, or taking pictures like me. He was just writing on the Web, now suddenly there's a court case and he's in jail."

As I spoke to him, I waited for Wael to ask why Washington had yet to pressure Mubarak on the government's crackdown on bloggers. But he did not. The difference with many in Wael's generation of political activists is that they have little desire for American help. In fact, they oppose it.

"I don't want American support. I want them to stop supporting Mubarak," he said. "I think we'd be OK if it was only us against Mubarak. But we're fighting Mubarak *and* fighting the Americans because they're supporting him. The Americans are not making it easy for us."

Sitting there, Wael gave me a run-through of recent American history from the perspective of a young Egyptian.

"America is not the same. In the 1970s, two journalists removed Nixon. Now Bush is doing worse things than Nixon did, and no one is removing him," he said. "America in my opinion is no longer for human rights, for freedom. America is for its own interests and its own security. It is paranoid."

Again, as in Jordan and Lebanon, I was hearing that sense of an America hell-bent on pursuing its interests with no regard for its own principles. Wael's blog often alleges that America is culpable for Egyptian government abuse because American aid money helps pay for the police trucks, tear gas, and guns used on protesters.

As we shared our thoughts over several months, I realized Wael's voice is the very kind many American officials and commentators have been clamoring for in the Muslim world. He is one of a few willing to criticize not only the government but also Islamic extremists. His and Ayman Nour's are voices that need protecting, but America appears either unwilling or unable to do so.

I asked Wael what advice he would give the next American president to change that perception.

"The damage is done," he said. "For the moment, it's not possible."

I pressed him. What about closing Guantanamo?

"Closing Guantanamo would enhance the image of the American government for the American people, but not in the Muslim world. The U.S. is now viewed as a colonial power. To be a *little less* colonial doesn't make sense."

Americans see the occupations of Afghanistan and Iraq as security operations, made necessary by fragile conditions on the ground. Wael sees them as examples of twenty-first-century colonialism, excuses for long-term influence and military bases. During the 2008 presidential campaign, when John McCain spoke of stationing U.S. troops in Iraq for a hundred years, he was articulating a prospect many here had suspected all along.

When I pressed him again, Wael rattled off a three-point plan for restoring his confidence in America.

"The U.S. should withdraw from Iraq," he said. "It should hold a trial for war criminals. And it should stop supporting dictatorships which it claims are allies, including Egypt."

Like the jihadis I'd met in Jordan, his demands, again, were neither outlandish nor religious. Calls for withdrawal from Iraq and for more public criticism of oppressive Middle Eastern regimes were not far off the stated positions of some of the democratic presidential candidates.

He left his harshest criticism for his own government. As with Gameela, it is America's support for President Mubarak that angers and disappoints him most.

"The U.S. should stop raising Egypt up as a democratic regime, portraying it as a country progressing toward democracy and freedom," he said. "The Egyptian record on human rights is horrible. We have a president in power for six terms, no presidential elections, no real parliamentary elections. One party wins all the time. The security services interfere in elections. People get killed trying to demonstrate. There's no free press, no privately owned stations. What kind of democracy is that?"

Gameela is equally angry and pessimistic. For her, the damage to America's image may be irreparable.

"It took them years to show they can't stop supporting dictatorships, and it will take them years again to reestablish any trust," she said. "Years and years."

She sees the warning signs in her two sons. They appear very Americanized. They wear American clothes, play American music, and watch American movies. They speak English first and Arabic as a foreign language. But they have no desire to live in America. In fact, they're afraid even to have contact with Americans.

"They've been complaining to me, 'Mommy, don't meet Americans,'" she said. "We are plagued by this."

With their father and mother portrayed in the press as American agents, they are driven partly by raw fear.

"They get into conversations with taxi drivers to see what's happening and what the public opinion is," she said. "And they're telling me that [their father's] image and our family's image is so bad. At the end of the conversation, they don't dare to say they are sons of Ayman Nour."

The Egyptian government—in her view, with tacit American support—has robbed her sons of both their sense of security and their father. More and more, Gameela fears they may never get him back. She worries that imprisonment may be killing Ayman.

In the summer of 2007, with his heart growing weaker and the symptoms of his diabetes becoming more severe, Ayman wrote to the National Human Rights Commission begging for help. His words took on a desperate tone far dif-

ferent from his usual defiance: "The situation is very serious. I can be killed anytime here."

Established with great fanfare in 2005, the rights commission has won few fans in the dissident community. No
one believes it has any real influence inside the government. But with her options running thin, Gameela was
eager to keep every official channel open. She met with the
head of the commission soon after Ayman sent his letter.

He was sympathetic, even hopeful. For the first time he
raised the possibility of Ayman's release on health grounds.
Not the full exoneration they were hoping for, but freedom
nonetheless.

At the end of the meeting he told Gameela there was a
way she could help her husband's cause. Taking an avuncu-
lar tone, he said she would do best if she followed his
advice.

"He told me, 'You have to relax and be quiet now, stop
protesting. A bit of silence will help your husband.' He said,
'Stop talking to the foreign press. Stop embarrassing us.'"

Exhausted and frustrated, she agreed. Four days later,
Ayman received the worst beating of all his time in prison.
One morning he was taken from his cell to a court hearing,
without his lawyers or family members present. He was
escorted to the staircase that led up to the court and
ordered to walk up. With his weak heart, he took deliberate
steps, pausing for a break on each landing. The guards were
not happy. So, grabbing him by his wrists, they dragged him
up three flights of stairs on his back. His body was bruised,
his knees twisted and swollen. Walking became painful.

"You can see the scars on his back now," she said. "It's a
way to break him."

Gameela called the head of the rights commission the

next day. He never called her again. "Every time we get a moment of hope," she said, "some big hand comes to crush it."

ON ONE VISIT to Cairo, a friend from the American Embassy invited me to an embassy-sponsored musical concert for street children. It was a gorgeous summer evening, refreshingly cool and with a clear sky lit by a giant, glowing full moon. The concert would be under the stars in a brand-new park overlooking the old city. I couldn't resist a break from Cairo's oppressive summer heat.

The event was more than charity; it was part of the embassy's community outreach intended, in part, to improve America's image in the Arab world. My jaw dropped when I learned that the band would be a Latino-funk group named Ozomatli. An eight-member, super-hip outfit from East Los Angeles, this was the last band I expected to be stumping for the State Department. Ozomatli was one of the first American musical acts to come out publicly against the war in Iraq, and they headlined one of the first antiwar concerts. They made the Dixie Chicks, who were excoriated for criticizing President Bush on stage in 2003, look almost Republican.

The band members were charming as they played their unique, upbeat brand of Latino-techno. I'm sure the kids had never heard anything like it. The lead singer and spokesman—a burly, goateed twenty-nine-year-old named Ulysses—told me he and the other band members decided they had a choice.

"We can either throw our arms up in the air and say we're all going to hell, basically, or we can do something positive," he said.

They chose the latter. Cairo was one stop on a Middle Eastern tour that would also take them to Jordan and the West Bank. Good for them, I thought. They certainly showed another side of America than the one many young people here see in the news—in military uniforms in Iraq or in dark suits meeting President Mubarak in Sharm el-Sheikh. On stage that night, they were good-natured American kids doing their part thousands of miles from home.

To get the children involved, the band members smiled and pulled a few of them on stage. The kids were having a ball. One little boy did a King Tut impression with the lead singer. Embassy staff joined in as well. I watched the embassy's cultural attaché smiling and gyrating as she led a conga line of eight- to ten-year-olds.

The sight was priceless, and depressing. With the leader of the Egyptian opposition in a prison cell just down the road—and the country's most prominent blogger fearing he might soon join him—were music concerts going to turn America from villain to hero? I was watching American public diplomacy at its most desperate: Ozomatli as antidote for tolerated repression.

I R A Q

STANCH THE BLEEDING

T HE SMELL WAS the first thing I noticed when I
entered Baghdad's bustling Yarmouk hospital. It was
subtle at first, but slowly enveloped me. Bitter and pun-
gent, I recognized it from an assignment years before at a
cattle farm in Iowa. It was the smell of a slaughterhouse.

The odor followed me up and down the halls as I went to
meet Dr. Jamal Taha. Dr. Jamal is chief trauma surgeon at
the busiest trauma center in all of Iraq. If you've ever seen
television pictures of emergency rooms filled with wounded
and dead Iraqis and their relatives screaming in sorrow,
you've probably seen the inside of Yarmouk. It is a broken
place: a 1970s-era hospital that looks as though it should
have been torn down and rebuilt years ago. The lights are
dim. The tiles on the floor are in constant need of scrubbing.
The medical instruments and X-ray machine look like
antiques. I don't think of myself as squeamish, but on every
visit I feel my stomach turning. I jam my hands deep into
my pockets to avoid touching anything, or anyone.

Dr. Jamal is a medical workhorse probably without equal
in all of Iraq. Since the invasion, he says he's treated more
than 10,000 victims of the violence. This is the simple
arithmetic of the bloodshed here, where bodies, bloodied

and broken, come in by the dozens every day. In fact, as I worked out the math in my head, I realized he might actually be underestimating the toll. In 2007, when Yarmouk received an average of 100 trauma patients a day, Dr. Jamal could have seen 10,000 victims *in a single year.*

I tried to come up with a benchmark to measure him against. New York during the murder spree in the 1980s? Beirut during the civil war? London during the Blitz? He is a living barometer of the suffering in Iraq. Today the violence can seem distant and almost indistinguishable from day to day. But for Dr. Jamal, it is his life, up close, every day.

Over the four years I've known him, I have watched the violence age Dr. Jamal. He is just thirty-four years old, but already looks well into his forties. Iraqis rarely look their age. As children, they inevitably look younger. I'll meet tiny, smiling boys and girls in the streets and guess they're eight or nine, only to be startled when they say they're already teenagers. As the years pass, Iraq seems to accelerate them unnaturally toward old age. Dr. Jamal's face is already wrinkled, and his skin has lost its color. He looks drained. He has the face of a man who sees more dead bodies in a day or a week than I'll see in a lifetime.

Somehow he maintains his energy, propelling his short, pudgy frame through the busy, stinking hospital hallways. His eyes reveal both his strength and his compassion. They are a piercing grayish blue, but forever shiny and wet, as if he's holding back tears. Despite all that he's seen, he isn't numbed to the pain.

"I think all the doctors working here need psychological therapy," he told me once with a nervous laugh. "You are under stress always. Our work is psychologically very hard." He is an expert in understatement.

Through more than a dozen assignments in Baghdad, Dr. Jamal became my living bellwether of Baghdad in crisis. Meeting him on each return trip, I watched the violence grow and evolve, ahead of each new plan to control it: the first small attacks on U.S. soldiers, the advent of mass suicide bombings, the scourge of targeted assassinations, and segregation of the city along ethnic lines. The hospital itself was also a living test case of the failed American-led reconstruction effort. Despite the many promises of the U.S. and Iraqi governments through the years, Yarmouk has always been alarmingly short of basic medicine and equipment: one aging X-ray machine to scan all the broken bodies, and too few antibiotics to fight infection in hospital wards.

Within the cacophony of opinions on the war, his accounts have been hard and incontrovertible. If he saw fewer dead and injured, Iraq was getting safer; if he saw more victims, it was not. If the power stayed on in the hospital for more hours in the day, Iraq was being rebuilt. If not, something was wrong. For a journalist like me, Dr. Jamal was an early-warning system, free of politics and propaganda.

By the time the American troop surge helped calm things down, it was too late for him. The war has killed an estimated 150,000 Iraqi civilians and injured hundreds of thousands more (as estimated by the World Health Organization through 2006). This is a consequence of the war often left out of our own calculations of success or failure. Insurgents and terrorists may have done most of the killing, but Dr. Jamal and many other Muslims blame America for unleashing the violence. The doctor measured the cost of the war in blood—and the cost was too high. I would hear the same logic from many Iraqi friends. One of them put it this way: "The U.S. brought us Pepsi and cell phones at the cost of freedom and security." To them, Saddam Hussein's police state was preferable to today's random violence. That may sound like insanity to Americans, but in their assessment of the war's usefulness, Iraqis and Americans are actually in agreement. Since the beginning of 2006, opinion polls in the United States have consistently shown that a majority of Americans, like Iraqis, now see the invasion as a mistake.

Dr. Jamal exemplifies what America has lost. He is supremely capable, with medical expertise Iraq desperately needs. And he truly welcomed the U.S. invasion. If anyone was going to greet American soldiers with flowers, it was he.

"The first day after the war, President Bush was my hero," he said. "I was telling my friends Bush would go to heaven directly with the prophets."

Five years later he is filled only with disappointment and distrust. He believes American failures here were not the result of incompetence, but of an orchestrated plan to weaken Iraq. He credited the apparent success of the surge to Iraqis, or else it was an American election-year ploy.

"I believe Americans could have controlled Iraq in just one month, if they wanted," he said. "But they don't want to. They never wanted to."

If he had told me that on the first day of the invasion, I would have dismissed him as another peddler of the Great Middle Eastern Conspiracy Theory. But as I followed his own riveting experience of the war, I came to understand the debilitating force of America's failure to live up to its own promises. Across the region, Iraq was the boldest advertisement for the aggressive use of American power. And in the eyes of many Muslims, it was a lousy one— more proof of America's plans to control their lives. If

America had undermined its own principles in Egypt, in Iraq it had blown them to pieces—as measured by the thousands of bodies that have crowded Dr. Jamal's ER.

DR. JAMAL BEGAN his life full of promise. As a young man, he was the hardworking boy who overcame humble beginnings to fulfill his parents' dream of becoming a doctor. I told him his family was probably the only one in Iraq that managed to live a version of the American dream under Saddam Hussein.

His parents, both teachers on modest salaries, pushed all five of their children—four boys and one girl—to better themselves the best way they could: through their studies. Even in Saddam Hussein's Iraq, medicine remained largely a meritocracy.

"I didn't get to play football with the other kids," he said. "I worked hard so that I could get the marks to go to a college of medicine."

I found it fitting that such an educated family came from Babylon. For more than a thousand years, starting around 1770 BCE, Babylon was one of the biggest metropolises in the world, and an early pioneer in education, laws, writing, and architecture. During Saddam's time, however, Babylon was exceptional for what it revealed of his regime's brutality.

I saw the evidence dug from the earth in May 2003. One of the first mass graves discovered after the invasion was located in the middle of one of Babylon's most important archaeological sites. The location was intentional. Under Saddam Hussein, it was illegal to visit protected areas, a fact that had helped keep the bodies hidden.

I arrived on a hot spring morning to find hundreds of anxious relatives swarming over the ground. Residents of

Babylon had long suspected that the fields concealed the graves of Shiite Muslims killed after a 1991 uprising. After the first Gulf War, the United States had encouraged the revolt, with disastrous consequences. Now the people knew for certain. Bulldozers churned up the ground to find hundreds of decomposed bodies in military uniforms. Medical teams searched remains for identification cards, which were still inside the pockets of many victims. The killers had no expectation their crime would ever be discovered. A man with a bullhorn announced the names of the dead to waiting family members. One by one, grieving relatives came forward.

I watched one man as he heard the name of his eighteen-year-old brother, missing for twelve years. "I'd still been hoping he might come home one day," he said.

In two days they found 2,000 bodies: men, women, children, some handicapped. Many skeletons were still blindfolded. All had bullet holes in the backs of their heads. Family members left carrying all that remained of their relatives in clear plastic bags.

In the months leading up to the invasion, I traveled across the region—Syria, Egypt, the West Bank—to gauge feelings about the war "on the Arab street." Warnings from the war's opponents that the invasion would fuel terrorism rather than starve it appeared plausible. Wherever I went, Muslims told me they already felt under attack by the West—from Palestine to Afghanistan. Condemnations of the September 11 attacks seemed forced. They often came with the proviso that America, after all, had it coming. A U.S.-led invasion of Iraq would only add fuel to the fire. But on that morning in Babylon, I wondered: Could America prove the doubters wrong by giving Iraqis the justice Saddam Hussein, a Muslim, had denied them?

Dr. Jamal remembers feeling panic when the grave was found. He is a Shia, born just a few miles down the road. It was only good luck that none of his relatives ended up there. He was raised in an atmosphere of fear.

"It was a very, very hard situation. The security apparatus of the government was everywhere," he said. "They would not even allow you to talk."

He escaped, gaining entrance to the second-oldest medical school in Baghdad, the respected Al Mustansiriya medical college. His four siblings followed him. I wondered how many families in Iraq, or even in the United States, have produced five doctors.

Like many of Iraq's best and brightest, they went to Baghdad to study and practice. Through the 1980s and into the 1990s, Baghdad was a magnet for the best doctors across the Arab world. Riding the oil boom, Iraq had built state-of-the-art hospitals and medical colleges. Admissions were extremely competitive.

Yarmouk was the first choice for many medical students. A teaching hospital, it was seen as one of the best in the capital. Many officials in Saddam Hussein's regime were treated there. That was the ultimate sign of respect. It was also dangerous. Treat one of Saddam's officials unsuccessfully and you could end up dead. Yarmouk's doctors had to be good.

"In Saddam's period," Dr. Jamal said, "Yarmouk was famous."

Later in the 1990s, while Iraq suffered under strict economic sanctions, the hospitals went into decline. Doctors' salaries were reduced. Medicine became a working-class profession. Dr. Jamal was paid ten dollars a month.

He was desperate for change. He was educated, dedicated to his work, and eager to make a real difference for his country, given the opportunity. With the U.S. invasion in March 2003, he thought he had that chance.

The months after the invasion were an electrifying time in Iraq. There was a palpable feeling of anticipation across the capital. Anything was possible. The city was sprouting new Internet cafés, hotels, and art galleries for the expected flood of international visitors. An Iraqi friend discussed the idea of buying a KFC franchise for Baghdad—the perfect business in a city with grilled-chicken stands on every corner. The café of the Sheraton Hotel was a hot spot for Iraq's budding new media; at every table sat the staff of a different newspaper or magazine. Young journalists wearing scruffy beards and chain-smoking cigarettes laid the groundwork for the country's budding intelligentsia. Iraq appeared ready to boom. The question was, how fast?

Dr. Jamal and millions of other Iraqis believed their lives were about to change for the better. Their excitement was real, and their expectations were exceedingly high. From their perspective, America would unleash all of its wealth and know-how to turn Iraq from a crumbling pariah state into a modern country, welcomed by the world. In early 2004, a nationwide "Where Things Stand" poll by ABC News, the BBC, and *Time* magazine found that three-quarters of Iraqis expected improvements in security, schools, availability of jobs, medical care, crime protection, clean water, and power supply in the year ahead. For Dr. Jamal, no other result was possible. America was too powerful, too rich, and too capable.

"After the war, I was full of hope and optimistic that something would change," he told me. "Bush promised freedom and democracy. I believed him."

As a journalist, I was tempted to get caught up in the

excitement. It helped that reporting from Baghdad was actually fun. The outdoor pool at the Al-Hamra Hotel was bar, restaurant, gym, and—sometimes—pickup joint. I swam laps there two or three times a week. Before we were dating, my wife and I spent our first afternoon together at the pool café. Every Friday and Saturday the entire ABC staff would be driven there for parties, dropped off at 8:00 p.m., and picked up at midnight like kids at a prom.

Still, in the midst of the euphoria, I remembered a warning that a Special Forces commander had given me during the invasion. As an embedded reporter with a unit of Green Berets from 10th Special Forces Group, I was with the first American forces to enter Kirkuk in April 2003—a diminutive vanguard speeding into the city in two dusty old Land Rovers. Iraq's third-largest city fell with a whimper, and I was lucky to be the first American television reporter on the scene. In the following days, everywhere we went we were greeted with smiles, honking horns, and shouts of "America!" in heavily accented English. Maj. Ty Connett, veteran of U.S. operations in Bosnia and Afghanistan, turned to me with a smile and said, "Today they're giving us the thumbs-up. Tomorrow they'll be giving us the finger." He had seen it all before. Patience was short with occupying armies.

It was just after the American invasion that Yarmouk received its first visit from an American government official (and, according to Dr. Jamal, the only one). The visitor was retired Lt. Gen. Jay Garner, the U.S. administrator appointed by President Bush to oversee postwar Iraq. At the time the Bush administration expected a large-scale occupation to last just a few months, with authority for security and reconstruction quickly passing to an interim Iraqi government, and that the biggest challenges would be humanitarian: alleviation of short-term food shortages, and care of refugees fleeing the fighting.

The White House appointed Garner for his experience in handling humanitarian crises, including directing aid efforts in the Kurdish areas of northern Iraq after the first Gulf War. For the first weeks after the fall of Baghdad, the highest-ranking American civilian in Iraq would not be an ambassador or a governor, but the director of a soon-to-be obscure Office for Reconstruction and Humanitarian Assistance, or ORHA. When Garner visited Yarmouk, he made a grand promise.

"He told everyone in Yarmouk that after a few months a brand new hospital would be built here," said Dr. Jamal. "And no one would be able to believe the change."

Dr. Garner's tenure would be as short-lived as the city's false sense of security. In Baghdad in the summer of 2003, violence was still sporadic—a nuisance more than a defining phenomenon. A small attack on an American patrol, with minimal casualties, would lead the evening news. The United States was taking steps that seem like fantasy today. I remember ending one report in May 2003 with the news that the military had begun broadcasting a message to Iraqis that it was illegal to own or sell guns. Soon, however, insurgents attacked and killed U.S. soldiers with greater regularity. And the many well-paid contractors hired to rebuild Iraq's infrastructure were finding the country in greater disrepair than expected. Postwar Iraq would not be a humanitarian effort; it would be nation-building on a massive scale. After just one month, Garner and his office were replaced by L. Paul Bremer III and the Coalition Provisional Authority (CPA).

"Then Garner disappeared with all his promises," said Dr. Jamal. "No one else came later."

The mood changed for good on the morning of August 29, 2003. A suicide bomber drove a Soviet-made flatbed truck into the UN headquarters and detonated 1,500 pounds of high explosives packed with mortar shells, grenades, and a huge bomb. Twenty-two people, including the widely revered UN Ambassador Sergio de Mello, were killed. It was the first mass-casualty terrorist attack of postwar Iraq—and the first time the ER at Yarmouk was inundated with wounded and dead.

"That sent a message to the UN and to the world that Iraq is not their business, don't interfere here," Dr. Jamal said. "It was a scary plan, and unfortunately the terrorists would succeed."

For Dr. Jamal, a more severe warning came a few days later, when a massive car bomb in Najaf killed Mohammed Bakir al-Hakim, the revered Shiite Muslim leader and by some measures the second most powerful man in Iraq, after Ayatollah al-Sistani.

"The real sign wasn't the target himself, or the city, but the site of the attack, right in front of the Imam Ali mosque, the most sacred place for Shia Muslims," said Dr. Jamal. "For Shiites, this is something that is impossible to be touched. You can kill a million Shiites, but don't touch this shrine. It was clear to me then that the terrorists were starting to spark sectarian war."

Three years before the attack on the sacred mosque in Samarra that is widely seen as the fuse that ignited civil war, Dr. Jamal saw the early signs of Iraq's self-destruction.

The bombings at the UN and in Najaf ushered in a wave of violence. I sensed things had changed when I returned to northern Iraq in early 2004. Our trip north started (and stopped) with new security checkpoints all along the highway. Iraqi police searched cars for weapons, explosives, and suspected terrorists. They wouldn't say how they distinguished terrorists from the hundreds of drivers they saw each day; most cars passed without more than a quick look through the windshield. Still, they were on high alert.

They had reason to be. Suicide bombings had come to define Iraq. The terrorists had created an entire new scale of destruction, killing first by the dozens, then by the hundreds. I was in Erbil, in northern Iraq, hours after deadly suicide bombings killed 200 people at the offices of the two main political parties. The city was left in stunned silence. Hundreds of men crowded outside the blast sites, somehow managing not to make the slightest sound. A memorial service at the city's main mosque was equally somber. Every mourner was frisked at the gate; guards looked even under headscarves. Erbil had lost any sense that the north was immune from the terror attacks that started in the south. Downtown, the obituaries for those killed in the bombings—hand-painted on thin black sheets—lined the fence around Erbil's ancient citadel.

There were occasional glimmers of hope. I remember the energy of the city hall, the feel of a government beginning to function fully. A hallway full of offices buzzed with activity—handling land disputes, business contracts, unemployment, and so on. Out front, professional scribes offered their services on antique typewriters set on wooden boxes. The fee was 500 dinars, or about thirty cents, per page. There was excitement in the pure monotony of it all. I remember pulling into Mosul in time for the first major snowfall there in fourteen years. As big, wet clumps of sleety snow fell on the town, our drivers joined the kids playing in the streets.

This was the trajectory of the war: severe and worsening violence interspersed with sporadic moments of brightness.

January 2005 was supposed to be one of those moments. Millions of Iraqis went to the polls to elect a 275-member National Assembly, which would be charged with drafting a permanent constitution. It was Iraq's first free election in more than fifty years. Voters chose from more than 100 party "lists," which comprised loose coalitions of parties and special interests. Altogether, more than 7,000 Iraqis were running for office. This was a sea change for a country where power had been won and lost exclusively at the point of a gun.

Still, fears were high that insurgents would unleash a wave of violence to sabotage the vote. International election monitors retreated to Jordan to observe the election from afar. But Iraqis continued to go to the polls. President Bush declared that Iraqis had embraced democracy, and rejected the "anti-democratic ideology of the terrorists." Many in the Muslim world shared his optimism. The elections in Iraq helped usher in what some described as an "Arab Spring," as the Iraqi vote was soon followed by elections in Palestine, Egypt and, later, Saudi Arabia and Kuwait—all places where democracy had been only a dream.

Dr. Jamal eagerly went to the polls as well. His choice was unusual: Ahmed al-Chalabi, the darling of American neoconservatives, who was mostly reviled inside Iraq as a tool of Washington. To Dr. Jamal, that was Chalabi's advantage. He believed Iraq needed a leader who could work with the United States and the international community. Better him than candidates running purely on the basis of their sects, he thought. Dr. Jamal was worried his fellow Iraqis would vote purely along sectarian lines—worsening rather than alleviating the brewing civil war he'd first seen coming after al-Hakim's assassination.

"I knew that democracy in Iraq was so new, the Iraqis didn't know how to practice it," he said. "I was hoping that they would at least do the minimum not by choosing the right people, but at least by choosing people who would not harm them."

The results were as he expected: Sunnis largely voted for Sunni candidates, Shiites for Shiites, Kurds for Kurds.

"People on both sides, Shiite and Sunni, chose the radicals, those who were fighting for sectarian benefits and never Iraq or the Iraqi people," he said.

American politicians and journalists ignored this crucial fact at first. It was only months later, as the newly elected leaders dug in their heels along sectarian lines, that outsiders recognized the danger. The new government was further dividing Iraq rather than uniting the country behind democracy.

"After the election, I start losing my hope in a better future, not only because the new leaders were not the right men, but also because I knew that neither the U.S. nor the UN would accept them or cooperate with them," he said.

HE SAW THE evidence of the country's divisions in his ER. After a brief period of calm following the elections, by April 2005, violence again escalated sharply. I was getting lessons every day that the risk was real for everyone. Many of us at ABC News had first befriended Marla Ruzicka in Afghanistan, where she began her work tracking civilian casualties of war. She had used the ABC bureaus in Kabul and then Baghdad as an informal office for her NGO, CIVIC (Campaign for Innocent Victims in Conflict). On April 16 she became a civilian casualty herself, killed by a roadside bomb while traveling on the Baghdad Airport road. A bundle of charitable zeal, she died on her way home. Speaking to soldiers at Fort Hood that same week, President Bush called Iraq "a central front in the war on terror" and said, "We are defeating them there where they live, so we do not have to face them where we live."

Of course, Iraqis were facing the violence right at home. On the ground, Iraq was experiencing a new and dramatic rise in suicide bombings. Dr. Jamal estimated that Yarmouk hospital was receiving, on average, about 100 trauma cases a day.

Traveling around the capital was increasingly dangerous for foreigners. We moved more quickly and less frequently than the year before. Iraqis themselves lived every day in fear. On our way to meet Dr. Jamal at Yarmouk, our security guards went first, checking the route for potential threats. We entered the hospital through the back door. As we walked into the trauma ward, we found mayhem. A handful of police cars had just pulled up. In the bed of a police pickup were three bundles wrapped in cheap oriental carpets. As I looked closer, I realized they were bodies, burned and still smoking. The police convoy had come under attack.

Inside, the doctors rushed to treat the injured, while policemen waited in the hall, angry and impatient. As the doctors attempted a haphazard triage, the police shouted at them, demanding treatment for their fellow officers. Then they shouted at us to stop filming them.

We were witnessing a new threat for Dr. Jamal and his colleagues. As Iraqi security forces fell victim to more and more attacks, they often vented their frustration on doctors and medical staff at Yarmouk. Just as under Saddam, failure could be fatal. Tiny signs in the ER said NO WEAPONS ALLOWED, but everyone seemed to have a gun.

"Once, when I told a policeman that his friend had died, he pulled his gun on me, right in my face, threatening me," he said. "He was shouting, 'Bring him back!' I remember taking a few steps backwards, slowly, and I told him, OK, just please wait outside."

In the ER, we watched as Dr. Jamal and his colleagues worked desperately to save one young victim. There was no privacy: no curtains between beds, no room for staff or family members to keep a polite distance. The lifesaving work took place in the middle of a crowd. As Dr. Jamal attended one patient, a janitor mopped the blood off the floor under another, undisturbed by the scene around him.

The effect of the equipment shortages was frighteningly clear. Dr. Jamal rattled off a list of things he was missing.

"There's no heart monitor," he said. "And no ultrasound to examine inside the abdomen."

I watched him and the other doctors slowly give up on their patient. For the victim's brother, it was too much. He broke into tears and desperate cries.

"It's painful for us to work on a fellow Iraqi, doing our best, and he just dies," Dr. Jamal said.

Painful and dangerous.

"For me and the other doctors, it is just so scary," he said. "You feel that death is always so close to you."

IN NOVEMBER 2005, I visited Dr. Jamal again. Across Baghdad, the violence had grown even worse. After the elections hadn't dampened the violence, many hoped the start of the trial of Saddam Hussein would. Justice for the former dictator would be a powerful advertisement for Iraqi democracy.

I was one of a handful of reporters inside the courtroom on the first day. Saddam was the last of several defendants to enter the room. He looked far healthier and more energetic than the bearded vagrant who had emerged from a hole two years before, but he still cut a pathetic figure, wearing a cheap brown suit and sporting what looked like a last-minute dye job in his hair. He surveyed the scene, taking note of the press behind the glass. He wasn't handcuffed like the others; instead, he carried a Koran. The fiercely secular dictator had found God.

Five judges sat in a top row of seats, with five clerks just below them, including two women. Over the judges' heads was a plaque bearing the inscription IF YOU MUST BE A JUDGER OF MEN, THEN JUDGE WITH JUSTICE. I watched to see if any made eye contact with Saddam. Only the presiding judge did. I also watched the Iraqi journalists in the gallery. If I was amazed to see Saddam facing justice, they must have been ecstatic. They didn't cheer, but smiled in giddy disbelief.

From the start, Saddam was defiant and unruly, refusing a dozen times simply to state his name.

"I am the president of Iraq," he said. "You know me, because you are an Iraqi."

The judge responded curtly, "Sit down." Judge Rizgar Mohammed Amin had earned my respect.

Saddam showed his old cocky self, smiling and joking with the other defendants. When one of the defense lawyers saluted him, he smiled and placed his hand to his heart in a sign of Arab respect. He was reveling in the scene. As the Iraqi guards tried to escort him from the courtroom, he made a show of refusing to be touched. The guards insisted; he shook his elbows away.

The trial was seen as another potential turning point in the war, just as Saddam's capture had been two years before. But the violence found its way even into the courtroom. Two defense lawyers were assassinated. Other lawyers resigned in fear.

The trial made little difference in Dr. Jamal's bloody routine. He and his colleagues were sometimes seeing twice as many trauma patients per day as in April.

On a visit to the ER, I asked how many shooting victims he'd seen that day.

"More than twenty," he replied.

"Now, two years ago, would you ever see twenty shooting victims in a day?"

"Before the war? No, it was very rare to see even one guy shot."

Shootings were responsible for a small percentage of trauma cases. Bomb blasts were the far more common killer.

Despite repeated appeals, the hospital was still short of basic medicines and equipment. There were only twelve beds in the emergency room, half the number needed on the day we visited. The hospital pharmacy posted a daily update listing of what it had run out of. On this particular day it was ointments, eyedrops, and medicine for children. In the medical lab, there was antiquated equipment and just one microscope.

"This is the only lab in the hospital? It must be very busy. When families come here, do they get very angry?" I asked.

"For sure. They ask, 'Why is the lab so slow?' They end up blaming it on the doctors," he said.

The front lines in Iraq's growing sectarian conflict did not stop at the hospital entrance. Sunni insurgents came to kidnap and kill Shiite patients. Seeking revenge, Shiite militias did the same with Sunni patients. More than once, Dr. Jamal heard shots fired in the trauma ward.

The doctors themselves resisted the ethnic tension. Shiite and Sunni Muslims worked side by side. But they began to fear they would be targeted precisely because they were treating patients from all sects. Several doctors at other hospitals had been kidnapped and killed. Desperate for help, Dr. Jamal and his colleagues staged a strike, demanding better security inside the hospital.

"We were just asking that we be able to do our work," he said.

They would gain little in return.

Around the country, confidence was waning. In another installment of the nationwide "Where Things Stand" poll conducted in November 2005, again by ABC News, *Time*, and other partners, two-thirds of Iraqis said they expected their lives to improve in the coming year, down from three-quarters the year before.

ACROSS IRAQ, 2006 would prove even bloodier than 2005. In the spring, I returned to the north, driving into Kirkuk over the surrounding ridgeline (the same one I'd crossed in early April 2003). I met with the police chief, Sherko Hakim. He was ashen-faced when he pulled up in a police pickup truck, six armed guards in the back. He'd just returned from the morgue, where he'd identified a relative killed two hours earlier by a roadside bomb. One of his guards still had blood on his shirt.

Sherko told me that Kirkuk was in the midst of a low-level civil war—Sunnis killing Shiites killing Kurds killing Turkmen. Kirkuk is effectively a miniature Iraq, a cauldron of ethnicities. I noticed during our interview that he was wearing an Idaho lapel pin. Why Idaho? I asked him. He said an American general gave it to him. He then told me he was applying for asylum in the United States for himself and his entire family—his wife, four sons, and a daughter. As police chief, he was a prime target for insurgents. From his front pocket he pulled a letter from the State Department, explaining in the boilerplate language of a form letter that the United States does not offer asylum purely for personal safety. The letter told him to ask his local police force for protection.

Everywhere the signs of chaos were becoming more pervasive. Iraqi authorities imposed a 24-hour curfew on Baghdad banning all traffic. Saudi Arabia announced it would build a fence running the length of its border with Iraq to prevent the fighting from spilling into its territory. Several more lawyers involved in Saddam Hussein's genocide trial were killed. In September 2006 in Washington, President Bush said war critics were buying into enemy propaganda.

Travel around Baghdad had never been more hazardous. Planning a meeting with Dr. Jamal became a full-scale security operation. On our way to visit him in September 2006, a gunfight broke out in front of the hospital just as our security guards arrived to scope the location for safety. So we decided to meet him at another hospital where he saw patients part-time. The surrounding neighborhood was relatively safer. Still, Dr. Jamal warned us to stay no longer than thirty minutes. Any longer and the word might get out to insurgents that an American reporter was there. These were everyday decisions for journalists in Iraq. But Dr. Jamal and other Iraqis went to work every day in spite of the danger.

Nationally, this was one of the deadliest months for Iraqi civilians since the start of the war, but emergency rooms in Baghdad were quieter. It wasn't because there was less violence; the violence was just deadlier. I followed Dr. Jamal on his rounds.

"Now people are arriving dead because of so many assassinations?" I asked him.

"Yes, yes, the violence is always changing in Iraq, and the new strategy for terrorists is kidnapping and killing people," he said. "That makes me as a doctor feel so sad because I will not go through my battle to save lives. This is bad. This hurts me as a doctor."

"They go straight to the morgue?" I asked.

"Straight to the morgue," he said. "As a doctor, you can do nothing—just watch the dead bodies."

On some days, Yarmouk took in as many as fifty dead bodies.

Baghdad had become a modern-day killing field. It was an urban murder spree on a scale greater than anything Americans had experienced, even during the most crime-ridden stretches of the 1980s and early 1990s. In 1990, New York's deadliest year, the city had 2,605 murders in a population of 7.3 million people. At the worst points of 2006, Baghdad, with a population comparable to New York's, had the same number of violent deaths in a single month.

The killing settled into a morbid rhythm: kill at night, dispose of the bodies in the morning. For Baghdad's police, the days began collecting the dead. The river was a favorite dumping ground.

I joined the Baghdad River Police on the grim mission of searching for the dead on the Tigris River. The insurgents liked using the river because the currents carried bodies downstream, away from the scene of the crime. A bonus was that the bodies were usually recovered long after they could be identified.

With Baghdad's morgue overflowing, Yarmouk hospital was another favorite dumping ground. Insurgents and security forces would drop bodies at the main entrance at the rate of twenty or thirty a day.

Inside, the hospital's equipment shortages had gotten no better. The trauma ward still had only twelve beds. And the lab still had only that single microscope. Blood was in such short supply that doctors imposed a harsh new rule. When a patient received blood, the doctors confiscated his or her ID card until a relative or friend donated an equal amount of blood to replace it. In all of Baghdad, there was only one blood donor center where blood could be taken and properly screened. Each hospital had a local bank as well, but no one bothered to donate blood anymore and even if they did, hospitals had no way to screen it.

"If we gave blood freely, we'd have no blood to give," Dr. Jamal explained. "It's not so hard to set up another big blood bank, but nobody cares."

Despite the doctors' best efforts, the sectarian battle lines finally began to divide the staff. Before the war, there was an almost equal mix of Sunni and Shiite doctors. But now most of the Shiite doctors have stopped showing up for work. That's because Yarmouk is in a mostly Sunni neighborhood, and it was no longer safe for Shiites. The violence precipitated citywide ethnic cleansing.

"I've started to notice that only the Sunni doctors are coming to work. It's so hard to me because I respect all the religions and the sects," Dr. Jamal told me with a sad look in his eyes.

He was rapidly becoming the only Shiite in the building. But he stayed.

"I am trying to help. You know, this depends on your loyalty to your country," he said. "If I don't do it, who will? If I just leave Iraq, just like the doctors who have left, who will treat those people?"

The answer was fewer and fewer doctors. Between 2006 and 2007, more than forty doctors resigned from the hospital. Dr. Jamal said that another forty or so didn't show up for work. Yarmouk's staff of doctors fell from 400 to 300 just after the invasion. During the same period, the number of trauma patients rose tenfold. Yarmouk was left desperately short of the specialists needed to treat basic trauma. There were too few orthopedic surgeons to patch together shattered limbs, and too few anesthesiologists for the operating rooms.

The brain drain was being felt across the country. By 2008, 75 percent of doctors, nurses, and pharmacists had left their jobs, with over 50 percent of them leaving the country entirely, according to a study by the UK-based health charity Medact. Iraq was left with an average of only six doctors per 10,000 people (compared with twenty-seven doctors per 10,000 people in the United States). The overall exodus from Iraq totaled at least 2 million people at its peak—the largest movement of refugees in the world in sixty years. Iraqis' earlier confidence was disappearing. They were voting with their feet.

ON EACH RETURN visit, I was hoping I'd see signs that the United States had come through. I knew there were dedicated Americans in the military and at the embassy who were familiar with Yarmouk's needs. I wondered, when would we send in the cavalry? But Dr. Jamal said he never saw the help he needed. So I went on the hunt, asking several U.S. agencies operating in Iraq—the U.S. military, the U.S. Army Corps of Engineers, USAID, the Iraq Reconstruction Management Office (or IRMO, a division of the U.S. Department of State)—what they had done for Yarmouk. Yarmouk would be a case study in the overall rebuilding effort by America and Iraq.

What I found seemed insubstantial in terms of the hospital's needs and as part of the $45 billion the United States has provided for Iraq's reconstruction: in 2005, $121,500 from the Multinational Division Baghdad to renovate the hospital; $50,000 from USAID to rehabilitate Yarmouk's Handicapped Vocational Institute and buy office and technical supplies, also in 2005; and between 2003 and 2007, one ultrasound scanner, one "microbiological safety cabinet," and 199 hospital beds. That was all for Baghdad's premier trauma hospital. The American military has often had a better record of putting reconstruction money into action in Iraq. But according to Dr. Jamal, American soldiers usually came to Yarmouk when they were looking for insurgents among the wounded and dead.

"They were not coming to help us," he said.

The Iraqi government was rarely helping, either. It was a problem nationwide. In January 2008 the U.S. Government Accountability Office (GAO)—the investigative arm of Congress—reported that Iraq had spent less than 5 percent of its annual reconstruction budget by August 2007, undermining Bush administration claims that Iraq was beginning to allocate a significant portion of its oil revenues to finance its own reconstruction.

Calculating the cost in lives is difficult—and depressing. In 2006 the Iraq Medical Association released a report saying that 90 percent of Iraq's 180 hospitals lacked essential equipment. The results are real. Doctors at Yarmouk estimate they lose about five patients a day owing to lack of equipment, adding up to more than 1,800 preventable deaths per year.

Like Dr. Jamal, most Iraqis had lost confidence in America's ability to improve their lives. In a nationwide poll by ABC News conducted in February 2007—the third installment of the "Where Things Stand" series—only 35 percent saw better days ahead, down from two-thirds in 2005 and three-quarters in 2004. Nationwide, 67 percent of Iraqis said postwar reconstruction efforts in their area had been ineffective or nonexistent. Iraqis' patience had run out.

I lost patience as well. From Afghanistan to Palestine to rural China, I had learned that attempting charity on assignment was more likely to soothe my conscience than to help. I convinced myself this could be a journalistic case study. If the United States couldn't help Dr. Jamal, how easily could I?

I contacted doctors in the States to see how difficult it would be to find the equipment Dr. Jamal was looking for. His wish list was long, but seemed fairly straightforward: pulse oximeters, chest tubes, portable X-rays, defibrillators. It turns out there's a glut of secondhand but functional medical equipment in the United States. Hospitals have little use for it once it is replaced. Within a few days I had found an American Muslim doctor with a long history of charitable work in Latin America. He contacted a group of doctors in Boston who sourced used medical equipment for charity. We found the machines; now we needed a plane.

The next challenge was getting the bulky, fragile medical equipment from a quiet neighborhood in Boston to a war zone in Baghdad. I contacted the air freight company, Pilot Air, which is a contractor for the U.S. military. Pilot Air ships military equipment for the army to Iraq, some of it very big. Business was booming. They told me they could ship the machines from Boston to Baghdad in a few days, safely and at a relatively low cost. In May 2007 we made our first delivery.

My ad-hoc team was nowhere near being an organized NGO—and we had no illusions that we'd made a long-term impact. I'd rustled together my brother-in-law and an old college roommate to make it happen. In the end, we had our challenges, but we'd gotten a shipment of supplies into Baghdad. That must have checked a to-do box somewhere in the category of "humanitarian aid." Why could we get Yarmouk some of the equipment it needed in a few weeks and for a few hundred dollars, but the U.S. government could not?

I asked Secretary of State Condoleezza Rice what she thought of Yarmouk's seeming invisibility to America's successive reconstruction efforts in Baghdad. The setting was the International Conference on Iraq in Sharm el-Sheikh, Egypt, in May 2007. With the situation on the ground in Iraq rapidly deteriorating, representatives of more than sixty countries had gathered to cobble together common goals for stabilizing the country. I wandered the convention halls, speaking with delegates and listening to foreign ministers' speeches. There was a sense of futility in the air. The speeches avoided grand promises. The goals were modest. Secretary Rice and her aides constantly reiterated that the simple fact that people were meeting meant progress.

Secretary Rice and I met in her hotel. After running through prepared questions on the U.S. troop surge and the summit, I put my notebook down and told her I was going to ask her a personal question.

"Iraqis always repeat to me that they're looking for positive changes to their lives," I said. "Does the power go on when they flip the switch? Does the hospital, when I take my child there, have basic equipment? They're not seeing those changes. When is it going to change for the better?"

"The interaction of security and reconstruction is a very important interaction, and it's a complex interaction," Rice said. "You need reconstruction in order to help provide security and security in order to help provide reconstruction."

This was a point that had long been clear on the ground, but how was the American government going to address it? Could it? Rice said that the United States was beginning to focus on more-localized efforts, in particular "emergency response funds," which were essentially cash handouts at the disposal of local American commanders. It was a strategy the U.S. military had implemented with some successes, but few that were visible beyond the micro-scale.

"Frankly, some of the more large-scale projects that we were engaged in, while some of them have delivered, it's harder to provide security for them," she said. "Doing it in conjunction with local and provincial leadership may be able to provide to the Iraqi people more near-term benefits."

More than a year later, Yarmouk, and Dr. Jamal, had yet to receive any money from the emergency response fund.

BY THE END of 2007, something surprising was happening: the violence in Iraq was diminishing. Beginning in April, the United States deployed an additional 30,000 troops to Iraq, bringing the total number of U.S. forces there to 168,000, the highest since the invasion. American forces then launched an aggressive military campaign to provide security in Baghdad neighborhoods. The troop surge soon showed results. Estimates of the monthly death toll vary, but by early 2008, most reports put the number killed at roughly 50 percent of the level one year earlier. U.S. troop deaths dropped from 126 in May 2007 to 30 by June 2008.

The drop was particularly steep in Baghdad. By September 2007, Yarmouk was seeing about fifteen trauma cases per day—a fraction of the number a year earlier. In December the number had dropped to six. By February 2008, the ER was receiving just five patients per day. Dr. Jamal had not been expecting this. I heard relief in his voice and something unfamiliar: happiness.

"Baghdad is much better. People are going now to markets even in the late hours," he said. "Government offices are actually doing their work. Families can even find places to go out."

Dr. Jamal did not question the numbers, but he did question the causes. He credited Moqtada al-Sadr for standing down his massive militia, the Mahdi Army, and Sunni tribes for turning against Al-Qaeda in western Iraq. His explanation wasn't outlandish or unfair. American officials identified both as significant causes of the decline. But Dr. Jamal doubted the United States had played any positive role at all.

"The changes happened out of America's control," he said. "The U.S. faced a different situation, so they have to prove they are not really the motivators of the violence here."

For him, the change had come too late and after too much bloodshed.

"All of us in Iraq have heard many promises, but none of them have been fulfilled. I think the Americans can win the war, but they don't want to win," he said. "They don't have the real intention to win the war."

I knew the war had been a disappointment for many Iraqis. But a conspiracy? Absolutely. To Dr. Jamal, and other Iraqis I have met, the continued instability is part of an intentional American plan to weaken the country and justify a long-term or even permanent military occupation. For Iraqis, there is history behind the suspicions. They remember American support for Saddam Hussein during the devastating war with Iran in the 1980s. And they remember America's call for a Shiite rebellion after the first Gulf War, to which Saddam Hussein responded by slaughtering thousands while America stood by. America's broken promises since the invasion seal the deal.

"With all the American capabilities and American soldiers, so brave, so qualified, the U.S. could control a country like Iraq," he said. "It's not even the size of one state in the U.S.!"

There it was again. The great paradox of America's position in the Muslim world: deep distrust of American intentions coupled with unrealistic confidence in American power.

The thinking was familiar, but for me this latest conspiracy theory carried greater consequences. Iraq was America's single most ambitious sales pitch to the Arab world. The United States laid all its principles on the line here: democracy, justice, and economic might, and over four years, each principle was betrayed. Democracy was shattered by violence and elections along ethnic lines. American justice was undermined by the abuses at Abu Ghraib and Guantanamo. And America's economic might was tarnished by plodding and inconsistent reconstruction.

Each successive failure led Dr. Jamal to conclude this was America's objective all along.

The suspicions were reflected in the February 2007 installment of the "Where Things Stand" poll (conducted jointly by ABC, the BBC, *USA Today*, and German television, ARD), in which 59 percent of Iraqis said they thought the United States "controlled things" in Iraq. Only 24 percent had said so in 2005. Four in ten Iraqis blamed U.S. and coalition forces or George W. Bush himself for the violence. Less than one-fifth identified Al-Qaeda and foreign jihadi fighters. Fifty-six percent now supported either a government headed by a strong leader for life or an Islamic state ruled by religious law. Only 43 percent still favored a democracy. It took five years of chaos, but many Iraqis now looked back to the days of Saddam with nostalgia.

Conspiracy theories are sport in the Middle East, so I had my rebuttals. My defense leads with the "get real" argument. If the CIA couldn't poison Fidel Castro's cigar, how could it stage 9/11 and get away with it, let alone destroy an entire country? America's good intentions are a tough sell in this part of the world. More seriously, I asked Dr. Jamal what we could possibly achieve by bogging down the U.S. military for years and spending trillions of dollars in a losing battle. Dr. Jamal's response was quick.

"It's not just for oil, but for selling weapons," he said. "Selling everything, soldiers need new tanks, new equipment, it's about money, not just oil."

The specter of the military-industrial complex had survived the Vietnam War and made it all the way to Yarmouk and my friend Dr. Jamal.

Throughout my friendship with Dr. Jamal, I've sensed his pain more than cynicism or bitterness. For us, Iraqi deaths may be cold measures of the violence. For him, they are the human cost of this war—and the cost was too high. Dr. Jamal bristles at suggestions that America showed resolve with the troop surge or by resisting calls to withdraw American forces. Did Americans show resolve back in the safety of the United States, he asked, or here in Baghdad?

Beyond the death toll, the consequences of the war are enormous and lasting. To Dr. Jamal, his country is broken, a shadow of its former self and a universe away from the country America promised. That was the essential lesson Dr. Jamal taught me. Iraq may rise from the ashes in Americans' judgment, but in the eyes of a doctor who had seen the consequences up close, the U.S. vision of a model country was gone. And, more troublingly, he believes that's what the United States intended all along.

I R A N

DEAF TO AMERICA

WHEN I FIRST met Babak Zamanian, I wasn't sure whether he was brave or reckless. He's the student leader behind one of the boldest public protests Iranian president Mahmoud Ahmadinejad ever faced. When the president came to speak at Tehran Polytechnic University on December 20, 2006, several students jumped onto their seats to interrupt him, burning his photograph and shouting, "Death to the dictator." They broke in several more times, chanting and throwing firecrackers. As he stopped and started his speech, Ahmadinejad was visibly unnerved. He shouted back, accusing the students of being "Americanized"—fighting words in Iran, even for dissidents. It was a courageous act of defiance, for sure, but I'd seen Iranians arrested just for showing up at a street demonstration. To organize this protest, cursing the firebrand Iranian president in public, Babak had to have a death wish.

That day, Babak told me he wanted to show the world that not all Iranians agree with Ahmadinejad's belligerent rhetoric. I started my report from Tehran that night for ABC with images of the demonstration. It was news to hear a chant here that began "Death to . . ." but didn't end with

"U-S-A." The protest gained wide coverage even in Iran, where the media rarely risks irritating the powers that be.

The government's reaction was swift and severe. The campus was soon crawling with dozens of Basijis— members of the Basij paramilitary force established by Aya- tollah Khomeini after the 1979 revolution, notorious for doling out beatings from the backs of motorcycles. They began showing up at every sort of student activity, from political organizations like Babak's to science clubs. They harassed students and shut down independent newspapers.

"We showed him to be nothing more than a straw man," Babak said, "so the little dictator showed his rage."

When I met him a few days later, Babak was on crutches after Basijis had broken his foot at another anti-government rally. The third time we talked, he had been expelled from the university.

I asked him why he kept at it. He told me, "The risks are inevitable, but we're determined to continue." As spokes- man for his student group, he was quick with the defiant catchphrase, but he also took me aside and made me prom- ise to tell his story if something worse were to happen to him. I knew he was scared. A few months later he was in jail, in solitary confinement at Tehran's notorious Evin prison, where Iran's most forthright thinkers, journalists, and political leaders are sent to suffer and die. He would spend a horrific forty days there.

Over the next two years, Babak and I became friends and undercover pen pals. We kept in touch even when I was outside the country, through a tortuous series of cryptic e-mails and phone conversations. This was not melodrama but necessity. We knew the Iranian authorities were listen- ing—and any political discussion could land Babak right back in prison. I lost any sense that he was in this for the thrill.

During numerous assignments there—from the presidential elections to the nuclear crisis—I have been encouraged by the young Iranians I have met. They are not the fist-wagging, flag-burning protesters we most often see from Tehran. I've always found those demonstrations deftly stage-managed by the government, right down to the televised cries of "Death to America." Many young Iranians are far more open-minded in the way they think, dress, and drink than most Americans are aware of. They are, in effect, more like us—right down to an intractable belief that they are always in the right.

Still, mention "the enemy" to Iranians and they know you mean America. Babak and I—like Iranians and Americans as a whole—are divided by diametrically opposed views of just about every fact of history and politics.

Americans remember the 1979 takeover of the U.S. embassy by Iranian students. Iranians remember the 1953 CIA-backed coup that overthrew the elected prime minister and brought them the dictatorial reign of the Shah.

We cite Iran's support for Hezbollah in Lebanon and Hamas in Palestine. They remind us of American support for Saddam Hussein during the Iran-Iraq War, which killed more than one million Iranians, and for the mujahideen who fought the Soviets in Afghanistan in the 1980s.

We condemn Iran's Seemingly indefatigable quest for nuclear weapons. Ever conscious of history, they remind us how the British, Germans, French, and Americans encouraged the Shah to develop that very know-how in the 1970s. When I interviewed the Iranian foreign minister, Manoucher Mouttaki, he brought a copy of a letter he said the Eisenhower administration had sent to the Shah in the 1950s, praising Iranian efforts to acquire nuclear technology.

Even more pointedly, they, like many in the region, say the United States not only has the bomb, but is also the only country in the world that has used it—twice. "Why can you be trusted with it and we can't?" they'll ask. My trips to Iran are always an exercise in the power of perspective.

The most striking difference is the Iranians' sense of who is standing in the way of peace. Babak dreams of an American-style democracy for Iran, but today he worries the United States is making it impossible. For Babak, the United States is contributing to the problem by seeking confrontation, rather than common ground, in a country where there is actually more common ground than many Americans imagine: more moderates, more democracy, more shared values than among many of America's allies in the region. If the United States was a beacon of hope for Soviet dissidents during the Cold War, for Iranian dissidents like Babak it is a mounting danger.

I came to Iran to assess America's standing in what many believe could be the next flashpoint in the wider conflict between America and radical Islam. When Americans speak of solutions, everyone agrees the United States should be courting dissidents like Babak. But in this country where America may need allies most, dissidents are telling us to keep our distance. I lost any doubt that solving America's image problem would be complicated and long-term.

BABAK IS A lanky twenty-two-year-old. At six feet two, he weighs just 160 pounds or so—his bulk stretched almost unnaturally along his willowy frame. Suffering from heart and thyroid problems, he walks with a plodding pace that gives him the air of a middle-aged man. When I first interviewed him, he limped in on crutches, looking almost embarrassed by his broken foot—the result of an attack by Basijis.

He has no personal memory of the event that still defines Iran for many Americans, the 1979 takeover of the U.S. embassy in Tehran. Like two-thirds of Iran's population, he was born after the revolution. To him, his country's defining historical event is a distant, ethereal idea—theory more than reality.

Still, Babak is a child of the revolution. His father, a student at Tehran University in 1979, cheered the U.S. embassy takeover and belonged to some of the same student groups as the hostage-takers.

"Iran's most prestigious Iranian university was a major hotbed of revolutionary activity," Babak said proudly. "My mother and father contributed to the success of the Iranian revolution."

Defying America was at the very root of the 1979 revolution—a tradition that continues today in the bombastic rhetoric Iranian leaders use to attack the United States and Israel.

Babak's father was the scion of a privileged, educated family from rural Nahavand, which has enormous cultural cachet in Iran. It is an ancient city, remembered as the site of the battle where Arab warriors overcame Persian armies to bring Islam to Iran. His grandfathers had been feudal landowners under the Shah. But Babak's early years were difficult times. He was born in 1985, in the midst of the Iran-Iraq War. Nahavand was a favorite target of Iraqi bombers.

The war and its aftermath were Babak's first introduction to American influence. It was an acutely damaging one. As a child, Babak asked his father why America—a country so far away—had supported the reviled Saddam Hussein. His father's answer was that the United States supported Iraq purely to weaken Iran. As Babak recounted the story, it occurred to me this was one Middle Eastern conspiracy theory that was actually true.

"My first sense of the U.S. was that it was ready to do anything to support its own interests," he said. "There's nothing it wouldn't do."

The war was ruthless on both sides. Iran sent tens of thousands of young volunteers in suicidal "human wave" attacks on Iraqi forces. Iraq used chemical weapons to repel the assaults, including the first ever use of nerve gas in combat. The United States learned of Iraq's deployment of chemical weapons in November 1983, one month before Donald Rumsfeld was famously caught on camera giving Saddam a hug. America would later block all UN Security Council resolutions condemning Iraq's chemical weapons use, and would even supply Iraq with chemical and biological weapons components.

Inspired by his father, Babak was already a political activist as a teenager. He found his heroes in Iran's burgeoning reformist movement. Nearly two decades after 1979, there was a growing sense in Iran that the revolution had lost its way. Even some of the revolution's architects argued that the country's current leaders were too conservative and too cut off from the West. In 1997, when Babak was only eleven, moderate Mohammed Khatami had been elected president. He soared into power on the backs of young voters, who were impressed with his calls for relaxing social restrictions and opening up to the West. Babak and many of his peers were intoxicated by a sense that young Iranians had a role in their country and a president who listened to them. Khatami put a friendlier face on what was still a devoutly Islamist government. But he instituted real change, nowhere more so than in U.S.-Iranian relations.

In January 1998, Khatami went on CNN, a network seen as an American mouthpiece by some in Iran, and called for a "dialogue among civilizations." Everyone knew he was talking about America and Iran. American officials later reciprocated. Secretary of State Madeleine Albright gave a speech in March 2000 in which she explicitly apologized for America's role in the 1953 overthrow of Mohammed Mossadegh—the first time an American government official had ever issued such an apology. She said the coup "was clearly a setback for Iran's political development." For Babak, these were truly revolutionary words—the equivalent of Japan apologizing for the attack on Pearl Harbor or Iran apologizing for the takeover of the U.S. embassy.

American and Iranian officials were making contact in ways they had avoided for nearly twenty years. Later in 2000, contrary to previous practice, Secretary Albright and President Clinton remained present while Khatami addressed the UN General Assembly. Still, even small gestures required grand diplomatic machinations—and both sides were hesitant. When Clinton tried to stage a handshake with Khatami, the Iranian president balked at the last minute, under pressure, it was thought, from Iran's hard-line clerics.

The September 11 attacks and the subsequent U.S. invasion of Afghanistan provoked other substantive signs of rapprochement. Iran's supreme religious leader, the true head of government in Iran, Ayatollah Khamenei, immediately condemned the attacks. Iran offered support to the U.S. military on search-and-rescue operations in

Afghanistan. After the Taliban were overrun, American and Iranian diplomats cooperated on the formation of a new Afghan government. The U.S. special envoy to Afghanistan at the time, James Dobbins, said that no one country had been more helpful than Iran. There was talk of broader negotiations, even the long-touted "grand bargain," covering all bilateral disagreements from nuclear work to economic ties to diplomatic relations.

At home, Khatami was making changes as well. Iranian activists spoke of a new golden age of Iranian civil society. Iran already had a more developed civil society than most of its Arab neighbors. According to a report by the Council on Foreign Relations, an estimated five to eight thousand NGOs were active in Iran, including Islamic charities, human rights groups, and legal aid societies, as well as student organizations such as Babak's. Now the government increased financial support to non-government organizations. Young people found new freedoms as well, some substantive, some symbolic. Women started wearing makeup again in public and pushing their veils farther and farther back on their heads until they were more fashion accessories than symbols of religious modesty. Energized by the mood, Babak openly criticized rule-by-mullah and was nearly expelled from school several times.

"It was during this time that I became ideological, believing that a completely democratic system could be built," he said.

Babak was drawn to Tehran, just as his father had been in the 1970s. He passed the extremely competitive entrance exam for the civil engineering school of Tehran's Polytechnic University. He joined the university's biggest student activist group, the Islamic Student Association. Despite the name, the association had nothing to do with religion. In Iran, students always found it easier to get a group approved by campus authorities if they included something religious in the title. For better or worse, Babak soon established himself as one of the most public faces of the opposition.

"I became the most recognized and newsworthy political figure among Iran's student movement," he told me proudly.

Some Iranians pinpoint the beginning of the end of this promising U.S.-Iranian diplomatic dance to President Bush's 2002 State of the Union address, when he dubbed Iran part of the "Axis of Evil" along with Iraq and North Korea. Babak was dumbfounded. Iraq was Iran's mortal enemy, and he'd never met a North Korean, let alone considered North Korea an ally. There were many failures at home as well; Iran's reformers delivered few of the changes they had promised. Babak wasn't surprised to see the goodwill with America fade, but he was disappointed. Accurate polling is difficult in Iran, but one poll found that 70 percent of Iranians wanted to normalize relations with the United States. They may not love us, but they don't want to go to war with us.

ANY AMERICAN WHO'S convinced Iranians are somehow programmed to be our enemies should spend some time with college students in Tehran. This is, after all, a country where you can have alcohol—anything from Russian vodka to cold beer to fine wine—delivered straight to your door.

I spent an evening two summers ago with a Tehran rock

band. The three members practiced in a sixty-square-foot garage next to one of their apartments. The walls were covered with posters time-warped from a 1980s American teenager's bedroom. Pantera. Black Sabbath. Nirvana. The band played me three songs, two American covers and an instrumental they wrote themselves. They were a garage band straight from central casting: the disinterested looks, the slow walks, the cigarettes tossed away without a thought. One Iranian friend described "a silent revolution" among young people. Frustrated by a government they see as fossilized, tiny rebellions are the only way they stay sane.

Take a trip to the ski resort in Dizin, just a two-hour drive from Tehran, and the skiers look like they hopped off the lifts in the Rockies or the Alps. Women show their hair under tiny ski hats and glide down the slopes in skintight suits. Men and women alike sport tanning-salon skin tones. I met a sixteen-year-old girl named Elham, who spoke perfect English. Sighing, she said it was a relief to have a place like Dizin. Several of the young skiers I met had lived in the United States. I was amazed they had decided to come home. A twenty-five-year-old named Reza told me, "In Iran, you can buy your freedom." Dizin is an expensive, snow-covered escape.

Young Iranians are forthright and friendly—open-minded and amazingly hip. They are better educated than their parents were. The number of state universities increased from twenty-two in 1978 to more than a hundred today. And they are largely urbanized: 70 percent live in large cities. Most important, they have a far more positive view of the United States than do people in nearly every other Muslim country in the region, except for

Afghanistan. A World Public Opinion poll in 2007 found that most Iranians believe it is possible to find common ground with America. Overwhelming majorities also reject Osama bin Laden and endorse democracy.

Still, Iranians' view of America is a complex mix of the exceedingly positive and dismally negative. The same poll found that a large majority see U.S. foreign policy as threatening, and very few believe the primary goal of the war on terror is to keep America safe from terror attacks.

As a student activist, Babak dreams of the freedom Americans have to speak up against their government. His student organization was modeled in part on American college activism during the 1960s, with bold public demonstrations (like the burning of Ahmadinejad's photo) intended to confront Iranian leaders directly and in public.

"'Throughout my life, there's always been propaganda against the U.S.," he said. "But I personally have never had any hard feelings."

It's America's foreign policy that drives him crazy. He believes the United States, in its relations with Iran and other Muslim countries, consistently violates its own principles—fighting terrorism with what he sees as state terrorism in Iraq and Afghanistan, or supporting dictators in Egypt, Saudi Arabia, and elsewhere while talking up democratic reform.

"I'm concerned because with the U.S. and other western countries, whenever national interests come into play, they don't pay attention to human rights issues," he said.

A pro-democracy activist who hates America is much more difficult to grasp than the stereotypical "Death to America" chanting demonstrator we usually associate with Iran, but he may be more representative of Iranians

today. Like most foreign reporters, I've made many stops—
rites of passage, really—at Tehran University for Friday
prayers. This was where Ayatollah Khomeini rallied the
young students who took over the U.S. embassy and
brought revolution to Iran in 1979. Today the Friday sermons still draw a crowd and are still injected with vitriolic
critiques of the United States. On my first visit, amused by
the sight of a visiting American, the mullahs invited me
onto the podium to watch. From there the mosque looks
more like a football stadium than a place of worship: a
huge, paved expanse open at the sides and covered with a
giant steel roof. Thousands of men sat on the ground in
neatly arranged rows, listening intently and bowing their
heads to the floor in unison. Women worshipped separately,
in their own section behind the men. When the services
were over, the crowd left quietly, until we took out our
camera. Seemingly on cue, a group of mostly older men
jumped into the shot and delivered the signature chant.
They were just a few of the several thousand who had
attended that day. Some of them could barely keep a
straight face. This was more performance than anger.

I went back to Tehran University again during the 2006
Israeli-Lebanese war. Outside the mosque, pro-Hezbollah
demonstrations were scheduled perfectly, just as worship-
pers were leaving. As they walked up the road to the main
bus station, the crowd chanted a little and then headed
home. In all, the "protest" lasted six minutes. Few of the
demonstrators I spoke with expressed much love for
Hezbollah.

"Iran has other problems," a twenty-four-year-old named
Armin told me. "We need to build our own country."

In Iran, dissent is not confined to the post-revolution
generation. Some of the very people who helped bring down

the Shah and establish an Islamic state believe the revolution has lost its way. During the presidential elections in 2005, I met Azam Taleghani. She is the daughter of the late Ayatollah Taleghani, one of the founders of the revolution and—at the time—a near-equal to Ayatollah Khomeini in stature. In her early sixties, she runs a community center providing training to rural women, one of the thousands of independent NGOs operating in Iran. A strict religious conservative, she greeted me in several layers of black chador and fought a running battle with her veil to make sure it covered every last strand of her hair. As we spoke, though, I got to know a tough, principled, and open-minded woman. She was an aspiring candidate for president herself, except the government had banned all female candidates. She launched a one-woman campaign against the ruling.

"They never gave a legal reason," she complained. "The Iranian constitution says nothing about a men-only presidency!"

She lost, of course, but she succeeded in holding the government to account. She had other bones to pick with Iranian leaders. She told me women should be able to choose whether or not to wear the chador. She also supported dating, as long as it's supervised and there's a serious prospect of marriage. With a government dominated by ideologues, these are progressive opinions.

At the end of our meeting, with a mischievous sparkle in her eyes, she broke out of Farsi and started chatting away in English. She'd just been to New York and loved it.

"Do you think it will be easier for Iranians to travel to the U.S. in the future?" she asked hopefully.

I found dissenters even in Qom, the "Vatican" of Iran and the ideological heart of the revolution. As we drank tea on the floor of his office, a well-known moderate mullah named Ayazi told me that faith, in his view, was a private choice and not to be imposed by the state. He wanted a truly independent legislature and true multi-party rule. However, his face had been banned from Iranian television. He could only speak to foreigners. Later I met Ayatollah Bayat, another close confidant of Khomeini during the revolution. His answers to my questions were half-hour sermons, full of criticisms of the current regime. Ayatollah Khomeini, he said, would not approve of today's Iran.

Many of the most open-minded, critical Iranians I met—including Babak—are still true believers in the 1979 revolution, not just as a religious event but as the watershed moment when Iran achieved independence from America. It's just that today's leaders have taken religion many steps too far.

"Religion has been taken advantage of for political purposes," Babak told me. "Religion has a role, but religion does not have the right role. It is being used and abused by the government."

Their differences may seem minor to us, but they provide an opening for America. The hard-liners hold most of the cards today—the presidency, the Revolutionary Guards, the oil money—but they don't hold Iranians' hearts and minds. More and more Iranians are acutely aware of the country's weaknesses, its decrepit economy paramount among them. And Iranians are willing to say so—in interviews and with their ballots.

The internal divisions are often exposed during Iran's elections. Democracy comes with severe limitations. All candidates are male. Men and women vote separately. Criticize the government publicly and you risk beating and arrest by Iran's security forces. More and more, they are choices between hard-liners and *harder*-liners, rather than conservatives and reformers. But they are at least more open than the often ceremonial votes held in countries such as Saudi Arabia.

I've seen Iranian democracy at its best and worst. In 2005, I was allowed inside the Interior Ministry to watch the final tally in the vote that would eventually bring Mahmoud Ahmadinejad to power. The Interior Ministry building had been the headquarters of the Shah's notorious security services. Now it was the power center of Iran's Islamic rulers. As I wandered the halls, I imagined the intrigue that took place behind each closed door.

The expected runoff between former president Hashemi Rafsanjani and former parliamentary speaker Mehdi Karroubi, both pragmatic conservatives by Iranian standards, turned into a near dead heat between Rafsanjani and a then little-known, hard-line Tehran mayor, Mahmoud Ahmadinejad. Inside a vast, high-tech counting center, the Interior Ministry's figures showed Rafsanjani and Karroubi finishing first and second, with Ahmadinejad lagging in third. But as the polls closed, Ahmadinejad suddenly catapulted into a strong first. There were allegations of fraud. Some suspected the Guardian Council had rigged the election in Ahmadinejad's favor.

It was a surprise turnaround, and many of my Iranian friends were nervous. Ahmadinejad was a former member of the Iranian Revolutionary Guards. There were even rumors he had delivered the coup de grace to prisoners at Tehran's notorious Evin prison. As we visited his offices that night, I found his staff surly and proud. A spokesman for the campaign echoed what Ahmadinejad had said earlier in the day: "We knew he would win long before the results were announced." Was this confidence or inside knowledge that a fix was on? As rumors of fraud circulated, the Guardian Council announced a "partial recount," though it counted just 100 ballot boxes out of the more than 50,000 that had been collected. Opposition politicians called the final result a sham.

Two years later I returned for nationwide elections for municipal councils. They were, in effect, President Ahmadinejad's midterm elections. And if this was a popularity test for the fiery Iranian president, he failed it. Most of the nearly 25 million Iranians who went to the polls rejected Ahmadinejad's hard-liners in favor of more-moderate conservatives and a handful of pro-reform candidates.

I'd learned that little happens here without the blessing of Iran's religious rulers. It's possible that the Guardian Council allowed the electoral defeat in order to undermine the president. Still, as I visited polling stations in Tehran, voters told me openly and confidently that they were using their ballots to send Ahmadinejad a critical message—attacking him for spending too much time antagonizing the West and too little improving the faltering Iranian economy.

At a polling station in downtown Tehran, a man named Amjad told me he had traveled 600 miles to deliver his one protest vote. "The leaders we have now are all talk, no action," he said.

Many of the regime's harshest critics had boycotted the presidential elections, but this time they mobilized their supporters, particularly young people. I met a twenty-one-year-old university student named Rama, who told me, with her mother smiling at her side, "It's very necessary nowadays to vote."

When I asked her why, she said, "Because Ahmadinejad is doing very bad things and we should do something."

At the headquarters of Iran's largest pro-reform party that night, there was relief that the reformers had made their first modest gains after years of losses.

"People are choosing us as a protest vote against President Ahmadinejad," one pro-reform candidate told me. "This shows we were never truly defeated."

His confidence was probably overstated. The reformers themselves had disappointed many of their supporters during a frustrating eight years in power. But the voters had spoken.

For Babak, the government's unpopularity is a double-edged sword. While it gives him confidence that Iranians support his acts of defiance, he sees the government as increasingly desperate and capable of doing anything to hold on to power. Ahmadinejad is, he says, like a cornered rat caught between dissatisfaction at home and U.S. threats abroad.

"The government sees itself going downhill fast," he said. "As an ideologically based regime, it believes any concession will puncture the ideological bubble and will inevitably lead to the end of the regime."

In the face of growing dissatisfaction, the government only grew more brazen in its attacks on the opposition. The threat of war with "the Great Satan" gave Ahmadinejad an excuse to crack down on domestic "threats" against the government. As the public face of Iran's student opposition, Babak himself was a high value target.

I'd seen Iranian security agents in action. During four assignments in Iran, I've only left once without getting arrested. For foreigners, encounters with Iranian police are usually brief and painless, the journalistic equivalent of getting pulled over for speeding. The first time was for filming inside the parliament building during a protest by pro-reform lawmakers (they eventually let us in). The second was for filming shoppers without the correct permission from the Information Ministry (that got us an hour or so at a Tehran police station).

The third time was more serious. During the 2005 presidential elections, I got a tip from an Iranian contact that police were harassing protesters in a public park in the north of the city. Security forces were out in startling numbers—plainclothes intelligence agents in their trademark dark suits, uniformed policemen in white, soldiers in olive drab. Several plainclothesmen tried to escort us away from the square, not knowing that my cameraman, Gary Shore, was still filming with his camera slung over his shoulder ("shooting from the hip," we call it). There, on a crowded street, we watched agents lift a young female protester off her feet and carry her to an unmarked van. She was screaming, begging people for help. A passerby, spotting a foreign television crew, whispered to us to keep filming.

When the agents spotted the camera, they rushed toward us. Gary quietly ejected the tape and slipped it into my pocket. We made it to our van, but more agents surrounded us. One reached in through the driver's window and took the keys. "Where are your papers?" he demanded. I was sure they wouldn't hold a western television crew for too long, so I focused on hiding the tape under the van's carpeting. Outside, police carried another protester away. Seeing us, he stuck his hand through the window and grabbed my shoulder, his eyes bulging with fear. A policeman ripped him away. After an hour or so, one of the agents received a call on the radio and smiled. We were now his friends. He apologized for the "mess" and told us we could go. Someone had decided we weren't worth the headline AMERICAN REPORTERS DETAINED.

But we still had our tape. Iranian state television is the only satellite transmission point in Tehran. Censors watch every second of video. I decided to sneak the protest video out in the middle of a random mix of shots: several minutes of downtown shopping malls, a feature on an Iranian fashion show. While the censor was still watching, I made a fuss, acting like I was looking for a particular sound bite, growing confused and angry as I shuffled through several tapes. I was hoping the sight of an angry westerner would distract him. It seemed to work. ABC broadcast the pictures that night.

For an Iranian dissident, life is an almost endless sentence of physical and mental abuse. Iran's security apparatus seems designed not only to scare the government's opponents but to break their will. As Babak described his treatment, an image grew in my mind of a twenty first century version of the East German Stasi. From Iran to Egypt to Myanmar, the security services seem to work from the same playbook. Even the look is the same: bad suits, cheap cigarettes, expressionless eyes.

Babak's punishment for confronting the Iranian president started with a beating by the Basijis at a campus protest. He left with a shattered ankle. Next he was expelled from his university and banned from pursuing higher education. That was an enormous blow to Babak and his family. Gaining admission to Iran's top universities is extremely competitive—as difficult as applying to Harvard or Yale. He was devastated.

He soon faced worse. On April 20, 2007, Babak passed by a small group of people in front of the city courthouse near his home. They were protesting a government home purchase plan that had turned out to be bogus. Just by talking to them, Babak put himself in danger. When protesters were arrested for gathering without a government permit, Babak was taken along with them. But when the officers at the police station recognized his name, they realized they had a much bigger fish. They moved him to a special cell of almost Lilliputian dimensions, three feet by eighteen inches. It was a closet-sized personal prison.

The next day he was moved to a larger holding cell for common criminals. He and the other prisoners lived together in medieval conditions—no food, water, or toilet. His feet were chained to a man who told him with a smile that he was in for murder.

"It was a truly painful experience to be near murderers, drug traffickers, addicts," he said. "Just the thought of being associated with them was disturbing."

When he finally appeared before a judge after several days in custody, Babak's "crimes" were identified as "political" and he was sent to the notorious Section 209 of Evin prison. Evin is full of painful memories for Iranians. It was founded under the Shah and run by his brutal security services. Many of the architects of the 1979 revolution, including Ayatollah Mahmoud Taleghani, whose daughter I met, were imprisoned and tortured there. Iran's new rulers took over Evin and today brutalize their opponents with equal relish. Even photographing the prison is a serious crime. In June 2003, Zahra Kazemi, who had both Canadian and Iranian nationality, was arrested taking pictures there. She was later beaten to death inside. More recently, in 2006, Akbar Mohammadi, a leader of the 1999 student-led pro-democracy demonstrations, died from injuries resulting from torture there. Babak had reason to be scared.

Babak has difficulty recounting the humiliation he faced over the next six weeks. He had no contact with his family or a lawyer. He laughed dryly when he told me his only recreation was going to the bathroom four times a day. He spent thirty-seven of his forty days in prison in solitary confinement.

"Even thinking about it is extremely painful," he said. "There was only a dimly lit lamp and no connection with the outside world. At times I really believed this was the end of the world."

He endured an endless string of interrogations, some as long as twenty-four hours. They came without warning—some in the day, some in the middle of the night. The element of surprise was part of the torture. Babak never felt remotely safe.

A team of seven men questioned him. Babak never saw their faces. In survival courses, I've been taught to make every connection possible with hostage-takers: eye contact, a few words, anything that would make them see you as a human being. Behind his blindfold, Babak could not.

The physical abuse was intense. His torturers were expert at doling out pain.

Babak wrote me this list of their methods:

- Intense hitting of the face by seven interrogators simultaneously, resulting in unconsciousness.

- Kicking of the arms, chest, back, and intense beating of the head, face, and legs until we fell out of our chairs or crashed into the wall.

- Being forced to lie flat on the floor while interrogators applied pressure by standing or sitting on our feet, waist, and back.

- Blows to the handcuffs, causing swelling that remained for weeks.

- Being forced to stand for long periods of time (forty-eight hours).

- Being forced to carry out unbearable repetitive movements for long periods of time, such as frequent sitting and getting up and bending over and grabbing one's ankles.

- Using cables and whips for lashing.

- Being forced to stand on one leg for a continuous period of time (eighteen hours).

- Withholding food for forty-eight hours.

- Transmission of loud sounds through the cell during hours of rest in order to prevent sleep.

Iranian friends reminded me that the U.S. government approved some of the same techniques for American interrogators, such as the standing for hours and the loud noises. What Babak faced was far worse, but the comparison was still wrenching. What had we lost by refusing to disavow torture altogether? In the eyes of some Iranians, we had lost the right to criticize without qualification.

After each session, Babak was broken. His wounds were sometimes so bad that even the guards noticed. Weakened by his heart and thyroid conditions—the Iranians denied him any medical treatment—he wasn't sure he could survive.

"I felt that my interrogators, being well aware of the fact of my physical condition, were aiming to purposefully harm me physically and emotionally in order to break my will," he said.

After each interrogation session, he would return to his six-by-seven-foot cell and dream of his family. I remem-

bered he was still just a twenty-two-year-old college kid.
His interrogators played on his weaknesses. They had a per-
vertedly playful and manipulative touch. They were toying
with him and enjoying it.

They first told Babak his parents had been fired from
their jobs—and brought him documents to prove it. They
later told him his parents had been arrested and beaten.
The government often punished dissidents' relatives. The
possibility was plausible. Babak was devastated at the
thought he was to blame for their suffering.

One day a solemn-faced guard came into his cell and told
Babak he had "grave news": his father had suffered a heart
attack.

"I knew this could be a lie, but the doubt tore at me," he
said.

And it was a lie, but Babak wouldn't know for certain
until his release.

"I was not allowed to contact my family the entire time
that I was in prison," he said. "I even went on a hunger
strike for twenty days to demand permission to contact
them and tell them that I was alive, but all of my requests
were ignored. This was the worst way to break my will."

For his interrogators, it was like a game. One day they told
him a judge had issued a sentence of eighty lashes. As he was
girding himself for the flogging, they confessed it was a joke.
On another day they informed him that he was about to be
released. Smiling as if they were happy for him, they told him
to pack his things, marched him from his cell, then turned
him around and sent him back to solitary confinement.

Though his family had hired an experienced lawyer, they
were told repeatedly that Babak had no right to one because
his case involved national security. Threatening national
security is one of the most serious crimes in Iran.

"The real reasons for my arrest were my activities as a student activist during the past few years," he said. "Someone made a decision to remove me from the scene."

After his release, he would learn he was also accused of making "foreign connections"—a charge the government frequently uses against dissidents. As in Egypt, the government likes to paint its opponents as agents of America. The accusation was widely reported by state-run newspapers and television stations, both to justify his detention and to tarnish his reputation.

Accusations of American meddling have surprising credibility here. The 1953 CIA-orchestrated coup against Iran's elected prime minister, Mohammed Mossadegh, remains an event that defines America for many Iranians, much as the 1979 revolution defines Iran for many Americans. The coup was a fascinating study in U.S. intelligence operations abroad. In April 2000, James Risen of the *New York Times* revealed the contents of the CIA's own secret history of the coup. According to the *Times*, Britain came up with the plan, fearful of Iranian plans to nationalize the oil industry. Iranians working for the CIA staged the bombing of a cleric's home to help turn the religious community against Mossadegh. The *Times* also reported that the American choice to replace him, the Shah, Mohammed Reza Pahlavi, nearly chickened out, until the United States sent General H. Norman Schwarzkopf, the father of the Desert Storm commander, to help shore him up. The coup would serve as a model for a series of CIA plots, from the successful coup in Guatemala in 1954 to the failed Bay of Pigs operation in Cuba in 1961.

To this day, many Iranians see the CIA behind just about everything. The conspiracy theories range from the uncorroborated (that it was the United States, not Israel, which bombed an alleged nuclear facility in Syria in September 2007) to the absurd (that a CIA "superbomb" sparked the 2004 Bam earthquake, which killed an estimated 26,000 people).

During his imprisonment, Babak says his interrogators forced him to confess that he was a U.S. agent. A government newspaper published his confession.

"This was conducted in the worst way," he said. "Never once did I take one cent from anyone, and never once was it offered to me. The only connection I ever had with individuals outside of Iran was limited to television reporters and journalists."

He was losing hope. In solitary confinement, he was given two blankets, one towel, and one Koran, but nothing else, not even plastic forks or spoons. His guards feared he was contemplating suicide. They were right.

"While I was in jail, I had no idea about the future, and if and when I would ever get out and when my future would start," he said. "At times I did think about suicide. The only things that would move me away from that decision were, first, the thought of my mother and father and, second, the negative effects it would have on the student movement."

On the morning of May 31, 2007, guards came to his cell for him once again. Babak was in pain. He wasn't sure he could survive another interrogation. They walked him along the same twisting path of hallways toward the interrogation room, then took him to the gate and let him go. Babak was suddenly free, but he began waiting, inevitably, for his next arrest.

"With the smallest level of activism, I will return to that

same place, and this is the most serious of my difficulties," he said. "I am completely prohibited from all political activities. I am under constant surveillance. I am a person who appears to be free, but in actuality, I am in prison."

During and after his imprisonment, I was hoping Babak would look to America for help—the way Soviet dissidents had during the Cold War. Without diplomatic relations or even an embassy in Tehran, I knew Washington couldn't free him. But I thought a word of support from a U.S. human rights group or a protest by a U.S. diplomat might have value. Instead, Babak told me the American government shared the blame.

"The more pressure outside powers put on the government, the government puts more pressure on the people," he told me. "Students are the first to feel it, since they're at the forefront."

Many Iranian dissidents inside and outside Iran share this view. Their message is: blunt force isn't helping. In fact, American support can put them in more danger. For Babak, even contacting me was sometimes risky. He believed police were monitoring his cell phone and e-mail. Speaking with an American might give police an excuse to arrest him again. For several months after his release, our communication tailed off. I struggled to find Iranian friends who could deliver questions to him in person. Several refused, including Iranians who had frequently worked with the western media before. They were more worried than I'd ever seen them. Contact with either Babak or me was a danger for them.

"In order to discredit and eliminate intellectuals, journalists, and students—who represent the fundamental voice of criticism in the country—and to back up talk about western designs for regime change, they have no other choice but to link Iranian activists to outside efforts for regime change," he said.

The Iranian government used American calls for a popular uprising against the current regime as an excuse to label everyone from student activists to women's rights campaigners to labor unionists, journalists, and political reformers as "agents of America."

Babak did not let the threats end our dialogue. Just as he had risked his safety by openly challenging President Ahmadinejad, he was willing to risk it again to spread the word about the widening crackdown. What he did not want, however, was support from the U.S. government.

Iran's crackdown leaves America with a delicate balancing act. Last year Congress allocated $66 million to help promote civil society in Iran. The programs appear harmless: funding for cultural and academic exchanges, public diplomacy efforts, and broadcast programs like Voice of America. The money that goes to civil society groups is channeled indirectly through undisclosed third parties, such as American and European NGOs, in order to avoid any connection to Washington. Conscious of the dangers for dissidents like Babak, U.S. officials say the money is not aimed at groups bent on overthrowing the current regime, but on groups seeking a more open debate. Babak says those promises are undermined by politicians' calls for regime change.

Even well-meaning moves carry risks. The U.S. government does not make public which groups receive the funds, but this has allowed the Iranian intelligence services to label any NGO or dissident an American agent, whether they receive U.S. support or not. While many Iran analysts support exchanges and dialogue between Americans and Iranians, some of them suggest limiting the role of government. For instance, the Iranian exile group, the National Iranian American Council, supports lifting U.S. sanctions barring American businesses and individuals from making donations to Iranian civil society and exile organizations, since private groups might be less open to charges of government interference.

Babak is wary of U.S.-based Iranian exile groups. Many Iranian exiles, most of whom live in the United States, are opposed to the government in Iran. Exile-run satellite television channels sometimes serve as valuable independent news sources inside Iran. Rang-A-Rang TV (which means "a colorful array of views") operates in a shopping center in McLean, Virginia—not far, as it happens, from the headquarters of the CIA. To Babak, however, they speak their minds from afar without any idea of how to effect real change—and without facing any personal risk of their own. The most glaring example, in Babak's view, was the boycott of the 2005 presidential election. Exile groups encouraged the boycott to protest the disqualification of dozens of reform candidates. The result was a record low turnout and victory for the hard-liners.

"The original architects of this policy were external opposition groups, and had this strategy not been followed, the result might have been something altogether different," he said. "We might have been able to avoid the terrible economic and social situation we face now."

Underlying his frustration is a sense that he and others bear the consequences for inconsistent, incompetent policies developed far away.

"The internal opposition groups are the ones that are on the front lines of government repression, and are feared the most by government," he said. "These groups have a more intimate and accurate understanding of Iranian society, and their style, approach, and behavior are more easily grasped by the Iranian public. But external opposition groups, who never possessed an accurate assessment of the internal situation in Iran, have taken Iranian society down the wrong path."

Of course, no option sparks as much emotion as military action by the United States or Israel. Unlike Iraqi exiles before the American invasion, Iranian exiles are not calling for war. And for people inside Iran, an attack would be the ultimate humiliation—another bloody colonial intervention. Babak takes a more pragmatic view—focusing on what an attack would accomplish and what it would not. As a child brought up during the Iran-Iraq War, Babak's first worry is that it would hurt the wrong people.

"I do not believe the system would be affected by any war. The people would bear the brunt, and of course it would affect the economy. All the pressures the regime would feel would be relayed to the people," he said. "I've lived through a war in Iran. We know from experience it doesn't change anything."

Even more, he worries that a military attack would strengthen rather than weaken the current regime. It might, in fact, be the one thing that could save it.

"Iranian society will fall further into an entrenched dictatorship, which is already taking place. With every day that passes, the Iranian government closes the remaining open spaces and allows only those who are closely associated with the ruling regime to enter the system," he said. "We are becoming a dictatorship in the full meaning of the word."

For Babak, war was never the answer. In addition to his

student opposition group, he led his university's Campaign
Against War. In Egypt, the democratic movement Kifaya
had also started as an antiwar group (this one opposing the
U.S. invasion of Iraq). It struck me that virtually none of
the pro-democracy groups in the region believed war was
the way to bring democracy.

Just after the U.S. invasion of Iraq, some young Iranians
told me quietly that they wished American tanks had
taken a quick right turn after Baghdad and continued on
all the way to Tehran. There was that surprising confidence in American power again: If the Americans had done
it so quickly and painlessly in Iraq, maybe they could do it
here.

But I don't hear that anymore. For Iranians, Iraq was a
poor advertisement for democracy-by-the-bullet. And I've
always found people here immensely proud. They believe
they deserve power and respect. That's one reason why
even some of my most pro-western Iranian friends fully
back Iran's nuclear program. It is a sign of pride and
restored power harkening back to Iran's illustrious history.
A Zogby International poll conducted in 2006 asked Iranians to rate their priorities. Forty-one percent listed the
economy. Twenty-seven percent chose nukes; they say, *If
you have them, why not us?*

For young members of the opposition, the government's
crackdown has worked in many ways. On each return trip,
I've watched young Iranians back further and further away
from political activity. It is part fear and part frustration.
Young Iranians swept pro-reform president Khatami to a
surprise victory in 1997 and gave reformist legislators a
majority in parliament in 2000. They were hoping for real
change—from guarantees of free expression to the right to

choose how to dress. But many say the reformers failed them on every count. The opposition is demoralized.

To some degree, the government has co-opted young people here with a deal. There is a tacit trade-off between young Iranians and the government that works something like this: enjoy yourself in private (drink, do drugs, wear makeup, watch western movies), but remain silent politically.

"In the last few years, the demands of Iranian students both professionally and politically have been lowered significantly, and this is the exact goal of a dictatorial government," Babak said. "By raising the costs of activism, fewer and fewer students are willing to pursue such activities."

Babak is part of an ever-shrinking minority of those willing to speak out.

I CALLED BABAK in December 2007, on the very day when U.S. intelligence agencies released a report reversing the American position on Iran's nuclear weapons program. The National Intelligence Estimate concluded with "high confidence" that Iran had suspended its weapons program in 2003. Though Iran was found to have repeatedly lied about its nuclear program, much of the basis of the Bush administration's case for further sanctions and a potential military strike had, according to the report, disappeared four years earlier. I reached Babak with the usual difficulty, routing a call to his cell phone first through London, then France, to avoid an American reporter's number showing up on his phone records. Though we were separated by thousands of miles, I could hear his frustration.

"It's just not clear what the U.S. is doing in the world,

and that's a huge problem," he said. "Speaking about diplomacy one day and war the next makes the situation in Iran very critical."

Babak had long told me inconsistency was one of America's biggest problems in Iran: inconsistency in policy and in applying our own democratic principles. The NIE reversal was more proof.

For me, the report helped reaffirm that change requires something longer-term, more complicated, and more time-consuming than war or sanctions. Babak granted that he could offer no easy answers, just steps forward. Among reformers inside and outside Iran, a consensus is developing, built in part on the nearly unanimous opposition to war. One is that the United States and Iran must resolve their differences diplomatically; even our best friends don't want military action. The other is that change in Iran must come from forces inside the country. The trouble is that many here, Babak included, not only don't want our help— they worry that our help may actually hurt them. And for him, it's not a problem specific to one American administration.

"It's difficult to say what the U.S. *can* do. There really isn't much," he said. "And while Democrats and Republicans have differences in public, in the end they're the same. They both have a hostile attitude. While they both say they want some sort of relationship, in practice it's completely different."

Three months later he was sentenced to another term in Evin prison. Division 15 of the Revolutionary Court had found him guilty of "action against national security," passing down a one-year sentence. He said his actual "crime" was simply speaking out so openly against the government. He was still defiant—and told me and other friends he would be fine.

For Babak, America was neither a source of hope nor a power with the ability to effect change. We were becoming irrelevant. According to Babak, changing that would require U.S. policy to be consistent, open to diplomacy, and committed to the democratic principles that—despite everything that separates our countries—still inspire him.

THE UK

BAGHDAD COMES TO BIRMINGHAM

I N BRITAIN TODAY, Islamic extremism can pop up on any high street. The men behind the July 7, 2005, subway bombings lived in Leeds and trained in the Welsh countryside. The doctors who attempted to blow up two London nightclubs in June 2007 had addresses in Liverpool, Newcastle-under-Lyme, Paisley, and down the street from me in Notting Hill. Men from Birmingham, which boasts Britain's largest Muslim population, concocted the plot to behead British soldiers returning from Afghanistan. All quintessential English cities and towns with quintessential English names. Around the country, British police say that they are tracking more than 2,000 known terrorists and 200 terror cells—thirty-five of them in London, another eighty in the Birmingham area. Police have a database of more than 10,000 other British citizens and residents around the country with links to known terrorists. I have to think that Americans would be terrified if a fraction of the number of Britain's known terrorists lived in the United States.

These British Islamists see both Britain and America as their enemies. In their view, there is little difference. Both are equal allies in a war against Islam in Iraq and

Afghanistan. Both have targeted European Muslims with arrests, harassment, and illegal "rendition" to secret CIA prisons. Both, they believe, have fabricated terror plots to justify a crackdown on Muslims. Today, I hear Muslims—born, raised, and educated in Britain—delivering the same conspiracy theories I've long heard in the deepest Middle East, only with sharp English accents. The head of Birmingham's Central Mosque, Mohammed Naseem, publicly questioned whether Muslims were behind the September 11 attacks and later accused the British government of "inventing" the terror threat. The former general secretary of the Muslim Council of Britain, Sir Iqbal Sacranie (he was knighted by the queen), demanded an inquest into the July 7 bombings to examine questions about the involvement of British intelligence. As absurd as the conspiracy theories are—such as the belief among many Muslims that America's government and news organizations are controlled by a powerful Jewish minority, for instance—they have resounded among some British Muslims. If there is a clash of civilizations, it is not just happening far away in the Middle East, but right here in Britain.

Hanif Qadir has placed himself right in the middle of the two sides—as peace emissary and anti-terror campaigner. Hanif sees Islamic radicalism as a twenty-first-century youth protest movement—a way for young men and women to rebel against their parents and a system they see as corrupt, violent, and intent on "breaking" their culture. It echoes 1960s black American militant activism in its convictions that "the man" (in this case, read "America") is behind every crisis facing the Muslim world.

"The recruiters tell them, 'You've got this problem and you've got to deal with it. It's your problem,'" he said. "'Whether you believe in it or you don't, this is your job.

And how are you going to answer when you see your brothers raped and plundered?'

"And that gets them thinking. Out of ten, you might get one, but that's one too many," he said.

Hanif runs a youth center for young Muslims in Waltham Forest, East London, where several men were arrested in the summer of 2006 for plotting to blow up airliners over the Atlantic with explosives hidden in soft drink bottles. For months before the arrests, he had been warning local leaders that local youths were being radicalized at an alarming rate.

"Our leaders need to take the blinkers off," he said. "Because once they take the blinkers off, they will see the reality. I tell the parents their boys are into extremism. They say, 'No, not our boys.'"

Hanif knew because he had been a jihadi himself. In 2002 he traveled to Afghanistan to volunteer for jihad against U.S. forces. He was quickly disillusioned. While their motives were different, he found the Taliban just as disrespectful of Muslim lives as he believed the Americans were. He returned to England—a jihadi turned anti-jihadi campaigner.

Sounding like a recovering alcoholic, Hanif speaks of philosophical "detoxification." Families are in denial about their sons' involvement. Recruiters for Islamist groups spread radical thoughts like drug pushers. Young men get hooked on small acts of rebellion (car theft, vandalism) and work their way up to the "hard-core stuff" (making bombs and planning for martyrdom). Hanif's center is a twelve-step program for terrorists.

"We are losing," he says. "But we can turn it around."

Simply by standing up to the ideology, Hanif has made a start—and as a former jihadi himself, he has something

American and British officials lack: credibility. Voices like his are rare. His solutions are simple and direct: confronting the ideologues, giving young people opportunities other than jihad, and bridging the gap in understanding that fuels hatred. From his tiny storefront in East London, a one-man fight against the hate.

HANIF LOOKS LIKE he can win the battle through pure physical strength. He is an intimidating presence. At five feet ten, he must weigh more than 220 pounds—his bulk concentrated in a wide barrel chest. He has deep-set eyes, wavy black hair, and a nose twisted by several well-placed punches. He was, by his own description, "a bit of a bad boy" as a young man—a member of a notorious criminal gang in south London. He is that someone you would not want to run into in a dark alley.

Hanif, a second-generation British Pakistani, grew up in the small town of Thornaby, near Middlesborough in northern England. Islam has a history in Britain dating back to the 700s (some even say the royal family has Muslim blood through intermarriage in Portugal and Spain, which were under Islamic rule up until the sixteenth century), but the vast majority of British Muslims, including Hanif's family, emigrated from Pakistan to England in the 1960s and 1970s. Tens of thousands of Pakistanis came to work in factories across central England's industrial belt. As native Englishmen left factory jobs for higher-paying work, Pakistanis filled their places.

"They came to make a better life for themselves," Hanif said. "They were involved only with hard work."

America was experiencing its own influx of Muslims at the same time. But the makeup was different. Muslim

immigrants to America tended to be wealthy and educated—and planned to stay—so they assimilated. Muslim
immigrants to Britain were poorer and initially planned to
work, save some money, and then go home. This helped
generate largely insular, culturally isolated communities in
Britain.

"They didn't think they were going to stay for long, but
of course they did," said Dr. Hisham Hellyer, a fellow at the
Centre for Research in Ethnic Relations at the University
of Warwick. "So they created a sort of subculture to protect
the culture they left behind."

Many new arrivals didn't speak a word of English. They
didn't need to. They worked in Pakistani shops, visited
Pakistani mosques, and ate in Pakistani restaurants. And in
the view of Britain's white population, they were visiting
workers rather than new British citizens. In a decade when
the U.S. civil rights movement was trying to break down
the barriers of segregation, Britain was creating a whole
new division. The insularity persists today, and it's one fac-
tor now identified as contributing to the growth of extremism.

Pakistani immigrants came seeking a better future. For
Hanif's family, though, the story didn't follow that script.
He lost his father at the age of seven. It was a devastating
blow. Hanif remembers him as a giant in their small community, a man of respect and generosity who helped neighbors and friends, even when he didn't have the means
himself. His father's death left the family poor.

Hanif's older brother went to London to find work. At
the age of just fourteen, Hanif left school to join him. His
mother and brother protested vehemently, but he was
determined. He wanted to help his family as he imagined
his father would have.

Life in London was not what he expected. In Thornaby he had little consciousness of his religion. In London he came face-to-face with discrimination. He felt shunned and unwelcome. He heard strangers calling him "paki"—a derogatory term for "Pakistani." For the first time in his life, he felt resentment toward white people. Hanif's frustration coincided with a wider coming-of-age crisis for Pakistanis in his generation.

"They didn't feel really British because the British wouldn't let them, and they didn't feel Pakistani, but they do have a sense of being Muslim," said Dr. Hellyer. "Plus there were political events at the time, the 1979 revolution in Iran, the Israeli invasion of Lebanon. The events mobilized a lot of Muslims to realize that they were part of a whole community of Muslims under attack."

Hanif tried to earn respect through sheer force.

"A day never went by without having a gang fight or a club brawl, and before long I realized how excluded I had become from white people," he said. "It wasn't good, I didn't feel right."

Oddly, it was a gang that provided a refuge. This was an old-fashioned street gang—defending turf, extorting money, selling "protection," and sometimes worse. He was involved in "all the major vices," including drugs and prostitution. Doing his best Tony Soprano imitation, Hanif claimed the gang made him "a man of respect." He had new power, a new identity.

"My gang used to control a few areas in south London," he explained. "A well-to-do guy—I won't name him—if he did dodgy things to make money, sometimes he would need protection, our services, to keep the other gangs away from him. We were enforcers."

Today, Hanif sees similarities between his old gang and

today's Islamist groups. They both sell themselves as anti-
dotes to young men's frustration and lack of purpose.

"Radicalism is a cause, and every young guy wants a
cause," he said.

The gang gave him something else as well: respect
outside the Muslim community. His gang was an equal-
opportunity employer, comprising blacks, whites, Poles,
and British-born Pakistanis. His "boss" was white. He had
a white girlfriend as well, a Polish woman named Helina,
whom he still calls a "love of his life."

This was too much for his mother. At age twenty-three,
Hanif's family staged a "cultural intervention." He had to
return to Pakistan, they told him. It was time to grow up,
time to find his roots.

For a British Pakistani his age, that meant it was time to
find a wife. His mother already had someone in mind for
him, a family friend he had met when he was fourteen and
she was eleven. The two families were already making
wedding plans. The burly British gang member was to have
a traditional Pakistani arranged marriage. When he saw
her, he was relieved.

"She was as pretty as I remembered," he said. "If you
asked me to choose one girl out of a group of fifty, she'd be
the one. She was truly a very beautiful and gentle person."

More meetings followed, always with their relatives
present. He found the thought of an arranged marriage
increasingly attractive. It felt right. It felt Pakistani.

"I liked the idea of something old-fashioned. I wanted to
make sure she was dedicated to having a family and taking
care of my mother when she got older. This is the tradition
for Pakistanis, more than for the British," he said. "We
wanted something more traditional and Islamic."

The trip was an education. He stayed for three months,

traveling the country and visiting his family's native village, deep in the countryside.

"I got to see and know many things, the huge divide between the rich and the poor, the lack of modern facilities, the corrupt authorities, the struggle for Kashmir [between India and Pakistan]," he said. "I experienced and learned a lot."

Some were issues he had heard British Pakistanis speaking passionately about since he was a child, but they had meant little to him. In London he had seen what separated British Muslims from British whites. Now, in Pakistan, he became more aware of what separated the western and Muslim worlds. He returned home determined to become more active in the Pakistani community—to become, he says, "more Pakistani."

The gang didn't fit this new image. Like a retiring mafia don, he wanted to become "legitimate." He and his brother opened an auto repair shop.

"This was something I was seriously excited about," he said. "I was feeling great. Money was coming in, and the people around me were OK guys."

He was now Muslim first, British second. The attacks on September 11 would solidify this new identity.

"Nine-eleven hit us right in the gut," he said. "I can safely say we were all very much confused. Attitudes changed immediately. We were hearing of minor incidents between whites and Muslims, although most were just rumors, but it seemed like the final hour was upon us."

He saw the attacks as brutal and disgusting, but he felt that America and Britain were blaming Muslims everywhere.

"The signs of being unwelcome became visible," he said. "Every household had the same old conversation going on:

'We must be careful now. Another Bosnia is going to happen.'"

Bosnia was the model for many British Muslims. A war that we tend to see as a messy ethnic conflict with many competing factions is viewed by many Muslims in Europe as the early stage of a western-led campaign against Muslims. It was, in their view, anti-Muslim ethnic cleansing in the heart of Europe, with barely a blip of European intervention to stop it. The fact that Bosnian Muslims are Caucasian, rather than Arab or south Asian, made the war even more threatening, in their view.

"People were saying, 'It will be just like Bosnia,'" he told me. "And the Muslims there were not even practicing and they were white, with light hair and blue eyes, so it's got to be even worse for us."

Enter one of the paradoxes in British Muslims' view of the West: they decry the lack of western intervention on behalf of Bosnian Muslims, but deplore the invasion of Iraq to remove Saddam Hussein, who killed more Muslims than Serbia's Slobodan Milosevic. Muslims downplay the contradiction and instead use it as evidence of the West's moral hypocrisy: If the Muslims in Bosnia weren't worth protecting, why were the Muslims in Iraq? Their answer: oil and western dominance of the Middle East. American-led intervention in Kosovo (when NATO air strikes helped stop Serbia's ethnic cleansing of the largely Muslim Kosovo Albanians) is forgotten—one exception in what they see as a global assault on Islam.

After 9/11, Hanif shared the fears of an anti-Muslim backlash, but he says he urged other Muslims to fight the perception rather than lament it.

"I said, 'Stand up and show that Muslims are not what they're perceived to be. It's your job to protect yourself and your children. You've got to stand up and say, "We're not evil."'"

The U.S.-led invasion of Afghanistan changed him. In principle, he believed the war was acceptable. It was understandable that America would go after the terrorists who had attacked New York. But he saw U.S. tactics in Afghanistan, especially the air campaign, as haphazard and deliberately dismissive of civilian casualties.

"It was the atrocities—the indiscriminate killing of whole families," he told me. "Whole families were being wiped out, by U.S. troops!"

Hanif found the "proof" on a growing number of websites, which displayed accounts and photographs of alleged atrocities by American soldiers. Like those that would later proliferate after the U.S.-led invasion of Iraq, these sites played a leading role in turning British Muslims against the Afghan war. It made no difference that many of the images were fabrications.

"I saw American soldiers standing on top of a guy, pulling his pants off," he said, his eyes widening. "Then, in the next one, you'd see the guy with his balls shot off."

There were others: U.S. soldiers allegedly beating civilians, villages razed by U.S. warplanes. To Hanif, America seemed bent on revenge. He recognized the reaction. To him, it was gang warfare on a geopolitical scale.

"You'd get sucked into it," he said. "And I'm sitting here thinking, 'I'm a bad boy, I should be going out there and protecting my brothers and sisters.' Those images could convince any human being to react."

Hanif began by bringing together several friends to send aid to Afghan war victims. They met in small groups, listening to readings from the Koran about how it was a Muslim's duty to "protect and aid fellow Muslims in their hour of need." They held their meetings in secret. Hanif feared they might otherwise attract the attention of British authorities.

"These meetings started to get more serious and clandestine," he wrote. "It felt good in a way. It made me feel we were actually doing something positive."

By attending these meetings, Hanif believes he first attracted the notice of Islamic extremists. In January 2002, three men approached him near his home. With an air of seriousness, they asked to speak with him in private. They told him to leave his cell phone behind as a precaution. "The British police can track you wherever you go," they said.

One, an Afghan, introduced himself as a Taliban fighter. Another, an Algerian, said he was a key ally of the Taliban.

"My first reaction was 'Thank God,'" he wrote. "I was made to feel an important person in the struggle against evil. In a very humble way, they thanked me for meeting them."

The men told him financial support was needed to help innocent women and children who had lost their parents in the American bombing campaign.

"One of the recruiters, he spoke Arabic," he said. "And for me, that was respect. He knew all about the Koran. He was guided by God."

Over the next few weeks they had several more covert meetings. Hanif sensed they were observing him, testing his commitment. "I had my doubts initially, but my suspicions were overwhelmed by their humble attitude and body language," he said. "In short, I thought I was 'in.'"

In early March he would find out for certain. His friends contacted him again and told him they were planning another meeting with a "very special man"—a personal friend, they claimed, of Osama bin Laden. This time secrecy was absolutely essential. They would not reveal the meeting location until ten minutes before the appointed time.   ·

When Hanif arrived, he was immediately taken to a second location. The first, they said, was no longer safe. Again he was told to leave his cell phone behind.

"This was the most exciting day since I first met these guys," he said. "I felt like we were really doing something very good and our rewards with Allah were accumulating immensely. And this new guy was a spitting image of Mr. bin Laden himself." Speaking in Arabic, he said he had a mission for Hanif. He was to go to Afghanistan to help those fighting jihad. Hanif agreed.

There was little time or preparation. Hanif told his wife and three children he might not be coming back.

"Sadly, I didn't think too much about my kids," he told me. "I only thought about these other Afghan kids getting injured."

Like the insurgents I met in Jordan, Hanif's route to jihad didn't follow some secretive underground railroad for terrorists. In late March 2002, he simply flew from London to Islamabad, Pakistan, then took a bus across the border into Afghanistan. Hanif had high expectations. He pictured a well-organized jihadi army with volunteers from all over the world united to fight the American invaders. He wanted to help the victims—the fighters and the civilians—and he was ready to die alongside them.

What he found in the Afghan hills quickly erased that heroic image. He saw untrained fighters, many of them young boys. They would be shipped off in trucks to engage American-led forces and return in the same trucks, in blood-soaked piles of the wounded and dead. To Hanif, this wasn't an army; this was cannon fodder. Scared and disappointed, he confronted Taliban commanders.

"These people—you can't argue with them," he said. "They get violent. They have no regard for human life."

His image of a vast Muslim brotherhood appeared equally naïve. A good deal separated the gritty Taliban fighters and the Thornaby-bred foreign volunteer. He felt different. In fact, he felt British.

"Looking into their eyes—it was like looking into a black hole," he said. "It was just not right, not right."

On his sixth day of jihad, he was on his way to the battlefield with several other fighters, packed into the back of a pickup truck. They stopped alongside another truck returning from the fight. As the drivers exchanged words, Hanif saw a young boy, wounded and bleeding, in the other car. Hanif guessed he was thirteen or fourteen.

"My own son was only four at the time, but there was something in this boy's face that reminded me of my son," he said.

Hanif knew the Taliban couldn't provide proper medical care, so he jumped out to see if he could help. Bleeding from a wound to the head, the boy told him he had been recruited in a village outside of Peshawar and sent into battle with no training or even a gun. This was definitely not the avenging army Hanif had imagined. He was thankful to have a reason, an excuse even, to turn around.

"That meeting was a godsend. It was like divine intervention," he said. "I wondered what I had been thinking."

Hanif had found himself a new mission, rescuing this one boy. In a nearby village he found a man with a car. Carrying the wounded child, he begged the man to drive them several hours back to Peshawar, the closest city with a hospital. The boy survived. After less than a week, Hanif's jihad was over. He returned to London, demoralized and angry.

He felt he had been duped. He went back to the men who had recruited him and demanded answers. They were disappointed in him as well. He must not be cut out for jihad, they said.

"I didn't trust these guys," he said. "They treated me like a piece of shit, sent me off to Afghanistan. Nobody accompanied me. Nobody was going to meet me. Meanwhile, if you're going to get shot, you're going to get shot. This wasn't what I'd bargained for."

Back home in England, Hanif struggled to find his way. There are no halfway houses for former jihadis. He opened a gym. Then he founded a youth center, focused on fighting juvenile crime. But on July 7, 2005, when four British Muslims carried out suicide attacks on the London subways, Hanif had found his new cause.

"I felt I had something to offer," he said. "The 7/7 bombers were people who got caught up in what I'd been caught up in. They were people being brainwashed into thinking they were defending Islam. They got sucked into something that was totally wrong."

TODAY, HANIF RUNS his one-man anti-terror crusade out of a tiny office on the ground floor of a community center in Waltham Forest. The neighborhood is, literally, at the end of the line—located just beyond the last stop of the Victoria line of the London Tube, in the northeasternmost corner of London. Until the 1960s, Waltham Forest had been in the center of white, working-class East London. Alfred Hitchcock was born there. So was soccer star David Beckham. One of its most famous local businesses was the

Matchbox Company, makers of the tiny toy cars. Now it is a burgeoning center of British Muslim life. As I got off the number 68 bus in front of the Jamia mosque, I was the only Caucasian in sight.

The shops are a discordant mix of British and Pakistani culture. Some would be at home on any English high street: a cell phone store called Bling Bling Telephones, a half-dozen fish-and-chip joints, and a few off-licenses (the British equivalent of the twenty-four-hour convenience store) selling everything from potato chips to scotch. But other businesses seemed transplanted from the soukhs of Damascus: a market selling colorful saris, a halal butcher, a spice market.

A group of adult men outside the mosque were dressed uniformly in white sharwal kamiz robes, speaking to one another in Urdu. Many older women wore veils and some even the full-length niqab, revealing only their eyes. The younger men and women, though, seemed plucked from the pages of an Abercrombie & Fitch catalog. They wore baggy jeans and British soccer jerseys, and spiked their hair with thick gel. They bantered back and forth in thick East London accents. Down an alley, three boys sat on the hood of a parked car smoking marijuana.

There is a paradoxical generation gap between Pakistanis who immigrated to Britain and their children who were born here. While the children look and sound more westernized, they often hold more conservative religious beliefs. Many seem to hate America and the West as viscerally as some of the angriest young Muslims I've met in the Middle East. They may dress like us, but they sound like our sworn enemies.

Hanif's center sits in an old brick row house just around the corner from the mosque. He calls it the Active Change

Foundation—a nod to his belief that it's up to Muslim communities to actively address the roots of radicalism themselves. It looks more like a boys' club than a reeducation center. Upstairs, the guys play pool and Ping-Pong, interrupted occasionally by fire-extinguisher fights and pot-smoking on the balcony. Downstairs, he counsels, prods, disciplines, and occasionally bails them out of jail. As I sat with him, I saw the young men treat him reverentially. They each shook my hand like teenage kids meeting their parents' friends—quietly, respectfully.

But behind their polite demeanor is the familiar anger. It only takes a question or two to draw it out. Malik, a lanky nineteen-year-old, sat down in Hanif's office and complained about how the police kept bothering him and his friends. He knew one of the boys who was accused of plotting to bomb airliners over the Atlantic. I asked Malik if he believed his friend was guilty.

"No way. It's all bullshit," he said.

Dr. Hellyer of the University of Warwick says the radicalization of young British men like Malik begins with a community searching for an identity. Not quite British, not quite Pakistani, they find their identity in their faith. They're pounced upon by extremist preachers. For years, Britain granted asylum to Islamist imams who had been expelled from other countries. Some came in surreptitiously, claiming to be political prisoners, but preached hate publicly, taking advantage of Britain's liberal free-speech laws.

"They find people in these communities who are vulnerable," Dr. Hellyer said. "Then they add their lethal component, which is their ideology. Putting those together, you create a window, a small window in a country with two million Muslims, but that small window is enough."

The Muslim communities in each country are different—American Muslims are relatively integrated, British Muslims more isolated—but could that change? Dr. Hellyer and others are doubtful, but he said the triggers are simple.

"You do have Americans who are not comfortable with the integration of Muslim communities in the U.S. If you have American Muslims who think they're not part of society, it takes them one step closer to thinking that society is their enemy," Dr. Hellyer said.

In Britain, the extremists' potential recruits are jarringly easy to find. The conspiracy theories are often a warning sign. When I was in Birmingham to cover the plot to kidnap and behead British Muslim soldiers serving in Afghanistan and Iraq, I met with a dozen men and boys, ranging in age from their teens to their late twenties. As police rattled off the details of how their schoolmates had planned to videotape the beheadings and distribute the images on the Internet, the boys described how the alleged plotters must have been tortured into false confessions. To them, it was just another story fabricated by the police as a justification to punish Muslims.

I asked them, "What about the July 7 bombers? They left videotaped martyrdom statements before blowing themselves up."

"The police can do anything on computers," one of them replied.

Indeed, there is a whole litany of urban myths about the attacks. One is that British police were planning an anti-terror exercise for that very day. Too coincidental, they say. Another is that the explosion came from under the tracks and not from inside the subway cars, so it couldn't have been a suicide operation.

One young Muslim explained the thinking to me best. Yassin (not his real name) is a middle-class kid from Ilford, a predominantly Muslim community near Waltham Forest.

Yassin's almost reflexive mistrust was rooted in humiliation. His parents came to England from Pakistan in the 1970s, but they were more highly educated than most Pakistani immigrants. His father was an engineer who had helped design and build tanks for the Pakistani military, a respectable career in a country where the army is held in high respect. His mother, the daughter of a famous Pakistani poet, was one of the first Pakistani women to study for a PhD in the UK.

When they arrived in Britain, however, they were immediately diminished in stature. His father got a job in a shop repairing televisions. His mother dropped her graduate work to become a high school teacher. Just as humiliation is a catalyst for the anger of Muslims in the Middle East, here in Britain, Yassin felt his family were being treated as second-class citizens.

"There was a sense of persecution," he said. "People would despise you for being Muslim. We were convinced that you could never have a normal relationship with a white person because they would be Muslim-haters."

Small slights became magnified. Yassin remembered the name-calling in his school, and the difficulty making friends with white students. His mother told him stories of verbal abuse by her students and disrespect from her colleagues.

He found himself becoming more conscious of his religion, even more so than his parents were. His family was liberal by Pakistani standards. His mother did not wear a veil. His father occasionally drank alcohol.

"In Britain, my primary identity was as a Muslim, more

so than my parents, because your position is unstable—you don't know who you are. We didn't have a predecessor. We were looking for identity and found it in Islam."

His mother encouraged him. She was worried she would lose her sons to a British culture she saw as morally corrupt.

"My mother was shocked by western morals, sexual morals, unmarried women, children brought up outside the family environment, old people left alone."

Her response was to raise her children as Pakistanis. They spoke Urdu at home. They would get married in Pakistan. They were willing to integrate—working, going to school, and socializing with non-Muslims—but not assimilate, which to them meant abandoning their own culture for a white, British one.

"My mom would say the English went to India and how many became Indian?" he said. "But they want us to become westerners. Bow down to the colonizers and say we accept your values, just brainwash us with your ideas, and we'll unquestioningly take everything you give us. Your clothes, your food, your ideas."

Yassin listened. His Muslim-ness became a source of strength—a way to stand up to the taunts and earn respect at school. This was a religious solution to every boy's adolescent crisis. Hanif found a gang. Yassin found God.

"Your entire life becomes centered on one identity: being Muslim, being connected to a group of people who are being victimized and who are under threat. Lots of issues all boiling into one: imperialism and one culture taking over another culture."

He was, he said, British in a purely legal sense. His culture, his values, his religion, and his identity were Muslim.

For Yassin, this powerful new identity extended beyond the borders of Britain. The suffering of Muslims in faraway countries became his own suffering, and that sense of shared suffering is central to the appeal of Islamic extremism. If Muslims are hurting, they say, we have to do something about it.

"The emotion was anger, constantly feeling angry," he said. "Just opening up the newspaper one day and seeing Afghans being bombed, Bosnian Muslims being killed, what's happening to Palestine."

At home, many British Muslims say they are growing up under the eyes of a modern-day Big Brother—monitored by ubiquitous CCTV cameras and hounded by arrests and interrogations. The numbers are staggering. According to Britain's Home Office, British police made nearly 1,200 arrests under the Terrorism Act in the first five years after 9/11. Of those, only forty-one led to convictions under anti-terror legislation, and more than half the suspects were released without any charge at all. On the streets are more than 4 million security cameras. Privacy advocates estimate that the average person in the UK is videotaped 300 times a day. It's always struck me as eerie that whenever there's a murder or a terror attack, the police and media have a video record of the victims' and attackers' final moments—shopping for dinner, hopping on a bus, carrying their explosives onto the subway. The system was first developed to fight IRA terrorism in the 1980s and 1990s, but Muslims feel it is targeting them.

Mohammed Abdul Bari, the head of the Muslim Council of Britain, has compared the atmosphere to the hostility toward Jews in 1930s Nazi Germany.

"The air is thick with suspicion and unease. It is not good for the Muslim community, it is not good for society," he told the BBC in November 2007. "Every society has to be really careful so the situation doesn't lead us to a time when people's minds can be poisoned as they were in the 1930s."

Equating Britain's surveillance program with the prelude to the Holocaust was offensive to many Britons. The feeling of persecution among Muslims, however, was real.

As with Hanif, Yassin's recruiters came to him. He first met them outside his family's mosque after Friday prayers. They handed out fliers to Yassin and other boys, telling them they needed to hear something different, something more proactive, than what they were hearing from their parents' imams. Yassin started attending prayers at a secret mosque, hidden in an upstairs apartment near his home. The imam spoke to Yassin of an Islamic empire, not just a state centered around the three Islamic holy sites of Mecca, Medina, and Jerusalem, but one extending across Europe all the way to Britain.

"This was fantastic," he said. "I couldn't wait for the day that Muslims got together and found an army and they could just sweep into Bosnia and liberate Muslims. There was so much injustice happening. How could anyone sit still? You had to be fighting. You had to be a revolutionary. You had to do something about it."

He studied Islamic history—and longed for a return to Islam's peak in the Middle Ages when it was a global power.

"This loss of pride, this recognition that Muslims are in the Dark Ages, pathetically disorganized, colonized, every Muslim country dependent on colonial laws, dependent on American aid to survive, and we can't even beat this tiny country, Israel. It created a serious lack of self-esteem."

Like Muslims I met in the Middle East, Yassin blamed the decline on western, particularly American, influence. He saw each American foray into the Middle East as an attempt to keep the Muslim people down while following a whole set of double standards: talking up democracy while supporting undemocratic regimes and killing Muslims in the name of saving Americans.

"We saw violence every day on television, saw people being killed and that Muslim lives are cheap, you know, so what's wrong with Americans dying? Why should Americans be superior, why should white people be superior? Why isn't it state terrorism when the U.S. has bombed fifty countries in the past fifty years, but when pathetic people pick up arms to fight, that is terrorism?"

Yassin was an angry sixteen-year-old being groomed for violence. He traveled to Pakistan and, with his friends, plotted small ways to inflict pain on the United States. He dreamed of killing himself and taking what he called "imperialists" with him. He was a middle-class British teenager dreaming of martyrdom the way his peers were dreaming of playing for Arsenal and Manchester United. He says there was very little that separated him from young men like the 7/7 bombers.

"It's about being in the right group, the right place at the right time," he said. "Being vulnerable, people saying, 'Just go for it, let's do it, don't think anymore.' It's quite easy to become one. I know what it's like to be angry. I completely identify with the anger."

Hanif recognizes the anger as well, and Islamic extremism allows young Muslims to put their anger to work, giving it a purpose as well as justification in religious terms. It is a difficult combination for him to fight.

In many ways, Islamic extremism is the protest movement of choice for a generation of young Muslims—with similarities to the anti-globalization movement, even the fight against global warming. The cause is not purely, or even principally, religious. It is in large part political. This help explain why terror recruits in the UK—Hanif and Yassin included—do not necessarily come from conservative Muslim families, or why a Christian in Lebanon—such as Sara—can also be attracted to the cause of standing up to America. Call it Islamic extremism as counterculture—Generation Y social consciousness juiced up on an insane interpretation of Islam.

Osama bin Laden seems aware of it. His statement on the sixth anniversary of 9/11 tapped into language reminiscent of a 1960s antigovernment manifesto—using news of the U.S. credit crisis as proof of capitalist rot.

"This is why I tell you," implored the billionaire son of a Saudi construction magnate, "as you liberated yourselves before from the slavery of monks, kings, and feudalism, you should liberate yourselves from the deception, shackles, and attrition of the capitalist system."

They are rebelling against both a western system they see as violent and hypocritical and against parents whom they see as ignorant of the problem.

"Young British Muslims are alienated from their parents, as happens with young people," said a U.S. diplomat serving in London. "They have no support network. So how do you rebel? You become more religious than your parents. What are the parents going to do? Tell you not to go to the mosque? To drink more?"

Their rebelliousness manifests itself in ways that make little sense in terms of Islamic culture. In Britain, women of Pakistani descent wear the niqab (the head-to-toe black robe covering everything but their eyes), although it is a form of dress that is traditional in Persian Gulf countries, such as Saudi Arabia, not Pakistan. Still, for British Muslims, it has become a sign of Islamic pride. Wearing the hijab, or head scarf (which covers the head but leaves the face open), is worn for similar reasons by a greater number of women.

To prove their allegiance, radical Islam's recruits don't necessarily have to blow themselves up or fight the Americans in Iraq and Afghanistan. Hanif has watched the growth of a widespread campaign of "uncivil disobedience" in Muslim communities in Britain. Hanif hears young Muslims justify everything from credit-card fraud to drug dealing to insurance fraud and even prostitution, as part of the anti-western cause.

"Recruiting to be a suicide bomber is just one weapon. Recruiting to damage the system is another," he said. "We have a state of war against the West. Steal a car, sell drugs, keep five percent. Whatever you can do. If you don't have the balls to fight, any kind of way you can damage the system."

Even inane gestures of rebellion take on meaning. Hanif told me the story of a friend of his wife's, a Polish woman who converted to Islam when she married a Pakistani British man. When she found a cell phone in a parking lot, she refused to turn it in to a police station.

"She says, 'I saw English names in the phone's address book, so this is an infidel's phone,'" Hanif said. "'I'm going to keep it. This is permissible. Muslims are in a state of war.'"

Hanif was incredulous.

Many young British Muslims get their first taste of radicalism on the Internet. I toured some of the most offensive Islamist websites with Glen Jenvey, who has spent several years infiltrating such sites for the British government. Glen is the perfect cyber-mole. In person, he is a mild-mannered British Indian, more English than the English, I thought, with an accent straight out of a *Fawlty Towers* sketch. On the Web, though, he plays an eager cyber-jihadi.

"It's real. They're not messing around just with words," he told me. "They're not playing. If they could hurt British or American people, they would, and they would not just use words."

Scrolling through the sites together, we found an abundance of angry anti-western rhetoric and terror know-how, all laid out in a friendly and glitzy way, a MySpace for terrorists. There were videotapes of the sermons of anti-western clerics, chat rooms discussing what worked and what didn't in recent attacks, and detailed instructions on how to build everything from a suicide vest to a car bomb.

Many of the sites had American domain names, which rely on web hosting companies based in the West, including the United States.

"Basically, all the files are uploaded on western companies' servers," Glen explained. "Then Al-Qaeda distributes those links on message boards all across the Internet. We're helping them. They're using our technology."

Hanif says some of the young Muslims he works with are surfing the same sites. It is similar to the way he was first recruited, shown images of alleged U.S. atrocities in Afghanistan.

"I showed some of the more mild videos to people in the government and they crapped themselves," Hanif told me. "I said, 'That's nothing.'"

Mosques are another recruiting ground—secret ones, hidden in apartments and storefronts and presided over by imams with dubious qualifications and training, or no training at all.

"You have these self-proclaimed imams," Hanif said. "They spout this totally distorted version of Islam."

Many of the imams are recruited in rural areas of Pakistan, financed with money from abroad. Policing them is a huge challenge. And it was only after September 11 that the British authorities started to crack down more forcefully.

HANIF FIGHTS BACK with a deft combination of religious re-education—going "toe-to-toe with the ideologues," he says—and big-brotherly social support. I joined him one night when he took one of his boys to an appearance at a police station. Malik—the same boy who told me he doubted the liquid bomb plot was true—had been accused of stealing a car from the taxi company where he worked as a driver. His accusers, the company's Pakistani owners, had already given him a beating. He was pale. With a broken rib and a stiff neck, he could barely move.

Hanif brought along two other boys from the center to act as Malik's character witnesses. They were Malik's extended family. This would be a team effort, though Hanif wasn't certain Malik was innocent.

"If I don't give them help when they need it, then I know who will," he said. "It's as easy as that."

When he's not in court, Hanif plays camp counselor. In the mostly homogenous communities where they grow up, many British Muslims have little contact with whites. So he forces them together. One of his programs takes British Muslims on camping trips in England's Lake District. There they spend a few days in the mountains with local white teenagers. Many of his boys have never been outside of London before.

"As soon as they are in the mountains, elderly folk, young folk, they were all, 'Hello, how you doing, where you from, ah great,'" he said. "There is so much cohesion."

The trips are simple but useful. Isolation is a powerful

recruiting tool for Islamic extremists. Hanif believes ending that isolation works wonders. His program has the support of the British and American governments. Hanif will
soon send young British Muslims to America on week-long
cultural exchanges.

Challenging the extremists at times requires a preacher's
skills and knowledge. The extremists believe they have
God on their side. So some of the most influential work he
does is intellectual: beating the radical imams at their own
game. One of the first things Hanif did when he founded his
center was to study the Koran. He wanted to be able to
counter the radical preachers point for point.

He laughs at the idea of a hardened former gang member
steeped in religious dialogue. But it's a language terror
recruits and recruiters speak fluently.

"Most of the recruits have a thug mentality, and they
bring that mentality with them into radical Islam," he said.
"So they're picking out of the Koran all the battles . . . and
statements made by the prophets when they were at war
and using that to justify jihad."

The Koran, he explains, is full of contradictory passages.
In one, it advocates peaceful interaction with nonbelievers:
"Invite [all] to the way of thy Lord with wisdom and beautiful preaching; and argue with them in ways that are best
and most gracious." In another, it seems to justify war in
the name of spreading the faith: "Fight and slay the pagans
wherever ye find them, and seize them, beleaguer them,
and lie in wait for them."

"Whether it's Christianity, Judaism or Islam, you can go
to different sections of the Bible, the Torah, or the Koran
and pick out statements that incite violence," he said. "It's
very easily done."

So Hanif tries to be smarter than the self-proclaimed imams—making end runs around them with a little bit of history.

"The Koran says, 'You cannot trust the Jews and the Christians. They will never be your friends,'" he quoted from memory.

"But that was revealed to a certain tribe at a certain time, for one particular battle," he says.

"So, I tell the guys, the Koran also says, 'Send your people to the Abyssinian king, a Christian, and they will find protection there.'"

Hanif is surprised by his own religious fervor. A large part of his fight is encouraging his boys to defend Islam against a damaging misinterpretation, even a bastardization, of the religion they love.

"When you have Muslims who should understand the religion, damaging it, in my view, that's the worst," he said. "I'm going to get angrier with them than with anyone else. My goal is to direct that anger at the danger that's within us."

His stand makes him unpopular with many British Muslims, who call him a traitor. He has faced criticism from fellow Muslims similar to that leveled at American opponents of the Iraq War: something along the lines of, *Yes, our side has made mistakes, but in this war, you're either with us or against us.*

"I don't expect any help from community leaders. I'm a thorn in their side," he said. "If I disagree with their understanding, then I'm an idiot. They say I'm damaging the Muslim community. I say, 'Let's address these problems ourselves, because if we don't, it's going to hurt us even more.'"

Hanif's is a rare voice. Many Muslim leaders refuse to

acknowledge the extent of radicalism in Britain. And if they do, they place the blame solely on British and American foreign policy. The relative silence of moderate Muslim leaders means there is no counterpoint to Islamic extremists from within the Muslim community. This creates a public debate that pits white, non-Muslim outsiders against non-white (mostly ethnic Pakistani) conservative Muslims. Like an exaggerated form of the vitriolic political divide in Washington today, the two sides cannot or will not find any common ground. That makes Hanif's stand even more crucial.

"You can't take the anger out of the kids," Hanif said. "Young kids are going to be angry just by nature of being young. And more so now when they see what's going on around the world. What I believe and try to do is to take the sting out of that anger and direct that anger in a more positive way."

Politics is one such way. For Hanif, that means challenging both the Islamists and the British and American governments, but with their voices and votes rather than violence. Muslims make up 3 percent of the British population, but there are only four Muslim members of Parliament. Out of a total of 648 MPs, that's a paltry 0.6 percent.

"I'm directing these guys to stand up, you know, have a voice," he said. "If you're really sensitive about the wars, then stand up and speak out. Let's challenge the policy makers. Vent your anger that way, in a political way. You cannot be going out there killing people in the name of Islam. It doesn't work that way. And you're not helping the religion. If you want to help your religion, if you feel so strongly about it, then set an example."

Hanif's intellectual insurgency inhabits the middle ground. He likes to tell his boys that it is possible to be against terrorism and not with America.

"I'm angry too," Hanif admits. "I'm angry at what's going on around the world. One, because I'm a human being. But, two, because I'm a Muslim."

Hanif argues this is another way in which President Bush's "with us or against us" mantra doesn't apply. In his work, it is essential to acknowledge the gray areas. So, for instance, when boys ask him the difference between a terror attack and a U.S. invasion that has killed thousands of civilians, he does not chastise them. In Afghanistan, he says he saw himself that—on the ground, from the perspective of those who have lost loved ones to U.S. attacks—there is little difference. This is a debate in which glib lines don't fit.

Hanif sees something inherently British in the attitude of the young Muslim radicals he encounters.

"They're more independent-minded. They feel more aggressive. Young people now, there's a change in our society that has crept up on us slowly. And we haven't adapted to it. Even now, parents don't understand the change with young people."

They are less respectful of their parents, more confident in themselves. Most surprisingly, they are more possessive of Britain than their parents. They see Britain as their own—and so worth fighting for—but in their own particular image of what Britain should be.

"I hear from the majority of young people that this is our country, and we're going to fight," he said. "I just have to help them realize what they should be fighting for."

HANIF QADIR BELIEVES AMERICA could make a huge difference by being honest about its mistakes. Just as he believes Muslim leaders in Britain should publicly condemn Islamic radicalism, he believes American leaders should publicly acknowledge what he sees as U.S. failures, such as in Iraq.

"What would blow the lid off this thing would be if Bush and Cheney said, 'You know what? We really made a mistake here. We'll try to make it better, but we really made a mistake. And all those lives lost, we have trouble sleeping at night, too.' That would take away any fuel that the radicals use."

Here in England, I had found a new kind of anti-westernism—a home-grown European one—and a new kind of ally. Hanif agrees our enemies are often flat wrong, but he believes dampening their anger will take more than waving the flag. As in Iran, the solution is more complex and longer-term. Hanif is clamoring for help.

"Young people are angry, but they'd accept an apology. They'd say, 'They came out with the truth.' But America is giving ideological weaponry to the radicals. America is, in effect, backing up the idea that this is an attack on Islam. Can't you see it?"

SEVEN

AFGHANISTAN

AN AFGHAN GIRL'S WILDEST DREAMS

T HE NUMBER 9 Elementary School sits on the out-
skirts of Kabul, where the capital's dusty urban sprawl
meets the foothills of the Hindu Kush. Kabul is a city
undergoing an explosion of growth, spreading into once-
empty fields with new homes, office buildings, hotels,
and—an Afghan obsession—elaborate wedding halls. The
Number 9 School was, like the city itself, bursting with
new arrivals, the children of Afghans drawn to the capital
from the countryside and from outside the country. Millions of Afghans have returned home after years away from
the grueling war here.

It was the summer of 2006, but five years after the fall of
the Taliban and the arrival of American troops and money,
the school was still a work in progress. The red brick classrooms were missing windows and roofs, so classes took
place under UN-issued canvas tents or outdoors, in half
circles of desks arranged neatly under shade trees. I sat in
on a girls' mathematics class. In keeping with Afghan tradition, the girls studied separately from the boys, though the
arrangement seemed especially silly when there were no
walls to keep the sexes apart. I expected the students to be
distracted—by the heat of the midday sun, or their broken

desks, or the boys nearby—but they weren't. They listened intently to the teacher, pressing their pencils into their notebooks as if they were etching each word in stone.

Four thousand boys and girls studied here, in two teeming shifts a day. Though the school is just a few minutes' drive from Afghan president Hamid Karzai's offices and all the foreign embassies and military bases, aid money somehow hadn't finished the job. Still, the students—from stumbling toddlers to giggling teenagers—kept coming in droves.

Memories of twenty-five years of war were still fresh. As the top of the hour approached, an old man walked to the center of the schoolyard carrying an iron rod and a spent artillery shell. A vagrant, I thought to myself, but no one else seemed to notice. He hung the shell from a metal pole and, raising his hand slowly, banged the metal rod against it, sending out a piercing metallic ring. The students jumped to attention, formed uniform lines next to their desks, and started walking to their next classes. I'd just heard the school bell, Afghan-style.

Walking through the grounds, I was showered with smiles. A construction site, the school was a living example of just how long nation-building takes in a country like Afghanistan, but it was also an oasis of enthusiastic ambition. For most of Afghanistan's recent history, dreams were figments of the imagination. But I sensed these students' dreams might actually have a chance. It was true at least for the girls. Banned from an education under the Taliban, the U.S. invasion had opened the school doors to them, even where there weren't any doors yet.

I wanted to talk to one of Afghanistan's new female scholars, so I asked the teachers to recommend a handful of outgoing and (hopefully) English-speaking students. As they scrambled through the classrooms searching for candidates, one young girl shot to the front of the class on her own and started asking me the questions.

"Why did you come to our school?" she asked. "What are you hoping to find here?"

She spoke in sharp, clear English, with the slightest British lilt—picked up, I guessed, from listening to BBC World Service on the radio. She told me her name was Homa, and she would speak for her country.

"It is clear [pronounced *clea-ah*] that when the Taliban were in our country, we couldn't do anything," she said. "Now girls can do anything we want. In the Taliban time, girls could not go to school and study. Now we can."

Homa was taking her new freedom and running with it. At fifteen, she was graduating from high school three years ahead of her class.

"Foreigners think of Afghan women as only sitting at home, but I look at you and know you're going to do much more than that," I told her.

"Yes, of course, we *should* do more than that," she said. "I think if a person wants to do something, he . . . she [quickly correcting herself] must have a goal. I want to study to become a good person for our country, for our government, for our people. I want to help Afghanistan become a modern country."

Homa had known the value of an education before the invasion. Under the Taliban, she studied in secret at home. Education was a top priority in her family. All eight children, five boys and three girls, had earned or were earning university degrees in the most competitive subjects: medicine, engineering, the sciences. Homa was the youngest, but she already had her sights on a loftier goal. She was going to college in America.

"I want to be a capitalist girl," she said.

She sounded to me like a Russian girl in a Soviet-era Hollywood film, but she was telling me something I'd stopped hearing virtually everywhere else in the Muslim world. She believed in the American dream, and she believed America was exporting it all the way to Afghanistan.

"When I see Americans, I feel happy," she said. "Of course, they are our friends. Our country is backward, and without their help we cannot build our country. I love them."

From Iraq to Iran to Palestine, even the sweetest-faced children seem to pick up an anti-American reflex early. In Afghanistan, though, large majorities of young and old believe the United States is helping to change their lives for the better. They are desperately afraid of a return to Taliban rule, "the dark period," as one teacher described it to me.

But so far America has failed to meet their expectations. Homa was a powerful example of what was right and wrong in Afghanistan. She was able to go to school, but four years after the invasion, her "school" was a collection of simple canvas tents. She and her family were safe from beatings by the Taliban for violating Islamic law, but they faced a growing threat of terrorist violence.

And yet, almost uniquely, Afghans continue to give America the benefit of the doubt—granting us credit for our successes and the chance to correct our failures. Following Homa's story, I wanted to find out why—and how much longer this window of opportunity would remain open for us. Just the simple fact that Afghans still like us is an enormous advantage. Even outside the country, this is the war Muslims are more likely to see as a justified response to Al-Qaeda and 9/11 than the invasion of Iraq. Afghanistan offers a rare and essential opportunity to help repair America's standing.

Homa was scarred by war before her life began. Her story

sounds tailored for dramatic effect, but it is real and, in Afghanistan, not extraordinary.

In 1992, when her mother was six months pregnant with her, her father was killed by a rocket in front of their home. Three years after Soviet forces withdrew, Afghanistan was descending into a destructive civil war—competing factions fighting for supremacy in the capital. The war touched nearly everyone. With her father's violent death, her mother became a thirty-two-year-old widow and Homa an orphan before she was born.

"I am such an unlucky girl that I didn't get to see my father," she told me. "I didn't get to see the kindness he was known for. It was when my father died that our suffering began."

Afghanistan was a broken country—alternating between a brutal Soviet occupation and a self destructive civil war. A coup in 1973 sent the Afghan king into exile in Italy. Another in 1978 unleashed a Marxist reign of terror by a Soviet-allied communist party, the People's Democratic Party of Afghanistan (PDPA). When tens of thousands of Soviet troops invaded in 1979, ostensibly to shore up the PDPA, Afghanistan descended into another decade of war. The resulting occupation and insurgency killed an estimated 14,500 Soviet troops and one million Afghans. When Soviet troops finally withdrew in 1989, the outside world largely lost interest and Afghanistan soon fell, almost invisibly, into another civil war. The relative peace of the 1960s and early 1970s, when Kabul was a vibrant city as well as a regular stop on the hippie backpacker trail, was a distant memory.

Her father's death brought immediate poverty for the family. A skilled carpenter, he had been the sole breadwinner. Giving his children an education had been his highest priority. Even Homa's older brothers, who would normally have been working by their late teens, were in university. Their parents had demanded it.

To earn money, Homa's mother began weaving carpets at home with the help of her daughters. This was too much for her eldest son, Nazir. At the time he was one year away from a graduate degree in engineering, but he quit his degree to find work in a bakery across the border in Pakistan, sending a few dollars home each month.

"Nazir didn't want my mother to go work," Homa told me. "So he dropped everything for us. In my family, nine people were now dependent on one."

The civil war dragged on for four years. Warlords ran sections of the country like private fiefdoms. Afghanistan was less a nation than a collection of warring tribes competing for turf. In the midst of the mayhem, the Taliban—a fundamentalist Islamic movement originating in largely Pashtun southern Afghanistan—gained ground. Educated in the religious schools, or madrassas, of neighboring Pakistan, they took the name "students" (*taliban* in their native Pashto). In 1994 they captured Kandahar, Afghanistan's second largest city. By 1996 they had taken Kabul. By 1998 they controlled 90 percent of the country.

At first, many Afghans welcomed the Taliban. They were desperate for someone to impose stability, and for a time the Taliban succeeded.

"When the Taliban came to power in Afghanistan," Homa said, "we thought they were good."

The fighting among Afghan's warring tribes was over. But the Taliban waged a war of their own on the Afghan people, imposing a vicious combination of ancient sharia law and old Pashtun tribal traditions. In meting out justice, they surpassed Afghanistan's own high standards for brutality.

They beat women for not wearing burkhas and men for not wearing beards. They issued the death sentence for everything from drinking alcohol to adultery. They banned music, television, and movies.

Many of the executions took place in macabre public spectacles. Kabul's national sports stadium was a favorite site. I visited the stadium for a soccer match just after the U.S. invasion, and found bloodstains and bullet holes still marking the walls of dark cells under the stands. When I went jogging on the stadium track (one of the few places a foreigner could venture outside in shorts), I measured my progress by clusters of bullet holes marking the surface.

The international community did not immediately identify the Taliban as a threat. U.S. allies Saudi Arabia and Pakistan supported them financially and ideologically. America itself occasionally praised the Taliban's success in reining in Afghanistan's massive opium crop, even as the Taliban were providing refuge for Al-Qaeda training camps. Inside Afghanistan, however, the Taliban were coming to be loathed. Homa's first memory of them is of half a dozen Taliban fighters bursting into her classroom and sending all the girls home. When she dressed for school the next day, her mother told her that she and the other girls wouldn't be going back.

"My mother didn't want her sons and daughters to be illiterate," she said. "You know, where we came from, my family was the only one that could read and write."

So every evening—when the lights in the capital were turned off—Homa's family waged their own private resistance campaign, studying by candlelight on the carpeted floor of their living room.

"It was very dangerous," Homa said. "We have all kinds

of books at home, so the Taliban would have thought we were Christian or something. At that time, the Taliban wanted every person to be alone and walk alone. You couldn't meet in groups."

Homa and her sister heard about a woman in the neighborhood, a former teacher, who was holding formal classes in her home. It was an underground elementary school—and a sign that there were other Afghans who opposed the Taliban's new rules.

"My mother encouraged my sisters and me to go there and study," Homa said. "It was like a school at home. It was very dangerous."

They were taking a tremendous personal risk. The Taliban killed girls, as well as the teachers who taught them, for violating the education ban. Homa snuck to school every morning, hiding her books under her dress.

"Once when I was going to the school, one of the Taliban came and asked me 'Where are you going?'" Homa said. She was only nine years old at the time. "I told him that I wanted to go to the mosque. He asked, if I was going to the mosque, what was I carrying?"

She froze. "If they saw any books in your hand other than the Koran," she said, "they would tell me I am not a Muslim and punish my family."

He let her go without checking under her clothes, but it would be months before she went to her secret school again.

Homa's family is devoutly Muslim, but secular by Afghan standards. They spent more time in school than in the mosque. Under the Taliban, however, her brothers were dragged from school and forced to pray five times a day. They were beaten in the street for not wearing their beards long enough. For the most conservative Muslims, a long beard is a tribute to the prophet Mohammed; short beards are a sign of creeping western decadence.

Afghanistan was descending further into poverty. For her other brothers, this meant splitting time between school and part-time work as street vendors—selling cigarettes for just a few cents' profit a day.

"In our house, there was just bread to eat, nothing else," she said. "I remember that when I wanted more from my mother, she would beat me. I have such bad memories, I can't control the tears."

This was Homa's life the day U.S. forces invaded Afghanistan—starved for food and education, desperate for someone to end the self-destructive cycle of violence.

"During the civil war, we didn't do anything without crying," she said. "Now we had a reason to be happy."

Was she telling me what she thought I wanted to hear? Afghanistan is a rare Muslim country where the sentiment is genuine. I asked a friend of mine in the Afghan government to explain why Afghans liked us. He said they welcomed the Americans into the country, in part, for the same reason they had first welcomed the Taliban. Things had gotten so bad that the invading army of a non-Muslim western power looked attractive by comparison. Everyone seemed to have personal experience of the Taliban's brutality. The day the Americans invaded, my friend was sitting in a Taliban prison, serving out his father's sentence for keeping a gun in the house.

"We were so beaten up by the Taliban that we preferred anyone to them," he said. "Even those who were ideologically opposed to the West, the communists, supported the American invasion, since it was the only way out of the claws of the extremists."

America had other advantages as well. Until 2001, the

most powerful foreign influence in Afghanistan had come from neighboring Russia, culminating in the Soviet invasion in 1979.

"Since the USSR had been opposed to the West and America," my friend said, "of course we thought that the West must be good."

In 2001, Afghans still remembered that America had supported the mujahideen against the Russians. As an American teenager following the war on the evening news, the mujahideen seemed like heroes to me—down-and-dirty "freedom fighters." I had no idea that a Saudi billionaire's son, Osama bin Laden, was among them—or that the insurgency would eventually give rise to Al-Qaeda. The law of unintended consequences worked in strange ways here. U.S. support for the mujahideen had given us both Al-Qaeda and the Afghan people's seemingly endless gratitude.

"It is so funny that many people, especially those in the countryside, believed that the Soviets were the worst type of infidels, and Americans were actually more Muslim than the Russians," my friend said.

In Afghanistan, the United States had an unprecedented and promising opportunity. To capitalize on it, though, America had to rebuild the country from the ground up. From my first visit in 2002, it was evident to me that this was going to be nation-building from scratch. Afghanistan was one of the poorest countries in the world, ranking at or near the bottom for every development indicator: life expectancy, literacy, nutrition, infant mortality. Three decades of war had destroyed the country's infrastructure, economy, and government.

At every turn, I found a country scarred by war—from the rusted hulks of Russian tanks still littering the highways, to the war amputees panhandling in the streets, to the crumbling ruins of western Kabul. Parts of the Afghan capital resembled an ancient city. Nothing seemed to work. If there was electricity, it came from gasoline-powered generators. The country's roads were dirt tracks with potholes that could swallow a truck. The drive from Kabul to Kandahar, a distance of 300 miles, took a day and a half.

Many Afghans were fearful, but they were willing to give the Americans a chance. I sensed something more experienced Afghan hands assured me was unfamiliar here: hope. One promising sign was the huge influx of refugees. Afghans were returning by the hundreds of thousands, most from neighboring Pakistan. According to the UNHCR, 450,000 came back in the first two months after the fall of the Taliban in November 2001. Soon more than a million returned home, one of the largest and fastest repatriations the UN had ever handled (though it would be dwarfed a few years later by the exodus of people from Iraq).

In early 2002, I visited a UN refugee camp just outside the capital, a way station at the time for the 4,000 refugees returning each day. Parked in a dusty field were dozens of elaborately decorated Pakistani trucks, covered with colorful designs and chains like wind chimes. One truckload at a time, they were bringing back the Afghan people from self-imposed exile abroad—those who had fled the Soviet invasion, the bloody civil war of the 1990s, the Taliban, and, later, the U.S.-led invasion. I followed a man named Shamsudin, who was coming home after sixteen years, bringing his entire family with him. His six children were seeing Afghanistan for the first time.

"In the past, peace never lasted long," he told me. "But we've never felt as safe as we do now."

In the camps, they were given food, medical care, and training on how to avoid land mines—a valuable skill in one of the most heavily mined countries in the world. But beyond the lure of home, Afghanistan had very little to offer these people. Jobs were almost nonexistent. Food was scarce. Schools were already overcrowded. And safe, decent housing was hard to find.

We followed Shamsudin back to the house he left in 1986. Ruined during the civil war, only crumbling earthen walls remained. It looked like an archaeological dig. Like most returnees, he was left to rely on the generosity of relatives. His family of eight, plus another family of six, lived together under one roof in a house with just three rooms. When a rare rainstorm greeted his arrival, Shamsudin turned to me and smiled.

"The rain is a good omen," he said. "There have been four years of drought. Now Allah is blessing us. We're finally home."

The Taliban were down but not out. Afghanistan was still suffering under their weight. In May 2002, I traveled to the Sheberghan prison near Mazar-e Sharif in the northern part of the country, where a Northern Alliance commander was holding hundreds of captured Taliban and Al-Qaeda fighters. An ancient building of mud and brick was bursting with people: 2,000 prisoners in a jail built for half as many.

As I walked inside the cellblocks, the conditions turned my stomach. Dozens of men crowded into a cell just a couple of hundred feet square. It was standing room only, twenty-four hours a day.

"I've seen several prisoners die right before my eyes," one inmate told me.

Several prisoners identified themselves as Al-Qaeda fighters. One was a towering, bulky figure, with darkly tanned skin and a thick black beard. His size impressed me, after what I imagined had been a harrowing few months of combat and incarceration. He smiled as he spoke to me. He seemed to be enjoying the chance to threaten an American face-to-face.

"It's our duty to kill Americans," he said. Another shouted at me from behind the bars of another cell, "I will fight jihad again, not just against Americans but against all infidels."

I was relieved these men were behind bars, but the prison's commanders did not have the resources to keep them. The prisoners were buying their way out. The price of freedom? One thousand Pakistani rupees, about sixteen U.S. dollars.

"None of the prisoners we release are dangerous," one commander told me. "We only release the young, the old, and the innocent."

The prisoners told me otherwise "Anyone can be released," one said, "as long as you have power or money."

As I left the prison, I wondered to myself which side would win: the Afghans, full of hope and desperate for change, or men like these, who were fighting to keep their country in the dark ages.

Four years later I returned to find the two sides still locked in battle. There were encouraging, even eye-popping signs of progress, as well as debilitating warnings of danger. Kabul was a city transformed. The first things I noticed were the cars, thousands of them. In 2002 there were mostly bicycles, donkey-drawn carriages, and dilapidated old Russian jeeps and Ladas kept running well beyond their years with sweat and tractor parts. By 2006, shiny new Japanese compacts dominated the streets. Kabul had its first traffic jams.

Under the Taliban, there were no newspapers, no television, few radios, and a total of six international telephone lines. Today there were dozens of newspapers, scores of television and radio stations, and hundreds of thousands of cell phones, as well as the ubiquitous new Internet cafés.

There was also a booming real-estate market. A real-estate agency seemed to sit on every streetcorner. Flyers in the windows advertised outrageous prices. A two-bedroom apartment with partially renovated bathrooms and kitchen for $1,500 a month—considerably more than the average annual income. A newly built two-story house for $6,000 a month. There were shiny new glass skyscrapers and at least one American-style mall in miniature. Inside, an atrium ran from the basement to the top floor, its levels connected by a shiny new escalator and crowded with brand-name shops—Diesel, Lacoste, Sony—and another café. Afghans, like the rest of the world, seemed to be developing a Starbucks-induced taste for high-priced coffee.

The city's real-estate boom was a promising opportunity for Homa's family. Her brother Nazir had returned from odd jobs in Pakistan to take up their late father's profession of carpentry. New homes and apartment buildings were going up all over town. Not the utilitarian Soviet-era housing blocks, but Afghanistan's version of McMansions. Nazir took me on a tour of one home he was working on. I counted seven bedrooms, four bathrooms, and a sprawling kitchen. From the roof, I could see dozens of similar homes being built. Though he was a late starter, he had inherited his father's reputation for quality and honesty. He shook my hand with the gnarled, muscular grip of a builder.

Homa's family had no hope of affording houses like these, and neither could the vast majority of Kabul's residents. One product of the country's crash course in capitalism was a rapidly expanding wealth divide between a tiny super-wealthy elite and the general population, whose per capita income remained below one dollar a day. Americans talk about the increasing wealth disparity between the richest and poorest Americans, but here the divide could be measured by many billions.

Homa, who dreamed of becoming a "capitalist girl," was getting an early lesson in the power of money.

"Without money, life is like hell," she said. "If a person wants to improve his life today, he needs money, more and more money. Without it, how can we?"

Many of the richest Afghans are warlords, government officials, and their relatives. Their neighborhood of choice is a new subdivision a few blocks from the American embassy. The Beverly Hills of Kabul takes conspicuous consumption to tacky new heights. The houses are architectural tributes to poured concrete, with imposing columns and crenellated façades. One had a huge swimming pool in the basement; another, a gigantic concrete falcon on the roof. This was Afghan warlord meets New Jersey mafioso.

"We have plenty of apartments, really good ones," a real-estate agent said as he gave me a tour. "Of course, price depends on security."

He wasn't talking about crime, although there is lots of it here. He was talking about terror attacks. These communities are gated to keep out bombers and burglars.

In the midst of Afghanistan's American-inspired boom, fear of the Taliban hung like a cloud over every home and business. Five years after the invasion, the Taliban ran rampant over southern and eastern Afghanistan. More and more, they were bringing the violence into the capital.

I saw the evidence just a short drive outside the capital in Logar province, where all these years after the American invasion, the girls of Qalaie Wazir village still have to study in secret, as Homa used to.

Their school was hidden in a barren field behind the

high, mud-brick walls of an abandoned family compound. Inside, their classroom is a thin strip of shade, with no desks, just a place to sit and listen. This was all they had left after the Taliban burned their school to the ground.

"They came at night," one teacher explained to me. "Four Taliban fighters told us the school was an American base. One pointed a gun at the watchman and the others poured gasoline on the school and set it on fire."

School by school, the resurgent Taliban were trying to turn back one of the most dramatic changes since the U.S.-led invasion. In the last two years, Taliban attacks and threats have disrupted or shut down hundreds of girls' or coed schools around the country. The attacks are worst in the south. In 2007, lack of security shut down 412 of 721 schools in the Taliban strongholds of Kandahar and Helmand provinces.

"This makes us worry," a female teacher told me. "We don't want to return to the time when we and our daughters stayed at home."

In Qalaie Wazir, at least, the attacks failed. The students kept coming back. Even the youngest sounded defiant. A six-year-old girl named Nour, with the light hair and tired eyes of creeping malnutrition, told me she felt lucky to be able to go to school. When I asked the students what they wanted to do when they grew up, they, like Homa, had only the loftiest ambitions: doctor, lawyer, government official. Afghanistan's future may depend, in part, on eager students like them, but I knew they would need a helping hand for years to come.

I sensed the fear even in the capital's sparkling new mall. Sipping lattes in the café, two boys and a girl looked around nervously, afraid of mixing the sexes in public. Ahmad wore a tight, designer T-shirt and faded jeans, and his hair was gelled into unbreakable spikes.

"Yes, the Taliban live in Kabul. They have changed their clothes and shaved their beards, but they're still here. Maybe foreigners think that the Taliban have run away, but everybody is scared in this country," he said. "I know women are scared. They can't go out after six or seven at night. [They're] worried maybe somebody will take them away."

Today, Afghans consistently rank security as a primary concern. In a national poll by ABC News, the BBC, and German television ARD in 2007, Afghans' confidence in the ability of American and NATO forces to provide security dropped to just over 50 percent from two-thirds the year before.

"If there is no security in a country, the people cannot do anything," Homa said. "If a country has security, the people of that country can do anything they want. So the first thing, our country should have good security so that we can do our work."

Homa, like many other Kabul residents, is clinging to the hope that the violence afflicting the southern and eastern parts of the country will not seep into the capital.

"Now, in the capital and some provinces, security is good," she said. "In other provinces, like Kandahar and Helmand, the security is not good and girls cannot go to school. The Taliban are the enemy of security. So the people who've come to our country should first help us ensure our safety."

Those "people" are, of course, the Americans. Many Afghans I talk to are reluctant to point directly to America's shortcomings. But even Homa, the bright-eyed supporter of all things American, is acutely aware of them.

"American soldiers can't control parts of Afghanistan,"

Homa said. "But if the U.S. works hard, I am sure adversity will never come again. I am sure."

Are we working hard enough? In the summer of 2006, as the Taliban was regrouping, I traveled the country with the U.S. operational commander for Afghanistan, Maj. Gen. Benjamin Freakley. Talkative and analytical, he is an officer in the modern mold for the U.S. military: open to the media and extremely well educated.

Traveling by helicopter, we saw the battlefield—the desolate terrain of eastern and southern Afghanistan. Here there was little government control and, until recently, just a few hundred soldiers in isolated bases resembling U.S. cavalry stockades from an old western. With American forces spread so thin, the power vacuum was being filled by Taliban fighters and a new campaign of violence.

The Taliban had never truly been rooted out of these hills and they were back in the thousands, better armed than ever, and organized into large-scale units. General Freakley described an enemy growing in strength and skill.

"We see better coordination. We see higher numbers. A year ago, we probably saw them in groups of ten to fifteen," he said. "Now, we've had fights with close to a hundred. But of course that makes them more vulnerable and we're killing them in those numbers."

We visited the U.S. base in Ghazni, just south of Kabul. Once a quiet province, between 2005 and 2006, attacks there had jumped 600 percent and the Taliban fighters in the area had increased their ranks from two dozen to several hundred. Nationally, the signs were equally ominous. Between 2005 and 2006, suicide bombings jumped to 139 from 27 roadside bombings doubled to 1,677 from 783; direct fire on coalition forces tripled to 4,542 incidents from 1,558.

I walked around the parapets of the U.S. compound, a mud-brick fortress that used to belong to a local warlord. Looking out over the plains rising into the mountains to the east, commanders told me they knew of several Taliban cells in the province, some of them possibly within sight of where we were standing.

The Taliban's model for success was Iraq. And they were copying the Iraqi insurgents' tactics with increasing skill, from roadside bombs to suicide bombings.

"They have seen what is happening in Iraq," General Freakley said. "They watch the news."

They were getting more than inspiration from abroad. They were receiving material support as well: Al-Qaeda bomb-makers, Arab fighters, and money—millions of dollars by the American military's estimate. Some of the Afghan soldiers I met told me they were utterly outgunned.

"The Taliban have new weapons, even satellite phones," an Afghan policeman said, recovering from horrific wounds in a U.S. military hospital back in Kabul. "We have old weapons left over from the last war."

Afghans, including President Hamid Karzai, have blamed neighboring Pakistan for standing by while the Taliban regrouped in sanctuaries just across the border from Afghanistan, training and arming its fighters. Afghan border control is more theoretical than real. At the main southern border crossing near Kandahar, people swarm across by the hundreds in buses, on motorcycles, and on foot, with no security screening at all. Afghan officials suspect this is where many of the suicide bombers cross over from Pakistan. But Afghans themselves are also a source of suicide bombers and safe houses.

The response of the United States and its allies came later in 2006, in the form of a huge increase in the number of combat forces deployed to the south and a series of large operations, some of the biggest since the invasion, involving (at times) 11,000 troops.

"We are going into valleys, into areas where the enemy has operated with impunity before," General Freakley told me. "And we are putting pressure on them. The local elders say, 'Where have you been?'"

Where had they been? At each base we visited, American commanders said they had asked for more troops. But General Freakley told us that was not the U.S. strategy. The United States already had an adequate force, he agreed. A surge here would make them seem like occupiers. In his view, the key was rebuilding.

"Reconstruction and security will be the antidote to the Taliban coming back," he said. "So, when the Taliban come, the response is, 'We don't want you here anymore. We want the government of Afghanistan.'"

An Afghan troop surge would come nevertheless. In April 2008, the United States deployed 3,400 U.S. Marines, bringing the total number of U.S. forces in Afghanistan to 30,000, the highest level since the invasion in 2001. I embedded with the U.S. Marines in southern Helmand province in June 2008. That month, Afghanistan passed a worrisome milestone when US military deaths for the month exceeded those in Iraq for the first time. The danger was immediately made clear to me when our convoy was hit by a roadside bomb on the way in.

In Afghanistan, security and reconstruction are indelibly intertwined. Where security is worst, reconstruction is nearly nonexistent. Where it's best, roads are more likely to get paved, schools built, power stations upgraded. The reverse is true as well. Rebuilt areas are less likely to tolerate the Taliban than ones where rebuilding has stalled. The equation would strike Homa and her family forcefully.

By late 2007, despite the increase in combat forces in the south, security across Afghanistan had deteriorated further. According to a report to the UN Security Council in March 2008, militant attacks rose 30 percent between 2006 and 2007, increasing to an average of 548 attacks per month, from 425 per month in 2006. There were 163 suicide attacks in 2007, the worst year of suicide bombings in Afghan history. More frighteningly for Homa, Taliban violence was spreading into the capital. One of the most sophisticated attacks occurred in January 2008, when attackers disguised as policemen stormed Kabul's Serena Hotel, the first-choice hotel for visiting diplomats and journalists. The assault killed eight people, including a well-known Norwegian journalist, Carsten Thomassen. When I heard the news, I could picture the lobby where a suicide bomber detonated his explosives, because my team and I had stayed at the hotel ourselves. It was a deftly calculated assault on what had been perceived as one of Kabul's most secure buildings.

The encroaching violence had an immediate effect on the construction industry. Building a home in a war zone is an enormous expression of confidence in the future. As attacks reached the capital, building fell off. Nazir didn't have the money to pay bribes to win the dwindling number of contracts. He lost his job. Homa's family faced poverty again.

"He can't find a job. We don't have anything in our house. We are poor people," she said.

In 2007, Kabul was experiencing one of the coldest winters in recent memory. Six years after the invasion, the city still had no reliable power grid. Homa's family, like many Afghans, relied on a generator for electricity. Rising fuel prices made them more and more of a luxury. Afghanistan had a host of amenities that had seemed unimaginable a few years before: malls, Internet cafés, cell phones. But basic necessities were often still hard to come by.

A September 2007 report to the UN secretary general found that national building was under severe pressure, if not failing. In spite of a bumper harvest, access to food was actually declining as a result of poor security and infrastructure. Efforts to create a civil service were moving slowly and faced an uncertain future. Many high-threat areas had little or no government presence. Anticorruption efforts in government were moving slowly or stalled entirely.

The lack of security threatened some of the major successes. One of the jewels of U.S.-funded reconstruction is the Kabul-Kandahar highway, a brand-new, asphalt-topped highway running nearly the length of the country. The new road cut the travel time between the two cities from a day and a half to five hours. But the road became a favorite target of Taliban ambushes. On our trip, we could only travel safely for a few miles outside of Kabul. Beyond that, it was considered too dangerous.

Afghans were increasingly expressing frustration at America's failure to match its good intentions with good results. According to the ABC/BBC/ARD national poll in 2007, only 42 percent of Afghans rated U.S. performance in Afghanistan positively, down from 57 percent in 2006 and 68 percent in 2005. Afghans were running out of patience.

Again, rebuilding was key. In areas where people rated reconstruction as "effective," two-thirds said Afghanistan was headed in the right direction. Only 40 percent of respondents said the same in areas where they rated reconstruction "ineffective." Afghans were judging America on results.

This is what is meant by the often-invoked battle for hearts and minds. Homa had expected the world from the Americans. But in many ways the United States had disappointed her. Her family's income was no more stable now than under the Taliban. Her house had no more reliable electricity. Her school still didn't have a roof.

"The people of Afghanistan have more expectations from the U.S.," she said. "The U.S. *can* help the Afghan people now. Afghanistan needs more rebuilding."

Afghans' overall views of America were tarnished as well. In 2007 the number of Afghans who viewed the United States favorably dropped to 65 percent from 83 percent in 2005. Two-thirds support is a tremendous achievement in any country (it was double George W. Bush's approval rating at home at the time), but the speed of the decline was disturbing.

"I won't say that Afghans have become anti-American, but I think the general view of America has greatly shifted toward the negative side," my friend in the Afghan government told me. "So, while they're not happy to hear that some U.S. soldiers were killed, and they don't want the Americans out, they do have doubts about American intentions."

For the first time I began to hear the telltale sign of brewing anti-Americanism: the conspiracy theory. It is the same logic I hear in Iraq today—disbelief that bad planning alone can be responsible for failure. Again, this reflected the paradox of America's position in the Muslim world: powerful and untrustworthy. Some Afghans were saying that if the United States wanted to solve their country's problems, it would have done so by now.

"They ask how come such a powerful country as the U.S. cannot defeat a bunch of hungry, bare-footed Taliban," my friend said. "The Taliban was overthrown very easily with only air raids, and now NATO and all western powers have soldiers here fighting the Taliban, and yet the Taliban are growing stronger by the day?"

Each rumor had its own perverse logic. Since the Taliban

tended to attack NATO and Afghan forces more often than American troops, some suspected the Taliban was cooperating with the Americans—even though the more plausible explanation is that U.S. troops were better protected.

Homa noticed the change in perception and it worried her.

"In our country, there are more people who don't want the U.S. to be in Afghanistan," she wrote me recently. "The Afghan people can't unite so they can help their country. The Taliban's supporters are more than we can count."

The United States has better intentions, she believes, than does her own Afghan government. Many Afghans see Americans as resistant to corruption in a way Afghan officials are not.

"I am happy with the U.S. government, not with the government of Afghanistan," Homa said. "They are not good people. What Afghanistan needs now are people who work honestly."

"It's been three years since the schools reopened," her English teacher remarked. "And three years is enough time for us to have reestablished our schools and classrooms. We have made many requests. Delegations from the ministry of education came here. We put our requests on paper, but no serious practical decision has been made."

Like Homa, the teacher reserved her harshest criticism for the Afghan government.

"Had the Karzai government asked the Americans, they would have helped us," she said. "We are a large country with thousands of schools all over. Perhaps many schools in the villages are much worse than this. But this is our capital. Sometimes I think if our capital is this bad, how bad would the countryside be?"

Indeed, the vast majority of Afghans want us to stay.

Homa's greatest fear is that the United States will give up and leave.

"If the U.S. leaves in the future, I am sure the situation in Afghanistan will get far worse," she said, "just like the old days."

I've ASKED HOMA what she pictures when she thinks of America. A lot of things come to her mind immediately: money, technology, greenery. But she always begins with "It works."

"Things work," she said. "The lights go on when you flip the switch. The roads are smooth. The cars start."

"The schools have roofs?" I asked, smiling. "Yes," she laughed.

Homa's American-inspired dream is an Afghanistan that works. This is what she believes the United States promised her at the time of the invasion. It's what she meant when she told me she wanted to be "a capitalist girl." She wants to live in a country where people set goals and then achieve them. That's something America still represents here.

"When I think about the U.S., I think of a benevolent country," she said. "All the bad things people say, I tell them they're wrong. The U.S. is a very good country."

Homa still wants to study in the States. Her first choice is a U.S.-run program, the Initiative to Educate Afghan Women, which was founded by an American, Paula Nirschel, to help young Afghan women attend American universities. It is a private organization, one example of what Americans outside the government can do to help bridge the distance between the two countries. It's important to remember just how unlikely such an idea was before the invasion.

"Like dreaming of going to the moon," she said.

That's what Afghans expect of America now: a moon shot in nation-building. We've set our own standards. Afghans expect us to meet them. In America, Homa wanted to learn something she could bring home.

"Afghanistan needs help, especially from people with a higher education," she said. "I want to study to become a good person for our country, for our government, for our people."

Getting Afghanistan right remains one of the most influential tests for America across the Muslim world. And Homa believed it was a test the United States could still ace—just as she herself had done so many times in her not-quite-completed American-made school.

SAUDI ARABIA

THE JIHADI TURNED ELECTRICIAN

J UST OUTSIDE JEDDAH, Saudi Arabia's second-largest city, Khalid al-Johani is making a fresh start. With a brand-new apartment, a spotless new Toyota, and his new wife of nearly a year, the thirty-two-year-old is living a Saudi version of suburban bliss.

"Next time we talk, maybe we'll have some children," he said. For now, he's saving his money.

A coastal town with a long history of traders, Jeddah is a world apart from the stiff capital of Riyadh, in the middle of the desert. Imagine a hustling, bustling Saudi San Francisco compared to an institutional Washington, D.C. The waterfront, or corniche, is full of life until well after dark—parents parading with their children, hawkers selling kebabs, and, during the Eid holiday that celebrates the end of the Muslim holy month of Ramadan, carnival rides that look as if they've been uprooted from an American country fair. Close your eyes and you might imagine you'd left Saudi Arabia, keeper of Islam's two holiest sites, for Omaha. Open them again and you see the many obvious reminders, like the separate men's and women's compartments on the cable cars snaking their way over the port. The men's are wide-open, the women's completely enclosed in thick metal, with only the tiniest slits to peer out of.

For Khalid, Jeddah is home—and the perfect place to raise a new family and settle into his new job as an electrician. He works the late shift at a small repair company, and the hours aren't easy. His shift starts at noon and ends well after midnight. But he'll take it. Until 2005, he spent twenty-four hours a day, seven days a week, as a prisoner at the Guantanamo Bay detention center, a self-confessed Al-Qaeda terrorist.

"The government's helped us get a new life," he said. "I'm focused on the future now."

That's what the Saudi government was hoping for. Khalid is a poster child for an elaborate program designed to reintegrate former terrorists into Saudi society. Of the more than 100 Saudis released from the Guantanamo Bay detention center by 2008, 40 had been "reintegrated," with others expected to join them. American officials maintain that the vast majority of them are dangerous terrorists. Officially, the United States set them free only with the proviso that they would remain in custody on their return to their native Saudi Arabia. But the Saudis prefer a softer touch. Some call it rehabilitation, others bribery—the good life as antidote to violence.

For his part, Khalid is convinced it works.

"When we came back, they understood us and tried to teach us what was wrong and what was right," he said. "They try to make it easier for us to stay away from the stuff we were into before."

By "stuff," Khalid means terrorism—and he was not just an ordinary fighter. He was a high-ranking member of Al-Qaeda and a graduate of Al-Qaeda training camps in Afghanistan, Pakistan, and the Philippines. When U.S.

forces barely missed obliterating Osama bin Laden in late 2001 in Tora Bora, Afghanistan, Khalid says he was with him. By the time he was captured on New Year's Day, 2002, Khalid was a seasoned professional. U.S. authorities considered him enough of a threat to hold him at Guantanamo for three years, before his release in July 2005. On his return home, he was held another ten months in a Saudi prison. Today, however, Khalid says his days as a terrorist are over.

Traveling the Muslim world, it's astonishing how often one can draw a line from some of America's most dangerous enemies back to Saudi Arabia. It's well known that fifteen of the nineteen hijackers on September 11 were Saudis. But today Saudi influence turns up more widely and in more surprising places. Hate-spouting Saudi imams, mosques, and conspiracy theories are conceived and distributed around the world—often backed up with healthy infusions of Saudi money. Look behind events such as the regional uproar in 2006 over Danish cartoons depicting the prophet Mohammed, and you see the hand of Saudi clerics. At home, the Saudi educational system is infused with the puritanical Wahhabi interpretation of Islam, from preschool right up to PhD programs in the sciences. We know Saudi Arabia as an ally and our biggest supplier of oil, but it is also a producer and exporter of people and ideas opposed to America.

To its credit, Saudi Arabia began tackling the problem head-on in recent years. But the change occurred only after the jihadis started to turn their attention inward against the Saudi government and royal family, which they see as subservient to the West and opposed to their goal of establishing an Islamic state. A rash of attacks across the country in 2003 and 2004 sparked a major crackdown, followed by a host of what the Saudis describe as longer-term, more preventive measures. They introduced "reeducation" for radical imams, in which they send hate-peddling preachers back to school, and "reintegration" for jihadis like Khalid. The Saudis say such programs are the best way to keep young Saudi men from becoming lifelong terrorists. "We can't lock them all up forever," goes the argument.

"This program is the best thing that happened to me," Khalid said. "If the government didn't do this, who knows what would happen."

I would need some convincing. Saudi Arabia wears its anti-American sentiment more openly and more proudly than nearly any country I've visited in the Muslim world. Even some Saudi officials don't hesitate to portray Americans as aggressors, and clumsy, ignorant ones at that. It's not a unanimous view. As in most Muslim countries, many Saudis have deep admiration for many things American. The United States is still by far the first choice for Saudi students studying abroad—and while student enrollment from other Muslim countries dropped after 9/11 owing to new visa restrictions, Saudi enrollment shot up (a Saudi government-sponsored scholarship program helped). But the hostility toward America, especially the American government, is pervasive and intense. As I watched the Saudi government attempt to shepherd Khalid from terrorist to model citizen, I had to ask myself, could *this* government really change? Could a jihadi truly become an electrician?

KHALID WAS BORN in Jeddah in 1976, two years after the oil crisis that brought the world economy to its knees. Times were difficult for working people in Saudi Arabia. Little oil money filtered down to most families. Khalid's family was lucky. His father had a steady job as a technician at Jeddah's huge desalination plant. (Saudi Arabia relies on the sea for much of its drinking water.) The al-Johanis were comfortably middle-class and a very close family. Today, he and his brothers and sisters all live near their parents.

"It's tough being away from your family," he said, sounding almost childlike in his devotion to his mom and dad. For five full years—partly while a terrorist in training and partly as a prisoner in Guantanamo—he didn't see them at all.

As a student, Khalid wanted to learn a technical trade like the one his father had. So he studied to be an electrician, finishing a one-year program at a vocational college. Jobs were hard to find for young people. So, at the age of nineteen, Khalid took a job at an electrical plant in the eastern part of the country. It was there—far away from his family and friends—that Khalid got his introduction to jihad.

It began with a five-dollar videotape—a glitzy promotional film issuing a call to jihad in Bosnia. Americans may have seen the 1992–95 Bosnian War as a confusing ethnic conflict, but for some Muslims it was a European-led massacre of Muslims. As when the Soviets had invaded Afghanistan, Muslims around the world were moved to defend their Muslim brothers in a new holy war.

"It was very exciting for a young guy to see different people from different countries who had no connection but their religion to come together and fight," said Khalid.

The video transformed Khalid. He had always viewed his faith as secondary, and wars as conflicts between nations and armies. To see average people like himself taking up arms in a far-off land to defend Islam was exhilarating.

"I was young, full of energy," he said. "I wasn't thinking of having a future."

By the time Khalid discovered the Bosnian war, it was too late. The war ended in November 1995. So he started looking for another cause. His attention turned to the Philippines, where the Moro Islamic Liberation Front, a militant extremist group in the Muslim-dominated south, was fighting for an independent Islamic state. The MILF had committed some horrible acts of violence, including kidnapping western tourists. But to Khalid, they were Islamic freedom fighters seeking only their right to an independent state.

Today, Khalid describes his early indoctrination playfully, as if he's talking about experimenting with pot or playing around with girls—a youthful indiscretion. I had to say, "Wait a minute! I used a fake ID to buy beers as a teenager, but it takes a special dedication to go on the Al-Qaeda world tour."

Khalid laughed. "Listen, in Saudi Arabia, I found all the doors closed to me except Al-Qaeda."

Al-Qaeda opened doors for him all over the world. Khalid spent much of the next five years in terror training camps in Pakistan, the Philippines, and Afghanistan. He tried and failed to get into Chechnya during the Russian invasion as well. Still, he was becoming a highly trained fighter, a true professional.

"I was learning all the things a soldier needs: artillery, bombing, electronics, explosives, guns, intelligence," he said, rattling off the list matter-of-factly.

Some of the camps had direct ties to Al-Qaeda. Others did not. In Khalid's view, the more terror organizations, the merrier. Like an ambitious college graduate, he was building his résumé and his network.

"When you go shopping, you don't go to just one market," he said with a smile. "You go from place to place."

Throughout, he withheld his involvement from his parents. He was sure they wouldn't approve. He says they didn't know until he sent them his first letter from Guantanamo Bay. I was not convinced. Young Saudi men have a long history of answering the call to jihad, going back to the thousands of Saudis, including a young Osama bin Laden, who went to fight the Soviet occupation of Afghanistan in the 1980s. The human export continues today, especially in the insurgency against American forces in neighboring Iraq. It would not have been difficult for his parents to guess where their son had disappeared to.

The truth is, Saudi Arabia and America have had a complicated relationship for more than seventy years, since oil was first discovered in the desert, and the king granted U.S. oil companies substantial control over the oil fields. From an early stage, the Saudi royal family has had a close relationship with the Wahhabis, long identified as a font of extremist sentiment. Through the years, Saudi kings have performed a delicate balancing act, nurturing the Wahhabis as a source of legitimacy at home while cozying up to the United States as an ally and trading partner abroad. More recently, there have been signs of an internal struggle between moderates seeking reform, such as King Abdullah, and others who sympathize with the extremists. Today, several years into the "war on terror," some view Saudi participation as contradictory. In the fight against anti-American hate, Saudi Arabia can be both friend and foe.

SAUDI ARABIA GAVE me one of my earliest and most jarring lessons in anti-American hatred. It was just a few months after the September 11 attacks and I was beginning a tour of the Arab world on my first overseas assignment for ABC News. Three religious teachers from one of the country's most respected schools had refused to be seen with me in public, so I arranged to meet them at a barbecue restaurant at my hotel. There, surrounded by diners feasting on Texas-sized portions of meat and potatoes, they told me calmly why they taught their students that killing Americans was justified under Islam. I struggled to maintain a journalistic distance as I listened to them. I sensed them struggling as well, squirming in the all-American surroundings. I couldn't help enjoying their discomfort. I could feel my temper rising. "I teach my students," one said, "that sometimes you have to do injustice to people who have done an injustice to you."

"You're telling your students that they can kill people because they're angry?" I asked.

"If someone kills my Muslim brother, I can kill him," he said.

"The people in the World Trade Center, they didn't kill your [Muslim] brothers," I said.

"If I can't target the enemy who did wrong," he replied, "then I can sacrifice other people."

That year, I would hear the same arguments from Pakistani teachers at a madrassa near Lahore. But the ultimate source was Saudi Arabia, which founded the school—one of many that Saudi Arabia set up since the 1970s in a campaign to spread Wahhabism. Oddly, Saudi influence in Pakistan came initially with the support of the United States, which saw it as a counterweight to Iran. Looking around the classrooms, I had wondered how many students would blow themselves up across the border in Afghanistan, where Pakistani madrassas were a leading source of suicide bombers. In many ways they were still giddy teenagers. But behind the familiar adolescent debates were hostility and ignorance. A group explained how they had learned to drink Coke instead of Pepsi. "So you buy an American soft drink?" I asked them. They said they had to, because Pepsi's profits went straight to Israel. "I think Pepsi is based in New York," I said. One of them laughed and replied, "Look—P-E-P-S-I. Pay Every Penny to Save Israel." The ideology didn't have to be intelligent to be dangerous.

SAUDI EXTREMISTS HAVE had some of their most profound effects on neighboring Iraq. By U.S. military estimates, Saudi nationals account for nearly half of all jihadis in Iraq. The Saudis going to fight and die there come from across the social spectrum—from young unemployed kids from the countryside to wealthy, well-educated urbanites. If Iraq is a cause célèbre for young men across the Muslim world, in Saudi Arabia it is a national obsession.

They go to Iraq with the tacit support of some Saudi leaders. In 2004, one of the country's highest religious authorities, Sheikh Saleh al-Luhaidan, was secretly recorded on tape exhorting Saudis to join the fight. More recently, Saudi officials have done the opposite, publicly discouraging young Saudis from answering the call to jihad. Some critics of the government wondered why they took so long.

Iraqis themselves are also wary. Many draw a direct connection between Saudi clerics and the sectarian violence that erupted between Iraq's Shiites and Sunnis. Saudi Arabia is a Sunni country; Iraq is largely Shiite. As late as 2007, Saudi clerics issued fatwas, or religious decrees, calling for the destruction of Shiite shrines in Najaf and Karbala.

In truth, Saudi ideological influence extends across the Muslim world and far beyond it. Visit Sarajevo and you'll see the imposing King Fahd Mosque in the middle of

downtown. Named after the late Saudi monarch who
financed its construction, the mosque looks out of place
among the shiny postwar skyscrapers and the neoclassical
buildings dating back to the eighteenth and nineteenth
centuries. Today it has become a center for Wahhabis,
including former mujahideen who fought in the Bosnian
war. The mosque, in fact, could have been transplanted
from Riyadh, and in many ways it is, as is the thinking dis-
pensed from the pulpit.

In London, many imams were recruited and paid for by
Saudis to bring Wahhabi theology to British cities and
towns. In 2003, a U.S. Senate subcommittee estimated that
the Saudi government had spent $70 billion around the
world to spread Wahhabism.

Wahhabi influence in Saudi Arabia dates back to the
country's founding, but some believe its more recent influence has roots in one of the boldest terror attacks ever
directed at the Saudi royal family. On November 20, 1979,
hundreds of Islamist militants seized Islam's holiest shrine
in Mecca, when more than 100,000 pilgrims were inside.
The number of militants involved amounted to a small
army, and the number of civilians made this one of the
biggest hostage-takings in history. Imagine terrorists seizing
St. Peter's Basilica in the Vatican during Christmas mass.

By attacking a regime they saw as subservient to America, the militants viewed the siege as a first step in a global
clash of civilizations between Islam and the West. It was
already a nervous time for U.S. policy makers in the Middle
East. Only two weeks earlier, Iranian revolutionaries had
brought down the U.S.-backed Shah of Iran and taken over
the American embassy in Tehran. Fifty-two American
hostages were just beginning their 444 days in captivity.

As recounted in Yaroslav Trofimov's *The Seige of Mecca*

(Doubleday, 2007), the fighting was intense. Over two bloody weeks, hundreds and perhaps thousands were killed. The Saudis were so worried about being overmatched, they asked for help from the CIA. According to Trofimov's account, Americans were on both sides of the battlelines— helicopter pilots firing on the militants, and a handful of African-American Muslim volunteers firing back. In the end, the Saudis put down the uprising, but victory came at a price.

In the view of some Middle East analysts, the Saudis, in effect, made a deal with the Wahhabis after the mosque takeover: You run religious matters. We run the economy and foreign affairs.

After Al-Qaeda's terror campaign inside Saudi Arabia in 2003–4, the government struck back against Islamic extremists, but the Wahhabis and other extremists retain significant influence today.

KHALID LEFT THE Philippines in 1997 after two months with the Moro Islamic Liberation Front. The rebels did not have their independent Islamic state, but he felt he'd done his part. He next set his sights on Afghanistan, Al-Qaeda's home base and the heart of its support. He spent the next two years in training camps there.

"You feel good learning how to help people, that you will be a martyr and sacrifice your life to help other Muslims," he said.

He tried to come home to Saudi Arabia to see his family. But he was nervous that the Saudi government was aware of his terror activities. So he returned to Afghanistan a second time, in the summer of 2001. Khalid's reputation as a fighter was growing. Osama bin Laden himself met with him several times. Khalid was honored, but he was not immediately impressed.

"He told me, 'We won't let you down, if you don't let us down,'" Khalid remembered.

Bin Laden asked Khalid to express his loyalty. He promised him a house in Afghanistan and a leading role in Al-Qaeda. Though many found bin Laden to be a difficult man to refuse, Khalid was reluctant.

"His words were magic to many people, but I didn't believe him," he said. "I mean, one day he says he wants to attack the Saudi regime, the next day it's America. And why should I tie myself to him? I mean, with Al-Qaeda, it's easy to get in, but it's hard to quit."

Khalid decided to keep what he called his "freelancer status," but he remained in Afghanistan. That's where he was on 9/11. The news of the attacks on American soil nearly took him off his feet. He was scared. He knew the United States would strike back hard.

"I thought, 'This will be horrible for Muslims,'" he said. "After I saw how many were killed, I felt bad. I wouldn't accept that happening to my people, so how can I say it can happen to others?"

He says he opposed the attacks from the beginning. His rationale was partly religious.

"In a place like Bosnia, it was clear-cut: Jihadis were there to help the Muslims. We can fight soldiers, but not people who had no involvement in what happened," he said. "It shows you as a killer, not as someone fighting for his rights."

Khalid had practical reasons as well. He felt the attacks would do more damage than good to Islam. I've increasingly heard this view in the Muslim world, even from some who have fought jihad. They still feel perverse satisfaction that America, in their view, got a taste of its own medicine on 9/11, but they also regret the attacks' impact on Islam. Today, this view is reflected in the declining popularity of Osama bin Laden. In 2007, the Pew Global Attitudes Project found that confidence in bin Laden has declined significantly among Muslims since 2003. In Jordan, for instance, just one in five expressed a lot or some confidence in him, compared with 56 percent four years earlier.

"This was not the way to get people on your side," Khalid said. "After this, who would want to be our friends?"

As the United States went on the offensive, bin Laden's aura faded further for Khalid. Bin Laden's prediction that Pakistan would stand by the Taliban turned out to be mistaken. Pakistan dumped its old proxy, and Al-Qaeda's hosts, to join America's war on terror.

"Bin Laden said Pakistan would stay behind the Taliban and Al-Qaeda, but [it was] only till the price got too high," he said. "It was like the stock market."

For now, though, Khalid's fortunes were tied to the Al-Qaeda leader's. As city after city fell, Khalid fled to Tora Bora along with bin Laden and hundreds of other fighters. When American forces surrounded them, dropping hundreds of tons of bombs, bin Laden told them this was going to be their last stand. For Khalid, that turned out to be another lie.

"He said we were going to fight to the end," he said. Of course, they didn't. Bin Laden escaped and Khalid was later captured by Pakistani forces, before being handed over to the Americans.

As Khalid tells it, the seminal moment for him involved a heated firefight and a tub of cream cheese. It was during the battle for Tora Bora in late November 2001. Under fire from American soldiers, Khalid led a group of fighters into a trench. As they huddled there, one of his men found an unopened tub of cream cheese. They were ecstatic. Cheese was a rare luxury for men who usually ate only dry bread and rice. Khalid joyfully distributed the cheese among his men. Soon after, another fighter came back to the trench looking for the cheese. Khalid recognized him as one of bin Laden's lieutenants. "This is the emir's cream cheese," he said angrily. "This is not for your men." The man berated Khalid and his men for taking liberties with their leader's food. Khalid was furious. He asked himself, bin Laden deserved cream cheese but not us?

"I couldn't forget that," he told me. "Who did he think he was?"

Listening to him, I tried to judge his sincerity. Had his transformation come before or after his "reeducation" in Saudi Arabia when he returned from Guantanamo? Was he telling me the truth or what he thought his Saudi minders and I wanted to hear? His disappointment with jihad did echo what I'd heard from jihadis in Jordan and Syria, even those who were still free. What is clear is that he and the others felt they had a mission beyond death and destruction for death and destruction's sake.

Khalid's jihad ended on New Year's Day 2002. After his capture by Pakistani forces, he was handed over to the U.S. military and sent to an American military prison, also in Kandahar. Today, when he speaks of his time there, his voice drops.

"They try to damage you," he says.

The mistreatment was physical and psychological. According to Khalid, prisoners were held in medieval conditions, denied blankets, and served unbearable food. Interrogators used extreme cold to get detainees to talk. In the middle of an Afghan winter, his captors had a natural advantage. They just sent him outside without clothes. Khalid says he was also subjected to electric shocks and beaten.

"I was smart. I only had two fingers broken. And I told them what they wanted to hear. I said, 'Yeah, I was fighter.' So they're like, 'At least he gave us something.'"

When he was sent to Cuba in the summer of 2002, Khalid was expecting even worse.

"I knew the Americans thought each of us was responsible for what happened on 9/11," he said. "I knew they were mad. So I thought we'd be beaten every day, not just once every few weeks!" he laughed.

By comparison to Kandahar, Guantanamo was a relief for Khalid. He was rarely physically abused, and there were a few small comforts. He received the first letters from his family. He was able to send them notes as well, though he thinks only about half eventually reached them. He even made some friends among the guards.

"I did meet some good guys," he said, before adding with a laugh, "but I don't want to tell you their names and get them in trouble!"

They were the first Americans he had ever met. They were not the monsters he'd imagined. They showed him pictures of their wives and children, and said they hoped he'd be released someday.

"They are human like us," he said. "They go with good intentions and find themselves forced to shoot people in Iraq or bomb some villages. The only difference is that some of us were betrayed by clerics, some of us by their government."

Throughout his three years there, his biggest fear was that he'd never leave. There was no talk of trials. He was never informed of the possibility of military tribunals. The guards supplied him little news.

"They only told us the news they wanted us to hear, like the war in Iraq, but that was three months after it started, or the capture of Saddam Hussein."

In Guantanamo, a defiant—even defensive—solidarity developed. The prisoners took care of each other. Khalid befriended a taxi driver from Afghanistan and became his protector. In Khalid's view, he himself at least had a reason to be there, but a simple driver didn't. He thought the driver had probably been in the wrong place at the wrong time. More important, Khalid felt he could handle it—the confinement, the isolation, the confusion—better than his friend could. But he was scared as well. He feared he might die there.

"It was like my life was stopped for years," he said.

In July 2005, almost three years to the day after he'd arrived, Khalid received a surprise. He was going home to Saudi Arabia—to a prison there, but home nonetheless.

He was returning to a different country than the one he had left. In 2003, Saudi militants had begun staging a series of bold attacks around the country. I was there during the peak of the violence in April 2004. In Khalid's hometown of Jeddah, Saudi security forces fought a pitched battle with militants in the streets. In Riyadh, police intercepted five trucks packed with explosives in five days. Another police raid turned up a bomb-making lab, stocked with dozens of weapons, stacks of cash, and women's clothing that the bombers allegedly intended to use as disguises. A bombing at the offices of the special security forces that week was the first ever on a government building. The Saudis were at war with a terror network that was bigger and more aggressive than ever.

"We expect them to appear every minute, every hour, every night, at any of our checkpoints, at any location,"

Gen. Mansour al-Turki, the head of internal security police, said at the time. "We will not be surprised when we catch anyone or when they succeed in committing one of their crimes."

The attacks shocked many Saudis. They may express sympathy for terrorism in the name of Islam outside their country, but not against Muslims at home. A policeman injured in an attack told me, "If the terrorists want to be martyrs, they should save Muslims in Iraq, Palestine, and Chechnya, not here." How magnanimous of him, I thought.

Facing terrorism at home, Saudi officials and imams were starting to dramatically alter their public rhetoric. During Friday prayers, the state-appointed cleric denounced terrorists as outcasts and criminals. For the first time, a publicity campaign instructed Saudis that it was their national duty to turn in terror suspects, though the government was willing to throw in a $2-million reward to encourage them. U.S. officials were pleased, but the timing was not lost on them.

"Suddenly their law enforcement agencies began to experience what it meant to be on the receiving end of very serious fire," U.S. Ambassador James Oberwetter told me at the time.

Saudi security forces unleashed a massive crackdown across the country, arresting hundreds of militants and killing others. But the bigger challenge may lay in confronting the ideology behind the attacks. Saudis may have bristled at the violence at home, but they still saw the war on terror as a ruse used by America and its allies to justify a war on Islam.

An American diplomat serving at the U.S. embassy in Saudi Arabia told the story of being invited to dinner at the home of a senior Saudi business executive in Riyadh in

2004. After the meal while drinking tea, his host leaned over as if to pass on a secret. He knew who was behind 9/11, he said. The diplomat had heard it all before: the CIA, the Israelis. No, no, the man replied, it was the Japanese. The Japanese had a history of kamikaze attacks, he explained, and they had to take revenge for losing World War II and they were angry at America for overtaking the Japanese economy after the 1980s. He may sound like a one-off crackpot, but on my assignments there I have met very few Saudis who fully accept our narrative of the September 11 attacks. The same is true outside Saudi Arabia. A poll by the Pew Research Center in 2006 found that fewer than half of Muslims surveyed in Egypt, Jordan, Turkey, and Pakistan believe Arabs were behind 9/11. Many Muslims still suspect American mischief in every event. If Saudis couldn't accept some responsibility for the deadliest terror attack ever, how aggressively would their country act to prevent the next one? Or would they focus purely on their own safety?

Saudi Arabia had an ideological mountain to climb. This is a country where the super-modern exists right alongside the antiquarian. At a posh new prep school near Riyadh, for example, boys and girls study in separate wings. To me, that much was understandable, a matter of tradition. However, when the school installed separate swimming pools for boys and girls, school officials later decided to fill in the girls' pool with sand. It wasn't because the boys would see the girls swimming—the wings were entirely separate— but because the boys might *think about* seeing the girls there. This is the kind of thinking the government was just beginning to address.

Much of the modernizing effort rests on the shoulders of

King Abdullah. I had met the king in Riyadh in 2002, when he gave his first-ever interview with a western journalist. At the time he was still crown prince, though he had been running the country since his older half brother, King Fahd, had suffered a stroke. When I asked him about the march toward war in Iraq, he answered sternly, almost scoldingly, "America should be very careful." Then his expression softened and he invited me to join him for dinner.

I'd met him on the day when the royal family invites citizens from around the country to come forward with their petitions. Sitting on a throne at the front of a grand palace hall, the modernizing king performed his feudal ritual. It was the march of the citizen beggars. One man asked for help sending his son to college. His wish was granted. Another asked for mediation in a business dispute. His wish was granted as well. I felt like I was watching a scene from a Disney movie—the benevolent king—but the scene seemed to belong in the Middle Ages, not the twenty-first century. At dinner, ABC producer Hoda Abdel-Hamid and I sat at the head table with the Crown Prince, an Arthurian feast laid out before us. His subjects were invited to dinner as well. At huge tables laid out before us, hundreds of them gorged on lamb, chicken, fish, rice, dozens of Arab mezze. I sipped my yogurt and drank in the scene.

When Abdullah officially assumed the throne in 2005, he soon solidified his role as a reformer. Part of his work was simply to challenge the extremists publicly, inside and outside the country. When he visited London in 2007, he encouraged British Muslims to avoid extremists, echoing my friend Hanif Qadir. Saudi clerics did the same. The same year, Grand Mufti Sheikh Abdul-Aziz al-Sheikh, the highest religious authority in Saudi Arabia, criticized young Muslims for allowing themselves to be exploited as "walking bombs." But change comes slowly here. Only a few weeks later, senior clerics would defend the flogging sentence given to a young Saudi woman who had been gang-raped along with her former boyfriend by seven men. Her crime was meeting a man who was not her husband. It was King Abdullah who pardoned her, but her conviction was never overturned. The law stood.

Some of the most important changes are economic. The country's biggest challenge may be giving young men like Khalid al-Johani opportunities more attractive than jihad. Dubai's ruler, Sheikh Mohammad bin Rashid Al-Maktoum, has estimated that the region needs to create 14 million jobs immediately and 74 to 85 million jobs over the next twenty years just to keep up with a population boom. King Abdullah's strategy is an education explosion. On the coast near Jeddah, he is building King Abdullah Economic City, featuring research centers, several universities, a cargo port, and the promise of one million new jobs. Abdullah is also addressing the country's antiquated school curriculum, reducing the number of religious courses necessary to graduate. Khalid said he'd joined Al-Qaeda, in part, because no other doors were open to him. King Abdullah is focused on opening those doors for today's young Saudis.

The reintegration of former jihadis is central to the government's reform plan. But this is reform Saudi-style, with a distinctly soft touch. Of the hundreds of jihadis arrested inside Saudi Arabia and others returned from Guantanamo, most will be released after reeducation.

"Their attitude is 'Don't beat them up, convince them, show them why violence is wrong and, especially, that attacking the royal family is wrong,'" an American diplomat serving at the U.S. embassy in Saudi Arabia told me.

Khalid felt the soft touch the moment he arrived back from Guantanamo. He still had to serve another ten months in prison, but this was a very different prison.

"When I arrived in the Saudi jail, the next day I saw my family," he said. "The government put them in a hotel nearby for one week. I got to see them every day for three hours."

He had other unfamiliar privileges as well. The man who'd been cut off from the world for three years now took delivery of three different newspapers every day. Instead of American soldiers, he saw a psychiatrist, who helped him cope with the stress of his long confinement.

"He kept asking me if I was OK or not," he said. "And what my plans were for the future."

The month before, he hadn't been sure he even *had* a future. The next step was his "reeducation." This, say the Saudis, is the most crucial part of the program. According to Khalid, the meetings took the form of conversations rather than interrogations. The imams didn't scold Khalid. They adopted a more practical approach.

"We would talk about 9/11 and the damage that it brought to Islam and to the Saudi economy," he said. "We also talked about the problem of terrorists attacking their own country." There was no talk about attacking America.

The imams steered the conversations toward the pragmatic. His intentions were good, but his method was wrong. In effect, the imams agreed with what Khalid himself concluded about Afghanistan—that he'd jumped into a local feud rather than a holy war. As for Bosnia, the Philippines, and Chechnya, Khalid still believed fighting was justified, but he didn't share his feelings with the imams. He knew contrition was a prerequisite for "graduation." And he didn't trust the imams anyway. In Khalid's mind, these were the same people who had told him as a young man that jihad was a noble cause, his religious duty.

"I blame them. They changed their minds. Are they going to take the responsibility for those kids who died in Iraq or killed civilians?" he asked. "Do they have courage to bear the responsibility? They should admit *their* mistake. But they say they didn't do anything wrong, only we did."

I asked him why he couldn't admit his own responsibility. No one forced him to travel the world from terror training camp to training camp.

"Listen, I know we caused trouble for ourselves and our government," he answered. "But the religious leaders encouraged us, they helped us. They told us it was right."

After six weeks of such conversations, the "reeducated" Khalid was officially welcomed back into Saudi society with a visit from a member of the Saudi royal family. Prince Mohammed bin Naif, the son of the interior minister and himself an assistant minister for security affairs, met personally with Khalid and his parents, greeting them the way a U.S. congressman might welcome home a soldier returning from war.

"This was a big honor for us," Khalid said. "He said to us, 'You did something wrong and we have a justice system that you went through, but you are our son and we trust you.'"

The Saudi government would soon prove its trust in more ways than Khalid imagined. He was about to get a taste of the good life. First he was released from prison and given a general pardon. After three years in Guantanamo and one year in a Saudi prison, his criminal record was clean. Then the money started rolling in. It began with a monthly stipend of $800. That's not a fortune in Saudi Arabia. On a yearly basis, it amounts to about half the per capita income. But for a working man—and Khalid did intend to go back to work—it was a generous gift.

There would be other, more lavish perks. A few weeks after his release, he received a call from his government contact—his "parole officer," so to speak, or (it seemed more and more) his concierge.

"He said, 'You are in Jeddah. You can go to the Toyota dealer and get a car. A Corolla,'" Khalid recounted. "I said, 'Are you serious?' I mean, this is a car worth maybe $15,000."

The man was serious. Khalid went to the dealer, picked out a white model, and drove it off the lot, no questions asked. The Saudi government's generosity seemed boundless. Another former Guantanamo inmate told Khalid that he called his government contact when he wanted to transfer his son to a school closer to his home. Changing schools is difficult in Saudi Arabia, but within a week his son's transfer was completed.

Khalid's mind was racing. The possibilities seemed endless. He didn't have any children, but he had recently been introduced to a female cousin, who his parents believed would make a nice wife.

"I called the government and said I want to get married, and they said, 'OK, once you show that you're serious, that you're not playing, we'll give you some money for a wedding.' So I got a license and they said, 'OK, take this money.' Twenty-two thousand dollars! It paid for a wedding party and all the furniture in our new place."

His past made finding a job more difficult. Many employers were understandably wary of a former terrorist. (As a returning prisoner from Guantanamo, his story was well known in Jeddah.) But after a call from the government, he also had a job.

"They would make a few calls, explain the situation, and

then the people in the company, they understood," he said. Again, his personal government concierge came to the rescue.

By 2007 the government had distributed an estimated $30 million to detainees and their families—to repay debts, cover health care and housing, and pay for weddings, cars, and those monthly stipends. The mercenary nature of it all struck even many Saudis as dubious. It all seemed as if jihad was good work, if you could get it. Still, as more jihadis returned home, the program grew even more generous.

"These guys are getting Corollas with automatic transmissions, not manual like mine," Khalid said, but only half-jokingly. "It took me one month to get the money for my wedding. Now it comes right away."

In Khalid's view, the incentives were working. The government's generosity proved that his country was on his side—that he'd made mistakes, but they understood his motivations.

"The most important thing that affected me was that this government was kind to us and our families," he said. "The government said, 'They were young. We'll give them a chance to start a new life.' Even they think we've been cheated by some clerics."

That expression of support has real value to him and other young men who sign on for jihad. As Khalid explains it, they all volunteer thinking they're going to be heroes. But when they see it's not what it's cracked up to be, they worry they can never escape it.

"You think you can never go home. You think you made a big mistake, mistake after mistake, and you're stuck with it," he said.

Today Khalid al-Johani is concerned for the friends he left behind at Guantanamo—Yemenis, Egyptians, Afghans like the taxi driver he befriended. He doubts their governments will treat them so kindly, if the Americans ever let them go home.

"In Saudi Arabia, if you break the law, they punish you for the crime," he said. "It's not like some countries, where you go to jail and disappear forever. The Saudis know punishment is not going to solve the problem."

American officials have maintained that the vast majority of prisoners released from Guantanamo remain a danger. That has not prevented Saudi Arabia from continuing the reintegration program. Public opponents of Guantanamo claim America's acceptance is a sign that the U.S. government exaggerated the danger posed by many Guantanamo prisoners. However, even if the U.S. does oppose the reintegration program, it may not have the influence with Saudi leaders necessary to end it.

The question is how much influence do we really have with Saudi Arabia? Are we going to stop buying oil? Are we going to stop selling them arms? As things presently stand, the United States has few good options.

I SPOKE TO Khalid again in early 2008, three years after he'd been released from Guantanamo and two years after his reintegration into Saudi society. Saudi Arabia seemed to have earned his loyalty—or bought it. But what had America gained? Had reeducation made him a friend?

Khalid says he learned powerful lessons on his own. Afghanistan didn't turn out to be as holy a war as he imagined. He thought he was helping the Taliban bring Islamic rule to the Afghan people. But to him the fighting was more about Pashtuns, who made up the Taliban, fighting a turf war with the Tajiks, who dominated the Northern Alliance.

"You find yourself in an ethnic war—the north versus the south," he said. "I was young, but I had knowledge of the politics. And this war was political, not religious.

"Now it's complicated," he said. "Like the situation in Iraq, that's *very* complicated. Why go there? To help who against who? Some people go to fight Americans and then end up fighting other Iraqis. Who wants to be used like that? They don't need Khalid."

Khalid was developing his own theory of good jihad and bad jihad. Good jihad was Bosnia, the Philippines, and Chechnya—where he believed Muslims had fought purely to live and practice their faith.

Bad jihad was Iraq and especially Afghanistan. He could see why America would attack Afghanistan after 9/11. He not only understood it; he expected it. And he also saw that America was doing some good there.

"The Americans brought democracy to Afghanistan. They let Muslims practice their religion. They weren't slaughtering Muslims like the Serbians [in Bosnia]," he said.

In Afghanistan, America had earned at least one jihadi's respect. But his love? Khalid laughed.

"Listen, Jim, you are my friend," he said, becoming more serious. "I have many friends there who sympathize with us. I respect the American people. But I don't respect this government and what it is doing, how it is spilling blood all over the world. That doesn't mean I hate all Americans. But I do hate the policy."

The motivation—the same cause that had driven him to risk his life for jihad—remained. His desire to fight did not.

"If my country was attacked, I would fight," he said. "But if not, why should I get involved? Other countries can take care of themselves. I've got a job and a future."

In this global battle for hearts and minds, one globetrotting jihadi appeared to have turned peace-embracing electrician. He had reversed the path taken by countless young men and women leaving homes and jobs for jihad. Khalid had come back to the other side, as it were—a model for what Hanif Qadir is attempting in Britain. Khalid may count, I thought, as a small victory.

EPILOGUE

PAKISTAN

IN FEBRUARY 2008, I traveled to Islamabad to cover Pakistan's parliamentary elections. Two weeks after Super Tuesday in the United States, it took an adjustment to watch 100 million voters who weren't obsessed about McCain, Obama, and Clinton. Still, even here, America was a dominant theme. Voters had to choose among a dozen parties with difficult-to-distinguish acronyms like the PPP, the PML-Q, and the PML-N. But the vote was in many ways a referendum on one man, President Pervez Musharraf, and his ties to one country, America, and its unpopular war on terror. Just as U.S. presidential hopefuls were competing to talk tough on terrorism, Pakistani candidates were falling over each other to talk tough on Pakistan's relationship with the United States.

This vote was very different from the one taking place in the States. It had been delayed six weeks by the assassination of the leading candidate for prime minister, Benazir Bhutto. And the threat of further violence hung in the air. I spent election day at a polling station in Harran Mehra, a small village an hour or so from the capital. There were almost as many policemen as voters at first. Tall men with Kalashnikov rifles and neat berets searched everyone, even the women in their colorful saris. There was no etiquette. The guards manhandled, frisked, and shouted at each voter with equal enthusiasm. This looked more like a police action than an election.

But something strange happened over the course of the day. Despite the danger, the voters came out in droves. There was palpable excitement. People talked about "a time for change." The theme had a familiar ring. By the end of the day, the spate of suicide bombings failed to materialize and a respectable 43 percent of the electorate turned out to deliver a convincing rebuff to President Musharraf. His party was trounced by the Pakistan People's Party of the slain Bhutto and the Pakistani Muslim League of former prime minister Nawaz Sharif, whom Musharraf had deposed when he took power in a coup in 1999. Voters had delivered their verdict on Musharraf and on the United States in uncompromising terms.

It was telling, how much anger Pakistanis had left over for America. They had a lot more to worry about than the fight against the Taliban and Al-Qaeda in the lawless tribal areas bordering Afghanistan. Across Pakistan, there were rolling blackouts and near hyperinflation for food and fuel. "It's the economy, stupid," applies just as well in Lahore and Harran Mehra as in New York and Ohio. But many Pakistanis saw an American connection to their misery. It was America, after all, that continued to back Musharraf despite his failures.

Their anger assumed the form of an odd new conspiracy theory: that America was planning to break up Pakistan, ceding the south to India and the north to Afghanistan. The United States wasn't just backing the unpopular Musharraf; it was plotting to end Pakistan as a nation.

As elsewhere in the region, conspiracy theories— particularly conspiracy theories about America—have a strange credibility here. I have my own theory that these fantasies are the unavoidable by-product of life under a broken system. When it seems impossible to get ahead in everyday life without a scam or a plot or a bribe, it's natural to assume the same rules apply to geopolitics. Throw in a deep belief in American omnipotence, and even far-fetched urban legends become real.

One person I did not expect to buy the story was Dr. Israh Shah, a veterinarian turned parliamentary candidate for Bhutto's Pakistan People's Party. Dr. Shah should be a natural American ally. He was devoted to Bhutto—and, after all, it was the United States that had backed a power-sharing agreement between her and Musharraf and likely forced Musharraf to allow her back into the country after an eight-year exile. Shah would also seem to have a brutally tangible reason to support the war on terror. In July 2007 his legs were blown off in a bombing outside PPP party headquarters. Nineteen people were killed. Lying on the ground after the blast, Shah was sure he would be among them.

"I was remembering my god," he said. "Because I was thinking that these are the last moments of my life."

He lost eight pints of blood. His heartbeat was barely detectable. But he survived and returned to politics more committed than ever, campaigning across Islamabad in his wheelchair. Sitting on the lawn outside his office the day before the vote, Dr. Shah told me he knew who was behind his attempted assassination. It wasn't Islamist fighters, as the government claimed, but the Pakistani security services, backed (of course) by the United States. And now America was at it again, this time to put an end to the whole country.

America wants Pakistan weak, he told me. "They support

the political process in public," he said. "But in private they're up to something worse."

I put my notebook down. I'd heard similar theories in so many places, I didn't need one more footnote. But then Dr. Shah smiled and asked me, "What can you tell me about this Mr. Obama?"

In his wheelchair, this angry, wounded politician lit up at the thought of the junior senator from Illinois. I reminded him that Obama had famously threatened to invade Pakistan, but he brushed off the thought with a knowing smile. "Politicians say a lot of things during the campaign. I think this one is different." Unquestioning Obama-mania had made it all the way to Pakistan.

Speaking with Dr. Shah and other Pakistani Obama fans, I sensed the infatuation was less personal than symbolic. Few knew much about him other than his name and his race. But for now, at least, that was enough. His candidacy seemed to prove that the ethereal, anything-is-possible America still survived. If a black man with the middle name Hussein could make it this far, maybe, just maybe, the American dream still had some life in it. Dr. Shah represented a willingness to give America another chance. Even as Pakistanis were voting to distance their country from America, the *idea* of America persisted. The question was, how could America live up to this idea? Here? In the region as a whole?

The stakes were particularly high in Pakistan. Within days of the election, the winning parties were already promising to back off from the assault on Islamist fighters and weaken ties with the United States. Dr. Shah and others told me the best way forward for Pakistan was without America.

"You don't have a friendship with the people of Pakistan,

I'm sorry to say. Your friendship is only with the dictators,"
he said.

From a U.S. standpoint, less U.S. intervention was an
alarming prospect. If there was a central front in the fight
against terrorism, Pakistan was it: a nuclear-armed country
bordering U.S.-occupied Afghanistan and a home base for the
Taliban, Al-Qaeda, and possibly Osama bin Laden himself.
During a trip to the Afghan–Pakistan border region with U.S.
forces in June 2008, I had witnessed how Pakistan's retreat
was contributing to increased violence in Afghanistan.

My Pakistani friends were brimming with ideas about
how America should recast itself here. Accepting the
results of this election was one step forward. Voters had,
after all, resoundingly rejected not just Musharraf but the
Islamist parties.

"If Americans have a friendship with the people of Pakistan, they will accept the popular leadership here," said
Dr. Shah.

Turning around Pakistan's debilitating economy was
another step. As he visited Pakistan to observe the elections,
Senator Joseph Biden suggested tripling U.S. economic aid to
$1.5 billion a year, a fraction of what America spends on mil-
itary aid to Pakistan.

Biden argued passionately about the importance of rural
development in the fight against radicalism. "The Taliban
begins where the road ends," he said.

I had strong doubts that money would be enough. With
few exceptions—American assistance after the devastating
2005 Kashmir earthquake was one—aid money rarely
seems to find its way into the right hands.

Many Pakistanis told me the change they were looking
for wasn't transformational, but straightforward—in particular, interacting with Pakistan on more than just military

terms. Pakistanis were tired of an America defined purely by the war on terror: invasions, renditions, air strikes. When American leaders describe an endless war, many Muslims hear this as an endless war *on Muslims.*

AS I'VE RESEARCHED and written this book over the last few years, friends have asked if it left me depressed. The answer, at times, has been yes. I know we have a deep, deep hole from which we need to extricate ourselves. And while it is not entirely of our own making, it is the product not only of extremists; it is something real, something grounded in experience.

Turning the tide of hate will take many different steps—big and small—in many different places. Sometimes it means aiding Muslims who are challenging the thinking from within, like Hanif Qadir and his one-man anti-terror campaign in London. Sometimes it means removing the obstacles to progress—for example, forcing Egypt to take the simple step of releasing its political opponents. Certainly it will mean questioning our friends: Is Saudi Arabia really reforming its jihadis by giving them new wives and new cars?

Most of all, what I keep hearing from Muslims is that America needs to remember what it means to be American: don't torture, don't engage in halfhearted nation-building, don't wage war incessantly as they increasingly believe we do. Here in Pakistan, even as voters were unequivocally rejecting the leader America had chosen for them, people believed America itself stood for something good. America the bête noire still had some red, white, and blue.

ACKNOWLEDGMENTS

M Y WIFE, GLORIA Riviera-Sciutto (who is also a London-based correspondent for ABC News), served as editor, critic, teammate, and occasional psychoanalyst throughout this project. She edited both the concepts and the text, encouraged me through the roadblocks and mental blocks, and—more often than she bargained for, I'm sure—tolerated me through the endless days of writing and editing.

I'm indebted to the men and women I profiled. They let me into their lives and their thoughts without hesitation—sometimes at a real risk to themselves. In many of their countries it can be dangerous to speak your mind. They were a living education for me and, I hope, for readers.

I'm grateful to ABC News for providing me with the extraordinary opportunity to cover the Middle East and many other parts of the world over the last six years. It's been an invaluable, traveling education.

I owe my thanks to a small but eager team of researchers. Shadi Hamid helped check the facts and the concepts throughout the entire manuscript. Najwa Mroue was my researcher on the ground in Lebanon, Chris Luenen in London. The Identity Project, by the London-based NGO

Forward Thinking, was also a useful resource. In addition, Mimi Daher conducted interviews in the West Bank and Sami Zyara in Gaza.

Fawaz Gerges, the Christian A. Johnson Chairholder in International Affairs and Middle Eastern Studies at Sarah Lawrence College and a far more knowledgeable analyst of the Middle East than I, gave me very helpful guidance throughout.

The manuscript was read in advance by my wife, my sister Nellie Sciutto (an actress and writer herself), and by Matthew Evans, a friend who also happens to be a member of the British House of Lords. They were tough and enthusiastic—just what an aspiring author needs on his first book.

A small amount of the material appeared briefly in reports I filed for ABC News, but all the profiles were built on relationships and interviews that I maintained over months and, in some cases, years. I made several reporting and research trips to each of the countries involved.

I knew my editor at Harmony, John Glusman, was right for this project the moment I met him. He had an understanding of the issues—and an interest in them—that was second to none. My literary agent, Gail Ross, and her editorial director, Howard Yoon, first spotted this as a viable and—as they both emphasized—important book. They were the first to read the material, and, thankfully, they didn't put it in the shredder.

I'm dedicating this book to my mother, Elizabeth Higgins Sciutto, who pushed me more than anyone to get it down on paper. She and my father, Ernest Sciutto (who is still keeping me in line today), were generous and dedicated parents to my three sisters and me—and always our best supporters. She was a journalist all her life, and from the very beginning of ours, she encouraged us to write—essays, stories, our dreams in notebooks by our bedsides. She was a pioneer herself in the early days of television news in her hometown of Louisville, Kentucky, and later a journalist with *McCall's*, *Newsweek*, and *U.S. News & World Report*. I carried what she taught me into my own career in journalism.

I wish she'd been able to read the final product. I'm sure it would have benefited from her red pen. I'll settle for her drive and inspiration.

Jim Sciutto
London
March 2008

INDEX

Abbas, Wael, 81–90, 93

ABC News, xi, 102, 108–9, 113, 119, 124, 145, 209, 214, 226

Abdel-Hamid, Hoda, 237

Abdullah, 6–8

Abdullah, King of Saudi Arabia, 225, 237–38

Abdullah II, King of Jordan, 4, 5, 6

Abu Ghraib prison, xiv, xv, 21, 22–23, 79, 123

Active Change Foundation, 175–76

Afghanistan, xiv, xvi, 13, 21, 26, 50, 53, 89, 108, 133–34, 136, 137, 163, 170–74, 180, 190, 193–218, 226, 239, 244, 248, 251

alleged American atrocities in, 170, 185

Al-Qaeda in, 220, 224, 229–30

civil war in, 197, 198, 201, 203

Kabul, 193, 197, 198, 199, 203, 205, 206, 207, 209, 213, 214

plot to behead soldiers returning from, 161, 177

refugees in, 203–4

Soviet invasion of, 28, 129, 197, 202, 203, 223, 225

Taliban in, see Taliban

Ahmad, 208–9

Ahmadinejad, Mahmoud, 127–28, 137, 141–43, 153

Al Arabiya, 66

Albright, Madeleine, 75, 133

Algeria, 28

Al Jazeera, 66

Ali, 5–6

Al Maktoum, Mohammad bin Rashid, 238

Al-Qaeda, xi, xii, xiii, xv, 2, 7, 9, 10, 14–15, 24, 28, 59, 65, 122, 124, 196, 202, 204, 248, 251

in Afghanistan, 220, 224, 229–30

al-Johani in, 220, 224, 229–32, 238

Hezbollah and, 42, 43, 53, 59

Internet and, 185

in Jordan, 4

Mustafa and, 19, 20–21

Nasrallah and, 47

Saudi Arabia and, 229

Taliban and, 199, 211

Amin, Rizgar Mohammed, 111
Aoun, Michel, 39, 47, 57
Arafat, Yasser, 42
ARD, 124, 209, 214
Argentina, xiii, 43
Assad, Bashar, 19, 32
Ayazi, 140

Babylon, 99–100
Baghdad, 97, 101, 102, 103, 104, 109,
    114–16, 122, 125
  Yarmouk hospital in, 95–97, 101,
    103–5, 109–10, 112–22, 124
Bali, 28
Barak, Ehud, 44
Bari, Mohammed Abdul, 180–81
Basijis, 128, 131, 145
Bayat, Ayatollah, 140
BBC, 102, 124, 209, 214
Beirut, 37, 39, 40, 42, 43, 55, 57, 58–59
Bhutto, Benazir, 247, 248, 249
Biden, Joseph, 251
Bin Laden, Osama, 10, 44, 77, 137,
    172, 183, 202, 221, 225, 251
  al-Johani and, 229–30, 232
  declining popularity of, 231
Bin Naif, Mohammed, 240
Bin Suweid, Salem, 2, 4
bloggers, 81–88, 93
bombings, 28, 43, 109, 112, 113, 161,
    210, 211, 234
  in Afghanistan theaters, 6, 7, 8
  Atlantic airliner plot, x, 163, 176
  car, x, xiv, 31, 32, 33, 105
  in London subway, ix–x, xii, 161,
    162, 174, 177, 182
  suicide, 5, 14, 42, 43, 47–48, 105,
    106, 109, 184, 185, 210, 211, 213,
    226, 238

Bosnia, 169, 180, 181, 223–24, 228,
    230, 239, 244
Bremer, L. Paul, III, 104
Britain, 11, 161–91, 228, 237
  history of Islam in, 164
  Pakistanis in, 164–68, 175, 176,
    178–79, 183, 184, 189
  subway bombings in, ix–x, xii,
    161, 162, 174, 177, 182
  surveillance program in,
    180–81
Buenos Aires, 43
Bush, George W., xiii, 18, 25,
    50, 53, 59, 60, 75, 88, 190,
    191, 215
  democratic reforms and, 68, 72,
    102, 107
  Iraq and, 98, 102, 103, 107, 109,
    114, 124
  2002 State of the Union address
    of, 135

Castro, Fidel, 124
Chalabi, Ahmed al-, 107–8
Chechnya, 14, 224, 239, 244
Cheney, Dick, 191
Christians, 32, 37, 38, 39, 52, 60,
    187, 188
  Hezbollah and, xv, 35, 36, 40, 46,
    47, 57
  Sara, 35–41, 43–44, 46–61, 183
CIA, xii, 5, 20, 86, 87, 124, 162,
    229, 236
  Iran and, 129, 150–51, 154
Ciccipio, Elham, 57
Ciccipio, Joseph, 56–57
Clinton, Bill, 133
CNN, 133
Connett, Ty, 103

conspiracy theories, xii, 13, 20, 98, 123–24, 125, 162, 177, 215, 221, 248–49
    Iranians and, 132, 150–51
    about 9/11, 13, 124, 236
    about Pakistan, 248–50

dictatorships, xiv, 137
Dizin, 136
Dobbins, James, 134
Dobriansky, Paula, 34
Druze, 32, 37, 38
Dying to Win: The Strategic Logic of Suicide Terrorism (Pape), 14–15

Egypt, xii, xiii, xiv, xvi, 11, 12, 23, 53, 63–93, 137, 252
    bloggers in, 81–88, 93
    elections in, xv–xvi, 107
    Kifaya in, 84, 156
    Muslim Brotherhood in, 65, 69, 71, 72, 76, 84, 85
Eisenhower, Dwight D., 130
El Ghad (Tomorrow Party), 66, 73, 84, 85
England, Lynndie, 23
Evin prison, 138, 141, 146–52, 158

Fahd, King, 228, 237
Fatah al-Islam, 59
Fedayeen Saddam, 15–16
Foley, Lawrence, 2, 4
Freakley, Benjamin, 210, 211, 212
Freedom House, 86
Free Patriotic Movement, 47

Garner, Jay, 103–5
Gates, Robert, 74

Gemayal, Bachir, 39
Gerges, Fawaz, xiii, xvi
Guantanamo Bay detention camp, xiv, xv, 89, 123, 220, 221, 223, 225, 232–34, 238–41, 243
Gulf War, first, 100, 104, 123

Haditha, 21
Hakim, Mohammed Bakir al-, 105, 108
Hakim, Sherko, 113–14
Hamas, 43, 72
    Iran and, 129
Hamid, Shadi, 71–72
Hariri, Rafik, 32, 33
Hellyer, Hisham, 165, 166, 176–77
Hezbollah, xv, 32, 34–36, 39–48, 50, 51, 53–55, 57–60, 138
    Al Qaeda and, 42, 43, 55, 59
    founding of, 42
    Iran and, 129
    welfare program of, 46
Higgins, William R., 43
Hirsi, Ayaan, 11
Homa, 195–201, 206–10, 212–18
Human Rights Watch, 73
Hussein, King of Jordan, 5, 72

immigration and visas, 51–52, 53, 222
India, 248
Indonesia, xii, xiii, 69
Initiative to Educate Afghan Women, 217
Intercontinental Hotel, 31
International Conference on Iraq, 120
Internet, 9, 184–85
    bloggers on, 81–88, 93

Iran, 24, 26, 32, 42, 46, 127–59, 226
    CIA and, 129, 150–51, 154
    civil society groups in, 153–54
    Dizin, 136
    elections in, 140–43, 144, 154,
        156
    Evin prison in, 138, 141, 146–52, 158
    Iraq and, 123, 129, 131–32, 135, 155
    Nahavand, 131
    1979 revolution in, 128, 129, 131,
        132, 138–39, 140, 146, 150,
        166, 228
    nuclear weapons program of,
        129–30, 156, 157
    security agents in, 143–45
    Shah of, 129–30, 131, 139, 146,
        150, 228
    Tehran, 127, 129, 131, 134, 135–36,
        138, 152
    U.S. embassy takeover in, 129, 131,
        133, 138, 228
Iranian exile groups, 154–55
Iraq, xii, xiv, 43, 68, 95–125, 137,
        227
    Baghdad, 97, 101, 102, 103, 104,
        109, 114–16, 122, 125
    chemical weapons in, 132
    civil war in, 23–24, 27, 105
    diminishing violence in, 121–22
    elections in, xv–xvi, 34, 67, 107–8,
        110
    exodus from, 117, 203
    Iran and, 123, 129, 131–32, 135,
        155
    Purple Revolution in, 34, 67
    reconstruction efforts in, 118, 119,
        120, 121, 123
    Saddam in, see Saddam Hussein
    Taliban and, 211

    "Where Things Stand" polls on,
        102, 113, 119, 124
    Yarmouk hospital in, 95–97, 101,
        103–5, 109–10, 112–22, 124
Iraq War, xiv–xv, 1, 2, 9–10, 12–29,
        43, 50, 53, 54, 60, 77, 89, 95–125,
        156, 169, 191, 196, 234, 237, 244
    American atrocities in, 21–22
    casualties in, 97
    claim of concealment of American
        casualties in, 17–18
    Egypt and, 75
    9/11 conspiracy theories and, 13
    plot to behead soldiers returning
        from, 177
    Saudis and, 225, 227
Islam:
    in Britain, 164
    and extremism as counterculture,
        182–83
    Hezbollah and, 46–47
    Koran in, 187–88
    misinterpretations of, 44, 188
    as political ideology, 11
    violence as part of, 53
Islamic Jihad, 56, 77
Ismail, Gameela, 63–67, 69–71,
        73–77, 79–80, 90–92
Israel, xii, 11–12, 36, 50, 60, 131, 151,
        155, 181, 227, 236
    Egypt and, 65
    as face of U.S. policy, 36
    Jordan and, 3
    Lebanon and, xii, 38–42, 44, 45, 48,
        54–58, 138, 166
    Palestinians and, xiv, 21, 25

Japan, 236
Jayousi, Azmi al-, 2, 4

Jeddah, 219–20, 223, 234, 238

Jennings, Peter, 58

Jenvey, Glen, 184–85

Jews, 5, 187, 188

Johani, Khalid al-, 219–25, 229–34, 238–45

John Paul II, Pope, 47

Jordan, xiii, 1–29, 53, 60, 72, 231
Swaqa prison in, 1–10, 18, 27, 28

Kabbani, Mohammed, 31–32

Kabul, 193, 197, 198, 199, 203, 205, 206, 207, 209, 213, 214

Karroubi, Mehdi, 141

Karzai, Hamid, 194, 211, 216

Kashmir, 14

Kazemi, Zahra, 146

Khamenei, Ayatollah, 133

Khatami, Mohammed, 132–33, 134, 156

Khomeini, Ayatollah Ruhollah, 128, 138, 139, 140

Kifaya, 84, 156

King Fahd Mosque, 227–28

Kirkuk, 15, 103, 113–14

Kohut, Andrew, xiii

Koran, 187–88

Kosovo, 169

Kurds, 108

Kuwait, 12, 67, 68, 107

Lebanon, 11, 14, 28, 31–61
Cedar Revolution in, 32–36, 54
civil war in, 37–39, 42–43, 45, 52, 53
elections in, xv–xvi
Hezbollah in, see Hezbollah
Israel and, xii, 38–42, 44, 45, 48, 54–58, 138, 166

Palestinians in, 42, 59
Qana Massacre in, 39, 40

Luhaidan, Saleh al-, 227

Madrid, 28

Malaysia, xiii

Malik, 176, 186

Manal, 78

McCain, John, 89

McCormack, Sean, 72

Mello, Sergio de, 105

Milosevic, Slobodan, 169

Misr Digital, 81–82

Moawad, Nayla, 32–33

Moawad, René, 33

Mohammadi, Akbar, 146

Mohammed, 10–19, 24–26, 28–29

Morocco, xii, xiii

Moro Islamic Liberation Front (MILF), 224, 229

Mossadegh, Mohammed, 133, 150

Mouttaki, Manoucher, 129–30

Mubarak, Gamal, 71

Mubarak, Hosni, xiv, 65–68, 70, 71, 73, 77, 83, 84, 87, 88, 89, 93

Musharraf, Pervez, 247, 248, 249, 251

Muslim Brotherhood, 65, 69, 71, 72, 76, 84, 85

Mustafa, 8, 19–24, 28

Nabil, Abdel Kareem, 87

Nahavand, 131

Najaf, 105

Naseem, Mohammed, 162

Nasrallah, Hassan, 34–35, 45, 47–48, 57

Nasser, Gamal Abdel, 23, 48, 76

National Human Rights Commission, 90–92

National Iranian American Council, 154

NATO, 209, 215

Nazir, 198, 206, 213

New York Times, 150

9/11, *see* September 11 attacks

Nirschel, Paula, 217

Nixon, Richard M., 88

North Korea, 135

Nour, 208

Nour, Ayman, 63–71, 73–77, 79–80, 82, 84, 85, 88, 90–93

nuclear weapons, 129–30, 156, 157, 251

Obama, Barack, 250

Oberwetter, James, 235

Ozomatli, 92–93

Pahlavi, Mohammed Reza Shah, 129–30, 131, 139, 146, 150, 228

Pakistan, xii, xiii, 51, 69, 167–68, 185–86, 247–52
  Afghan refugees from, 203
  Al-Qaeda in, 220, 224
  conspiracy theory about, 248–50
  economic problems in, 248, 251
  elections in, 247–48, 250, 251, 252
  Saudi influence in, 226
  Taliban and, 199, 211, 231, 251

Pakistanis, in Britain, 164–68, 175, 176, 178–79, 183, 184, 189

Palestine, xiii, 11–12, 43, 180
  elections in, xv–xvi, 72, 107

Palestine Liberation Organization (PLO), 42

Palestinians, 37, 38
  Israel and, xiv, 21, 25
  in Lebanon, 42, 59

Pape, Robert, 14–15

Pew Global Attitudes Project, xii–xiii, 231

Pew Research Center, xiii, 5, 236

Philippines, 220, 224, 229, 239, 244

Pinochet, Augusto, 83

prisons, 146, 232–33, 239, 240
  Abu Ghraib, xiv, xv, 21, 22–23, 79, 123
  Evin, 138, 141, 146–52, 158
  Guantanamo, xiv, xv, 89, 123, 220, 221, 223, 225, 232–34, 238–41, 243
  Sheberghan, 204–5
  Swaqa, 1–10, 18, 27, 28
  torture in, xiv, 22, 23, 78, 79, 82–84, 146, 147–48, 233, 252
  Tura Mazraa, 77–80, 82

Program on International Policy Attitudes, xii

Project on Middle East Democracy, 71–72

Qadir, Hanif, 162–76, 179, 181–91, 237, 252

Qutb, Sayid, 76

Rabin, Yitzhak, 44

Rafsanjani, Hashemi, 141

Rang-A-Rang TV, 154

Rania, Queen of Jordan, 4–5

Rice, Condoleezza, 68–69, 72, 73, 75–76, 120–21

Risen, James, 150

Riyadh, 219, 234

Rumsfeld, Donald, 2, 132

Ruzicka, Marla, 108–9

Sacranie, Iqbal, 162

Sadat, Anwar, 77

Saddam Hussein, 21, 98, 99, 100, 101,
  123, 124, 129, 132, 169, 234
  Al-Qaeda and, 20–21
  trial of, 111–12, 114
Sadr, Moqtada al-, 122
Sandia, Liran, 58
Sara, 35–41, 43–44, 46–61, 183
Sarajevo, 227–28
Saudi Arabia, xiv, 12, 14, 21, 51, 53,
  67, 68, 137, 183, 219–45, 252
  elections in, 107, 141
  Iraq and, 114
  Jeddah, 219–20, 223, 234, 238
  mosque takeover in, 228–29
  Taliban and, 199
  Wahhabis in, 221, 225, 226, 228,
  229
Schwarzkopf, H. Norman, 150
Seige of Mecca, The (Trofimov),
  228–29
September 11 attacks, xii, xv, 28, 48,
  49–51, 54, 100, 133, 196, 230–31,
  233, 239, 244
  bin Laden's statement on sixth
  anniversary of, 183
  British and, 162, 168, 169–70,
  180, 186
  conspiracy theories about, 13,
  124, 236
  Qana Massacre compared with, 40
  Saudi Arabia and, 221, 225–26
Serbia, 169
Serena Hotel, 213
Shah, Israh, 249–51
Shamsudin, 203–4
Sharif, Nawaz, 248
Sharif, Sayid Imam al-, 77
Sheberghan prison, 204–5
Sheikh, Abdul-Aziz al-, 237–38

Shiite Muslims, 23–24, 32, 35, 36, 38,
  42, 44–47, 60, 100, 105, 108, 113,
  116, 123, 227
Shore, Gary, 144
Soviet Union, 38, 47
  Afghanistan invaded by, 28, 129,
  197, 202, 203, 223, 225
Sri Lanka, 14
students, international, in U.S.,
  48–49, 50, 51, 222
Submission, 11
Sunni Muslims, 23–24, 32, 37, 38, 59,
  108, 112–13, 116, 122, 227
Swaqa prison, 1–10, 18, 27, 28
Syria, 10, 18–19, 21, 24, 28, 151
  Lebanon and, 32, 34

Taha, Jamal, 95–99, 101–5, 107–10,
  112–19, 121–25
Taiwan, 46
Taleghani, Ayatollah Mahmoud,
  139, 146
Taleghani, Azam, 139
Taliban, 134, 163, 171, 173, 193–96,
  198–201, 203–16, 243–44, 248
  Al-Qaeda and, 199, 211
  Nasrallah and, 47
  Pakistan and, 199, 211, 231, 251
Tehran, 127, 129, 131, 134, 135–36,
  138, 152
  Evin prison in, 138, 141, 146–52, 158
  U.S. embassy takeover in, 129, 131,
  133, 138, 228
Thomassen, Carsten, 213
Time, 102, 113
Tomorrow Party (El Ghad), 66, 73,
  84, 85
torture, xiv, 22, 23, 78, 79, 82–84,
  146, 147–48, 233, 252

Trofimov, Yaroslav, 228–29
Tura Mazraa prison, 77–80, 82
Turki, Mansour al-, 235
Turkey, xiii, 14

United Arab Emirates, 51
United Nations (UN), 39, 58, 105,
    132, 133, 203, 213
USA Today, 124

Van Gogh, Theo, 11
Vietnam War, 35, 42, 124
visas, 51–52, 53, 222

Wael, 79, 81
Wahhabis, 221, 225, 226, 228, 229

Washington Post, 47
"Where Things Stand" polls, 102,
    113, 119, 124
World Health Organization, 97
Wright, Robin, 47

Yarmouk hospital, 95–97, 101, 103–5,
    109–10, 112–22, 124
Yassin, 178–80, 181–82, 183
Yildar, 1–3, 8–10, 12–16, 18, 19, 24,
    28, 29

Zamanian, Babak, 127–29, 130–32,
    134–35, 137, 140, 143, 145–59
Zarqawi, Abu Musab al-, 2, 5, 6,
    19, 21

ABOUT THE AUTHOR

JIM SCIUTTO is the senior foreign correspondent for ABC News, the first correspondent to hold this position since Peter Jennings and Pierre Salinger. He has reported from more than forty countries in Europe, Asia, Africa, Latin America, and the Middle East, including thirteen assignments in Iraq. In 2007 he won the prestigious George Polk Award for Television Reporting. He lives in London with his wife, Gloria Riviera, who is also a correspondent for ABC News.